"For a male psychiatrist *Using Textile Handcrafts in Therapy with Women* presents a unique cross-cultural journey into unfamiliar feminine territory, ably guided by Futterman Collier who weaves Jungian psychology, contemporary mental health practice and the media of textile arts in a style that is both entertaining and enlightening."

—*Peter Aitken, Consultant Liaison Psychiatrist, Royal Devon & Exeter Hospital and Director of Research & Development, Devon Partnership NHS Trust, UK*

"I met Ann Collier, her husband and their three lovely daughters one summer afternoon during a rainy visit to the Saint Mary-of-the-Woods College campus. Meeting Ann for the first time was like seeing an old friend who was so excited to talk with you about her love for textile arts and the value of the creative process for personal and spiritual growth.

In this book, Ann has woven her two natural callings as a psychologist and fiber artist. She has created the likings of a Brook's Bouquet where the weft yarn (psychology) is wrapped around by several warps (creative art making) to draw them together. The result is a weaving that is layered with textile art metaphors that inspire the reader to use the creative process for self-renewal. The golden thread that is interwoven throughout the book is the call to listen to your creative spirit and enjoy where the textile journey takes you."

—*Kathy Gotshall, ATR, LCSW, Director of the MAAT Program and Assistant Professor, Graduate Art Therapy, Illinois*

"The author has chosen the medium of fiber as a path to encourage her clients to discover and create meaning out of what often appears as senseless and traumatic. She encourages people, whether they are helping professionals or clients, to not hold themselves back through some expectation of having to be artistic but rather to explore and, through some of the guidelines she has developed over her numerous years of practice and careful observations, regain a liberating sense of self-esteem and integrity."

—Sheila Hicks, artist, and daughter Itaka
Martignoni, gestalt-therapist, Paris, France

"By writing this book, Ann Futterman Collier has encouraged therapists to understand and use their skills to enrich women's lives, by expanding their horizons, and giving them tools to cope with their journey through life while exploring textile mediums. I heartily endorse this endeavor."

—Anne Field, international teacher, weaver, spinner,
and writer, Christchurch, New Zealand

*Using Textile Arts
and Handcrafts in
Therapy with Women*

of related interest

Art Therapy Techniques and Applications
Susan I. Buchalter
ISBN 978 1 84905 806 3

Trauma, Tragedy, Therapy
The Arts and Human Suffering
Stephen K. Levine
Foreword by Shaun McNiff
ISBN 978 1 84310 512 1

Art in Action
Expressive Arts Therapy and Social Change
Ellen G. Levine and Stephen K. Levine
Foreword by Michelle LeBaron
ISBN 978 1 84905 820 9

Creative Expression Activities for Teens
Exploring Identity through Art, Craft and Journaling
Bonnie Thomas
ISBN 978 1 84905 842 1

Expressive and Creative Arts Methods for Trauma Survivors
Edited by Lois Carey
ISBN 978 1 84310 386 8

Drawing from Within
Using Art to Treat Eating Disorders
Lisa D. Hinz
ISBN 978 1 84310 822 1

Using Textile Arts and Handcrafts in Therapy with Women

Weaving Lives Back Together

ANN FUTTERMAN COLLIER

Jessica Kingsley *Publishers*
London and Philadelphia

Artwork in Chapter 10 reproduced with kind permission from Neta Amir,
Bo Breda, Rebecca Cross, Christine Marie Davis, Elizabeth Harris, Kathleen
Holmes, Lisa Klakulak, Elaine Quehl, and Erica Spitzer Rasmussen.

First published in 2012
by Jessica Kingsley Publishers
116 Pentonville Road
London N1 9JB, UK
and
400 Market Street, Suite 400
Philadelphia, PA 19106, USA

www.jkp.com

Library of Congress Cataloging in Publication Data
Collier, Ann Futterman.
  Using textile arts and handcrafts in therapy with women : weaving lives back
together / Ann Futterman Collier.
    p. cm.
  Includes bibliographical references and index.
  ISBN 978-1-84905-838-4 (alk. paper)
  1. Textile crafts--Therapeutic use. I. Title.
  RC489.A7C66 2012
  616.89'165--dc23
                                  2011025723

British Library Cataloguing in Publication Data
A CIP catalogue record for this book is available from the British Library

ISBN 978 1 84905 838 4
eISBN 978 0 85700 337 9

Printed and bound in Great Britain

To Dr. Barb Lozar.

You told me I could do it. You found ways to share in my excitement through your heritage of Slovenian lace. You read 891 qualitative surveys to help me sort out what women were saying, only because you were my friend and you knew I was working solo and you wanted to offer me your quiet support. Then your brain shut down half-way. And as I sat there knitting fervently by your bedside, first waiting for you to recover and then waiting for you to cross over, I knew whenever you looked up and saw me knitting that we both silently acknowledged the more than 891 women before us that had done the same thing. And I, as with the women before me, will now wear this cardigan with sad, sweet, and grateful memories of everything you have been in your life, felted into the very fiber with tears. I did surprisingly finish my book and publish my study before the tapestry of your life so suddenly ended. Now that your flame has danced on to somewhere only your soul knows, I will be forever thankful that you brightened my path with your colors before you left. And I am reminded, once again, that this is why we women need to create with fibers while participating in the process of life. This book is dedicated to you, Dr. Barb Lozar. For everything you have brought into my life.

*I dedicate this book to my husband, Jay, and to my
Irish triplets, Abby, Sophie, and Emma.*

*To Jay, for your love and for sharing our adventurous life.
For appreciating my never-ending curiosity, intensity, and
passion. And most of all, for supporting an atmosphere where
all forms of creativity are imaginable and acceptable.*

*To my girls, for bringing me your magical, transformative love. You
were real little fairies; now you are becoming real goddesses. You
challenge me every day to become a better person. And to figure out
how to be a realistic role model so that you can each do an even better
job of integrating motherhood with your passions and your loves.*

Contents

Preface

For decades I have been trying to find a way to blend my passion for creating with fibers together with my expertise as a clinical psychologist. I am not sure which came first, being a natural textile artist or being a natural shrink. I think it is in my constitution to do both as these abilities became apparent to me at a very early age. My earliest memories are filled with making craft projects *and* trying to fix the people around me who were emotional wrecks. Believe me, no one in my world was very good at either, so there were no role models to look to. I found that making textiles allowed me to escape from my childhood reality and, later, gave me a creative outlet to feel renewed and restored.

I taught myself to sew when I was 11 after I had walked into a fabric store and became mesmerized by the colors and textures. I was practically over-burdened by the knowledge that I could pick out fabric to create my own vision of clothing; it was like opening a psychedelic door of possibilities in the universe. I became an avid seamstress by the end of junior high school and made most of my clothes while in high school. I apprenticed at a costume shop in a summer-stock musical theater in Northern California at 15; by the time I was 17, I was the chief dresser and had been offered a job at the American Conservatory Theater. I was convinced, however, that there was no stability in clothing design as a career, and that being a psychologist was my one true calling.

As I do with most things, I pursued becoming a psychologist passionately. But, of course, I also continued to work with textiles, fervently. Learning to weave at 21, I began making my own fabric to sew with. Weaving solidified my life-long need to make textiles. I wove my way through graduate school, grounding myself in my tiny "loom-room" filled with colors and images. When I could no longer take the fatigue of reading hundreds of pages of psychology articles each week, I worked into the wee hours of the night playing with whatever colors seemed to make me happy. Somehow the hypomanic sleep deprivation caused by "creating" cloth until 4:00am often gave me *more* energy, not less. In my own little world, with control over my ungraded projects, I was revitalized in such a way that I could continue studying clinical psychology. When I had no time to make fibers, I day-dreamed about them; I invigorated and transformed myself by picturing what I would make later. My countless clothing doodles led to orders from my class-mates and, before I knew it, I was selling my wares.

After graduate school, my life began to change dramatically. I down-sized and moved into a tiny efficiency in Manhattan to pursue a post-doctoral fellowship in psycho-oncology. Then I settled into Colorado, living as a young professional and working as faculty at an urban university. And then I down-sized again as my new husband and I opted for life outside of the mainstream. We began a seven-year journey of working and living in the Pacific Rim. Every place we moved or traveled to, I learned new textile techniques, typically from everyday people around me. Although most of the fiber arts I created during those days were portable, I still managed to transport my 54-inch counter-balanced loom to Micronesia, New Zealand, and then Alaska (much to my new husband's dismay). I found a universal, non-verbal language to connect with women: from remote villages in Laos along the Mekong River, to small hamlets in rural Indonesia, to sheep farms in the far south island of New Zealand, to isolated Pacific atolls in Micronesia and Polynesia, to dirt pathways behind storefronts in Ubud. I sat with pre-adolescent girls, young women, and old women, and learned different ways to weave and shear sheep and felt and use a kajip and batik and spin and sew. And while I openly learned and watched, I created personal connections with strangers who had very little in common with me aside from our shared humanity, love of textiles, and archetypal connection with cloth.

Ironically, as my fiber-making skills developed, my clinical skills also developed. I became better and better at creating relationships and more and more comfortable with using textiles as an entry-way to connect with women. For example, I once re-channeled a discussion on quilt-making to explore the past, present, and future with a client who had breast cancer. After I had walked with another client through a casual discussion of our shared passion for fibers I found that I could access parts of her world not open to many people, let alone mental health providers. To this day, one of my most treasured possessions is a book of art deco design plates gifted to me by a young woman who died of breast cancer. Her gift was a true acknowledgment of what she had shared with me during her final days of living and a testament to her ability to find loveliness during an abhorrent disease process.

Through all of this, I still thought that I didn't know how to blend my love of textiles with psychology. And then it came to me like a flash of brilliant light. I had already been doing it, for years in fact. I knew then that my calling was to formalize the integration of textiles and psychology into my own clinical practice.

Now I bring to you in this book my compilation of a deeply rooted knowledge and experience in both worlds: textiles and psychology. Combined with an insatiable curiosity and voracious quest for knowledge, I hope my approach and passion for this area inspires you to find the same in your practice.

Chapter 1

Introduction

WHY FIBER IS GOOD FOR YOUR PSYCHE

Purpose of the book

There are three overall goals of this book:

1. To review the role of fiber and textile handcrafts in women's lives, and to integrate the life-issues women face with the therapeutic making of fiber art.

2. To provide counselors and therapists with specific suggestions for how to use fiber arts in their practice.

3. To provide a psychological synthesis for how to use textile handcrafts to enhance psychotherapy goals.

What is unique about this book?

The majority of art therapy books and journal articles emphasize the visual arts and expressive arts. A "PsycInfo" search on art therapy and psychotherapy for publications between 1995 and 2010 indicated that were 1797 items available: 516 published books and book chapters; 1195 published journal articles; 47 dissertations; and 39 electronic collections (American Psychological Association 2011). Although the visual arts and expressive arts do theoretically include textiles and fiber-making, there were shockingly few studies and no books dedicated exclusively to the use of textiles in art therapy. The majority of articles generally explored reasons why people create with textiles and dealt mostly with quilting (about 100). There were only a handful of peer-reviewed, published studies on the role of knitting, weaving, embroidery, and tapestry.

In my own practice and in conversations with other therapists and artists, I have found that the use of textile-making presents an amazing opportunity for growth, development, and psychological wholeness in women. As will be reviewed in Chapter 2, textile words, metaphors, and idioms are deeply entrenched in the English language. As such, they naturally avail themselves to symbolically describing our inner psychological and outer social lives and can be used to explore key issues. Chapter 2 will also review how women around the world and throughout history have created with textiles to clothe the body, and to protect, to soften, to beautify, and to adorn it (Barber 1994). What is known from the literature on how women use textile-making to cope with life will be reviewed.

Who is this book for?

The book will be useful to the textile handcrafter who wants to explore personal issues via textiles, while its theoretical orientation is mostly geared towards mental health professionals who already have background knowledge and training in counseling. Textile artists who offer workshops and classes might also find this book helpful. In my experience, multiple psychological issues can and do arise in people while taking fiber-related workshops, and most artists (other than art therapists) are not trained in how to deal with these issues. I have taken dozens of textile workshops over the years, and, because I was usually on vacation, I have not wanted to cross boundaries that weren't meant for me to cross—that is, I have typically kept my psychology training under wraps. Instead, I talk with pride about having lots of kids and being a part-time stay-at-home mom, which is only partially true! And I have silently watched individual women display their emotional issues for all to see. I have seen entire classes participate in recapitulating an unhealthy member's personal dynamics onto their confused teacher. I have seen women completely interrupt the learning and leisure of other participants because of their own insecurities and personality disturbance. I have seen students so derailed and caught off guard by the interpersonal dynamics of their class-mates that they leave early and claim the instructor was poor. Because I have rarely seen teachers who know how to deal with these kinds of issues, I hope that this book will provide an important resource.

Chapter 3 reviews specific types of mental health problems that women face, globally and in the Westernized world. More severe psychological problems may preclude the use of textile therapy, and clinicians must recognize this before embarking on the journey or it will be a misguided one. The classic medical model is first offered, and then an alternative approach which emphasizes conceptualizing "passages" in a woman's life is discussed.

Chapter 4 reviews the literature on what to assess before beginning. This includes explicit suggestions for brief mental health screening tools and tools that specifically focus on female issues. Chapter 4 also provides ideas about how to determine the types of textiles to use with women.

Women all over the world use fibers and textiles. Chapter 5 provides the clinician with a framework for how to explore textile art therapy in a culturally competent and sensitive manner. Leaders are given suggestions for how to "tune in" to ways to integrate textile mediums within and across cultures, within and across generations.

The theoretical foundation of this book (Chapter 6) takes a unique approach. Art therapy classically emphasizes psychodynamic and psychoanalytic models. Instead, my approach will integrate techniques and research from a variety of theoretical models. Key concepts in metaphor psychotherapy are presented, and justification is provided for exploring rites of passage, folklores, stories, and mythology when using textile art therapy (Brenner 2007; Burns 2007; Young 1996, 2001). Art therapy also typically encourages women to express and vent negative feelings through their artwork. This is consistent with Freud's use of catharsis in psychotherapy. Textile art therapy will encourage women to use their handcrafts as a way to bring about positive mood, relaxation, and pleasure. I believe that this, in turn, reinforces their continuation of textile-making, which subsequently continues to promote positive coping (Collier 2011).

I will also encourage the therapist to help transition women from creating functional textile handcrafts to non-functional pieces. Through my research and discussions with both professional artists and women who make handcrafts, I can say with confidence that most textile handcrafters do not use textiles to create specific metaphors. Of course, their work may unconsciously represent inner feelings and thoughts, but the product is not created with a conscious metaphoric intent. Using the textile mediums for metaphorical expression will come as quite a challenge for many women, but will allow for the most growth. Finally, narrative therapy, expressive writing, and guided imagery are also incorporated. Where applicable, some principles from cognitive behavioral therapy are applied.

The translation of these theories into practice does require some expertise in the application of guided imagery and expressive writing. The mechanics of how to use these techniques are explored in Chapter 7. Chapter 7 also explores ideas about how the therapist can tune into the design process.

Chapter 8 shows how, with the support of a mental health provider, textile art-making can take personal growth to an entirely new level: by building and constructing metaphorical objects with textiles and fiber—not to dissociate, but to engage and to be present. The chapter provides quite a few projects that can be adapted or modified for different life issues. The reader will find a variety of psychosocial issues identified, and matched with corresponding fibers, objects, and topical metaphors.

As mentioned earlier, using textile art therapy in group settings requires sensitivity, awareness of group process, and care. There are many examples of leaderless textile "groups" (e.g. quilting circles). Fiber art-making is naturally interdependent, intergenerational, and affiliative. How to engage women in groups is the emphasis in Chapter 9.

Finally, there are more and more female textile artists who have been using textiles to specifically reflect key feminist issues. Chapter 10 examines examples of artists' work, and finds out how they perceive using art for mood change.

Chapter 2

Threads of Time

WOMEN AND TEXTILE-MAKING

A brief definition of textiles

For thousands of years, women have created with textiles. Although the root of the word *textile* (*texere*) means to weave, the term actually encompasses a variety of fiber-related materials. Fibers come from plants (e.g. cotton, linen), animals (e.g. wool, alpaca, silk), vegetable matter (e.g. bark cloth, hemp, linen), chemicals (e.g. glass, asbestos), and, more recently, synthetic materials (e.g. nylon, spandex, rayon, acrylic). The range of fibers has increased dramatically in the last hundred years, since the first synthetic fibers were made in the 1920s. Once the type of fiber is selected, techniques to work with it include matting, felting, twisting, spinning, and plying into yarn. Fibers can also be knit, crocheted, looped, braided, knotted, or woven into fabric. Fabric can be further modified by sewing, hand-stitching, and tying knots, and subsequently embellished and decorated with various methods including embroidery, beading, and additional surface design (e.g. batik, shibori). Frequently textiles are dyed (at any stage of the process), although there is an increasing value placed on natural colors. Textiles can also have color removed, such as in bleaching. Any combination of these techniques can be used together. For example, wool roving can be spun, knit, and then felted; wool batts can be felted on lightweight silk and then sewn and embellished into clothing; braided rope can be incorporated into beading and then pieced together for traditional clothing.

In addition to the techniques used to create textiles, there are multiple *objects* one can make with textiles; many of these can be made by a variety of methods. For example, rugs, household objects that are used for ground and wall coverings, can be made by weaving on a loom (with warp and weft), by tying knots on a warp (e.g. Turkish and Persian single and double knots), and by hand-tufting or hand-hooking (pushing yarn or wool through a dense fabric). The most obvious type of textiles is *household objects*. These are frequently practical, serving to insulate, yet also aesthetically appealing, thereby decorating living spaces and surfaces. Other household textiles include afghans and throws, quilts, upholstered fabric for furnishings, window shades, bed coverings, and table coverings. Textile objects are also made into clothing. Just as with household objects, clothing is typically practical, serving as protection for the human body. Clothing can also be made to adorn and for ornamentation. Veils are a type of clothing used to hide and protect, to disguise, and to separate.

Another category of textile objects is *containers and vessels*. These can hold anything from food to gifts to children. Vessels are typically made from twine and tree parts, but they can also be made from fabric, leather, felt, weavings, and mixed-media, as well as unconventional materials such as up-cycled plastic and clothing. A purse is also a vessel and contains valuable and personal items ranging from currency to identification. Textiles can be made into items for *play* (e.g. dolls, play silk blankets) and for *sport* (e.g. horse blankets, backpacks, tents, kites, and temari balls). Another class of textile objects relevant to the handcrafter can be seen in *transportation devices*, or items designed for movement, for example balloons, nets, kites, sails, and parachutes. Additional textiles used in industry, but not typically by textile handcrafters, include *geo-textiles*.

Textiles and their associated meanings

Expressive idioms, similes, and metaphors that include textiles are all around us. Fiber-related phrases are incorporated into every aspect of our speech. Examples include "the worldwide web," "spinning a tale," "a thread of discourse," "a network of ideas," "threads of time," "she has come unraveled," "unveiling the techniques," "interwoven lives," "loosening the thread of her waiting," "crafting humanity," "of the deepest dye," "hanging by a thread," "on pins and needles," "wear and tear," "at loose ends," "no idle hands," "the thread that binds," and "a coat of many colors." Many words associated with textile-making techniques and objects are also homographs (words that are spelled the same but differ in meaning, derivation, or pronunciation), homophones (words that are pronounced the same but differ in meaning, derivation, or spelling), and homonyms (words that are spelled and pronounced the same but have different meanings). These literary references can be easily incorporated into textile art therapy as metaphors (see Chapter 6). What follows are some examples of the symbolic meanings associated with different fiber techniques.

Basketry

A basket is a container made of interwoven cane, rushes, or strips of wood that is open at the top. Usually baskets are made from organic materials, and they typically serve a functional use as a receptacle for dry food (gathering, storing, and serving) and liquids. Nevertheless, the techniques for basket-making can be applied to clothing, mats, and headgear. Baskets are frequently beautifully made and serve as decorations in many cultures. They range from rigid, box-like carriers to mesh sacks. Although sometimes woven, in basket-making, fibers are frequently twisted together (not through warp and weft). Tension is not placed on length-wise threads because the fibers are less flexible than threads.

In the English language, a "basket case" usually refers to someone who is a nervous wreck, crazy, and unable to organize his/her life. The expression apparently originated during World War I in Britain, and was used for a soldier who had lost all four limbs in combat and had to be carried in a litter ("basket"). Later, this term was picked up by American soldiers and the expression was applied to an emotionally or mentally unstable person; eventually it came to mean anything that failed to function (Ammer 2003). The word *basket* has also been used in the expression "put all your eggs in one basket." This means to risk losing everything (materially, emotionally, etc.) all at one time and is probably based on the idea that if all the eggs you have from your chickens were placed in one basket (container) and that is dropped, you will probably lose all your eggs.

In many native populations, basket-making symbolizes life's course, and patterns found in baskets frequently have a symbolic meaning. For example, Navajo ceremonial baskets (ts'aa') are a metaphoric representation of the individual life course. The basket tells the collective history of the Navajo, and expresses the interconnection of individuals with their culture and natural environment. The traditional ceremonial baskets always include an open pathway from the center to the periphery, which symbolizes both the Navajo people's exit from one world and re-emergence to the next, as well as the ever-forward progression of individual human thought. The Warao of the Orinoco Delta consider basket-making to be shamanic, transforming the crafts-person into a plant-ancestor spirit. The Hupa, Karuk, and Yurok Indians of Northern California use baskets in their "Jump Dance," also known as a "world renewal" ceremony; baskets in this ceremony receive blessings from the spirit world.

Baskets are also associated with ancient stories and myths. Baskets have a womblike form, and are frequently connected historically with the cycles of life, death, and rebirth. The womb, or uterus, has fallopian tubes on the top and narrows towards the cervix as if it were an overturned triangular vessel. The Easter basket carries the egg, which foretells the coming of spring, which also leads to rebirth and fertility. Basket-making naturally integrates the idea of maternal containment, and as such, the rejuvenation of body and soul.

Beadwork

Beads are typically small and round, made of glass, plastic, or wood, and pierced for stringing or threading. They can also be made from fiber, such as thread, felt, and yarn. Beads can be made into jewelry and can be incorporated into textiles with intricate patterns on apparel, handbags, and shoes. At the most practical level, beads have been used in everyday life to weigh down scrolls, on saddle blankets, on tablecloths, to serve as an abacus, and curtains. In some societies, beads signify status and value, even monetary value.

Beads have played an important role in almost every civilization. In the English language, one expression for beads is "to draw a bead on" or "to get a bead on" someone or something. This originally meant to locate someone or something in the sights of a gun. Later, it came to mean to prepare to deal with or obtain someone or something.

During the Qing Dynasty in China, officials, army officers, and their wives and children were required to wear strings of court beads. The Asante people of West Africa, kings, and other great people get the privilege of wearing Bodom beads. Western society wears beads of pearls, gold, and precious stones as symbols of wealth and prestige. Beads also are traded as money, for food, gold, animal pelts, and spices. In some other societies beads denote strength and courage, bravery, and accomplishment. Beads have been used to offer protection from enemies, as well as magical protection on journeys. Amulets and talismen, or lucky charms, are made of beads. For example, the Magical Eye bead of Turkey is believed to ward off evil. In parts of Asia, beads were scattered like seeds at temples to induce bountiful harvests. Religions around the world use beads to reflect spirituality and prayers with the making of "prayer" beads.

Cloth and fabric

As described above, fibers can be knit, crocheted, looped, braided, knotted, or woven into cloth or fabric. Cloth is derived from an Old English word and means fabric. Fabric is a Latin term (*faber*) for an artisan who works with hard materials, such as a carpenter. By the mid-eighteenth century, the underlying definition of "manufactured material" gave rise to the current meaning. Today, *fabric* is defined as the material made by connecting a network of fibers, through weaving, knitting, crocheting, knotting, or felting (pressing the fibers together). *Cloth* is the finished product that can be used for multiple objects (e.g. clothing, quilting, curtains).

The word *cloth* is to *textiles* as words are to *text*. Interestingly, both the words *text* and *textile* share the root "to weave." And, cloth closely resembles words in many legends. The Dogon myth combines weaving and speech, where the mouth and vocal cords are a loom, and words and cloth produced. The Odyssey portrays women as obtaining their voices through weaving. There are many cloth and fabric idioms. One well-known idiom is "cut from the same cloth"; this implies sharing a lot of similarities, seeming to have been created, reared, or fashioned in the same way. "Take the cloth" or "man of cloth" means to be a man (or woman) of priesthood. In this circumstance, cloth has a holy connotation.

Cloth can also be used as a metaphor for skin (Valoma 2010). The word *skin* comes from the word *skinn*, of Norse derivation. Technically, skin refers to an outer covering, just as with cloth. Our skin allows us to comprehend pain, pressure, and temperature. It protects us and cushions us, and it provides information to and from our hormonal, vascular, immune, and nervous systems. Touch is the first sensation to develop in unborn babies, and the last sensation to disappear in the elderly. We need the contact of touch. Without it babies fail to thrive; adults feel less content and connected. Skin can also serve as a mechanism to depict information around the world, such as through scarification, tattoos, and even make-up. We use terms associated with skin to suggest depth of personality (e.g. "skin-deep"), mental and physical toughness (e.g. "thin skinned"), irritation (e.g. get "under one's skin"), and survival (e.g. "save one's skin"). Stories refer to a human having the skin of an animal; Inuit lore has animals pulling back skin to reveal a human. Most cultures use skin color to make ethnic distinctions and racist classifications.

Interestingly, Shakespeare frequently used clothing as a metaphor to symbolize morals, stature, violence, ambition, and admiration. In Macbeth, one of Shakespeare's darkest plays, there were numerous references to blood-stained clothes. Additional metaphors used throughout the play were light and dark (to communicate evil and danger), and clothing, which did or did not fit (to represent titles gained honestly, or by force and treachery).

Dyeing

When dyeing textiles, color-producing agents are applied to fibers in order to impart a degree of color permanence. Thus, to *dye* means to use a substance to color a material, or to impart a color (American Heritage Dictionary 2009). Dye, when added to a textile, will make it vibrant, and when removed will increase its mystery. The origins of the spelling appear to be unknown; however, the conventional spelling of the word *dye* was not established until the nineteenth century, and even then, the word *die* was used for some time. These homophones are easy to confuse, but of course, the word *die* means to cease living life. And with death comes the need to change and revitalize. Thus both spellings of the word *dye/die* will have metaphoric meaning when applied to textiles, and can be used interchangeably.

One common idiom is the expression "dyed-in-the-wool." This suggests a person has very strong opinions that will not change; it puts forward that something is permanent or extreme. Color idioms include seeing someone's "true colors," suggesting a person's true attitude, opinions, and biases. To "lend color" to something is an expression that means to provide an interesting accompaniment. To "sail under false colors" means to function deceptively, being not who you seem to be. This expression actually comes from pirates sailing under the national flag of the ship they planned on attacking, so that they could mislead people.

Color holds its own meaning, personally and culturally; this will be discussed more in Chapters 4 and 5. Cycles of light and color observed in nature are the bases of traditional Navajo belief and ceremonial practice. These light and color phenomena and associated beliefs structure the designs found on Navajo beaded baskets. In the Hindi literature, similes and metaphors abound with the use of color. For example, the red lips of the beloved have been compared with the red flowers of kachnar (*Bauhinia variegata*) and of the silk cotton tree.

Felt

The noun *felt* means matted or compressed animal fibers, such as wool or fur. Felt is a non-woven fabric where the fibers are locked together in a process utilizing heat, moisture, and pressure to form a compact material. Felt is also a homonym for the past tense and past participle of *feel*. Given that mental health providers are concerned with feelings, these two words can be used interchangeably to suggest the matting of feelings into confusion (felt) as well as clarity. An example is with the expression "make your presence felt," which is to have a strong effect on other people or on a situation. However, if a presence is made into felt, it could be a manifestation of a feeling.

Historically, felt has been particularly important for its ability to absorb: sound (e.g. a piano, television, or loudspeakers can be covered in felt), fat, dirt, dust, and water. Felt can represent positive attributes such as protection, healing, and spiritual warmth; and negative attributes such as isolation, suffocation, and the inability to communicate.

A new type of felting process was developed approximately 15 years ago by Polly Stirling, called *nuno* (Japanese for cloth). It involves bonding loose wool fibers into an extremely lightweight sheer cloth, such as silk or cotton chiffon and gauze. The result has a wide range of textures and colors. Some images of nuno have a scar-like appearance, where the material is transparent, but lines run through it. The transparency yet toughness of the fabric holds many metaphoric nuances.

Knitting and crocheting

Knitting means making a fabric or garment by intertwining yarn or thread in a series of connected loops either by hand, with knitting needles, or on a machine. Fibers are closely joined and united securely. Crocheting is quite similar, except the tool used is a single hook.

Expressions using *knit* typically convey this intertwining. To "knit one's brows" suggests that eyebrows come together in wrinkles or furrows, as with knitting. It usually refers to deep contemplation and thought. The expression "cast pearls before swine" means not to waste something precious or time-consuming on someone who will not value it. The expression comes from the New Testament, Matthew 7:6: "Do not give what is holy to dogs, and do not throw your pearls before swine, or they will trample them under their feet, and turn and tear you to pieces" (NASB 1997). Simplified, it means do not waste something valuable—like weeks of knitting or crocheting—on someone who is not going to appreciate it!

The steps involved in knitting and crocheting can also be seen as a metaphor for life. The primary symbolism in knitting is that of creating something new out of available material. It can mean that a project or idea is beginning to come together, or it can mean it is unraveling, and needs reconsideration.

Perri Klass is a regular columnist for *Knitter's* magazine. In one of her columns, she commented on knitting as a metaphor for life:

> For my children, life is like a cardigan sweater. We cast on—we follow the pattern or we improvise—we choose the best materials we can, but sometimes we learn, to our sorrow, that we have not picked the perfect yarn for the task at hand. We embark on complex multi-stranded patterns, or try to work designs in intarsia with no gaps and no puckering. We must decide, at times, whether to pause and rip back, and redo our mistakes, or whether to rush on past them and hope that time and stretch will be forgiving. (Klass 2008)

Kumihimo, braiding, and knotting

There are a variety of ways to make rope, cord, and string. All involve the interweaving of three or more strands of fibers, strips, or lengths in a diagonally overlapping pattern. A *braid* (also called a *plait*) is a complex structure or pattern formed by intertwining three or more strands of flexible material such as textile fibers, wire, or human hair. Kumihimo is a Japanese form of braid-making where cords and ribbons are created by interlacing strands on a disk that has notches. The braids can be flat, four-sided, and hollow. Historically, the kumihimo cords were used by samurai as both functional and decorative ways to lace their armor. They are currently used in Japan as ties on jackets and kimonos, as well as haori jackets and obijimes, which are used for tying on an obi (kimono sash). Kumihimo braiding has made its way into the beader's arsenal, as well as that of handcrafters.

Knots are a method of fastening or securing linear material such as rope by tying or interweaving. A knot is used to bind ropes, strings, webbing, twine, straps, or chains to themselves or to some other object. Knots have been the subject of interest for their ancient origins, their common uses, and the area of mathematics known as knot theory.

Braids are often used figuratively to represent interweaving or a combination of thoughts, such as in "He braided many different ideas into a new whole." In some river and stream systems, small streams join together and redivide in many places, and are referred to as braided. Knots invariably weaken the rope in which they are made. When knotted rope is strained to its breaking point, it almost always fails at the knot or close to it, unless it is defective or damaged elsewhere. The bending, crushing, and chafing forces that hold a knot in place also unevenly stress rope fibers and ultimately lead to a reduction in strength. Thus the expression "tie a knot and hold on" is probably not the ideal survival mechanism, as it will likely not sustain you!

Lacework

Lace is a delicate fabric made of yarn or thread in a web-like pattern. It is typically lightweight and has an open-hole pattern. It unites ornament with structure, in which the patterns of its spaces are as important as those of its solid areas. Lace creates holes (white space) by the removal of threads or cloth from a woven fabric, or by building up the fabric from a single thread. Lace can be created with needle and thread, bobbins that hold threads which are woven together and held in place with pins stuck in the pattern, cutwork where threads are removed from a woven background, crocheted, or knit. There is also *tatting*, in which lacework is made with a shuttle.

The word *lace* originates from the Latin word *laqueus*, or noose or snare, which comes from *lacere*, or to lure and to deceive. Thus lace originally meant entrapment or enticement. By the mid-sixteenth century, lace referred to a fabric made of threads. In addition to this definition, in the English language it also connotes several different meanings. It can refer to a small amount of something added as in a flavor (e.g. the soup was *laced* with basil), an intoxicant, or color. It can also mean to hurt or abuse someone (e.g. she *laced* into him when he was late). Lace can also mean to bind up or tie something or someone.

The interesting feature of lace is that it is actually both strong yet delicate. It is not easily unraveled by a broken thread, and it is both practical and frivolous. The metaphors associated with lace include both hiding and exposing at the same time. Lace can be used to veil and to cover, but as in lingerie, to reveal. Lace consists of inherent oppositions—the open–closed, light–dark contrasts of the patterns—as well as the interconnectedness and intricacy of the overall designs.

Needlecrafts

Needlecrafts entail a number of different techniques all involving needle and thread. These can include embroidery, needlepoint, cross-stitch, tapestry, and quilting. Embroidery is decorative needlework that is usually made on loosely woven cloth or canvas; it is frequently a picture or a pattern. Needlepoint and cross-stitch are essentially subtypes of embroidery. Needlepoint refers to uniformly spaced patterned embroidery on canvas and typically uses the tent stitch. Cross-stitch uses a double stitch to form an X in embroidery.

The word *embroidery* can also be used to mean to elaborate or exaggerate, in a falsifying way, for example embellishment with fancy (fictitious) details. Tapestries, which typically depict visual images in the form of a story, are sometimes thought of as needlepoint, but are actually more often made by weaving.

Tapestries use complex and rich images and typically tell the story of the times. Tapestry has been used quite literally as a metaphor for who we are as people. Cervantes, in *Don Quixote*, said it this way: "Still it seems to me that translation from one language into another, if it be not from the queens of languages, the Greek and the Latin, is like looking at Flemish tapestries on the wrong side; for though the figures are visible, they are full of threads that make them indistinct, and they do not show with the smoothness and brightness of the right side."

Another metaphor associated with tapestry is seen when comparing the front (image that we see) with the back. The front shows what people want you to see and understand; the back is full of the threads and knots that hold the meaning together. It is obviously less organized and attractive. A literary idiom of tapestry, "be part of life's rich tapestry," suggests that you must accept the parts of life that you cannot avoid.

Quilting

Quilting refers to the process of stitching through two layers of fabric, sandwiched between a filling of wool, feathers, or down, so as to create a warm, protective covering for sleep or clothing. The fabric is pieced together and sewn (historically cross-stitched) in a decorative design.

The word *quilt* comes from the Latin word *culcita*, meaning mattress. It eventually evolved from a mattress, which you lay on, to a cover that you lay under. One expression, "piecing for cover," implies making something serviceable, for everyday use. Another expression is to "run for cover," which means to run for protection or camouflage oneself. One author, Janet Berlo (2001), used quilting to cope with depression. She suggested that quilting provided her with a shelter, a comfort as if under a big quilt and surrounded by swathes of fabric. Berlo stated: "When I wasn't quilting, I wasn't alive. On most days, I felt that I literally needed those vibrant hues in order to breathe. My body craved the colors and the kinetic act of cutting and piecing, cutting and piecing."

Recycling textiles

Textile recycling is a way of re-using and reprocessing textiles, including clothing, fibrous material, and clothing scraps. Textiles in municipal solid waste are found mainly in discarded clothing, although other sources include furniture, carpets, tires, footwear, and nondurable goods such as sheets and towels. To up-cycle is to transform used everyday materials, including trash, into something personal, expressive, and attractive. Fiber artists who up-cycle focus on both the surface texture created and the message conveyed. Materials can be as simple as dental floss and Band-Aids, to dog hair, sausage casings, tea bags, plastic packaging, and even left-over medicine bottles. Inexpensive materials can also be found in kitchens, backyards, pharmacies, beauty shops, hardware stores, liquor stores, and even groceries. This is true for dyeing fabric as well: you can look to your kitchen for red wine, beet juice, rusty washers, tomato paste, coffee, and cocoa.

Several artists have commented on repurposing textiles created by unknown female artists. Lace, needlepoint, and clothing are typically not labeled and hence the artist is frequently anonymous. Women re-using these materials can be very validating for the artist. Other artists (e.g. Nancy Rakoczy) have commented on feeling a need to use materials that are cast aside and unimportant, as a way of acknowledging women. Rakoczy uses discarded plastic in her work (see www.nancyrakoczy.com).

Berlo (2001) also talks about women's unfinished art: "Old quilt squares, those small fragments of the past, are oddly moving. They are remnants of other women's hopes and aspirations, glimpses of the colors and patterns that inspired gluttony and hope, a link with our female ancestors."

Detrixhe (2005) refers to the necessity of mending, altering, and remaking things. When materials were scarce, expensive, and difficult to obtain, re-using fabric was common and everything, including sheets, was fair game. Clothing is now so inexpensive that if a garment tears, it can be discarded. The expression "wear and tear" refers to our history of making do.

Spinning

Hand-spinning is the art of twisting fiber into a continuous thread by hand, using a drop spindle, or with a spinning wheel. Any type of fiber (animal, vegetable, synthetic) can be used. Yarns are spun with a Z-twist (usually for single ply) or an S-twist (typically for plied yarn); the twist depends on the direction of spinning. The tightness of the twist is measured in twists per inch (TPI). The fiber can be spun thick or thin, plyed or unplyed, and dyed or undyed. Handspun yarn can also be combined with commercially made yarns. Handspun yarn can be used for any textile handcrafts, such as knitting, crocheting, weaving, basket coiling, and felting. Hand-spinning is thought to have originated as long as 20,000 years ago, by simply taking animal hair or plant fiber and rolling it on one's thigh by hand. Eventually a spindle whorl was created to steady the speed and promote the fiber's rotation. The first spinning wheels were invented in the mid-1700s, and produced a consistent yarn much more quickly. These eventually became mechanized with a powered waterwheel, and then electricity. Small spinning wheels are still available and used widely today; they can be operated by foot pedals, hand, or electric motors.

The origin of the word *wheel* comes from Chakra, where the Sanskrit *cakra* means wheel or circle; it is sometimes referred to as the "wheel of life." Today the term *Chakra* refers to energy that is channeled by most "new-age" healers, holistic medical practitioners, and alternative therapies such as reflexology, reiki, and yoga.

Some expressions used with spinning include "put a spin on something" to twist a story to one's own advantage, or to interpret an event to make it favorable or beneficial to oneself or one's cause. The expression "spin one's wheels" refers to wasting time, being very unproductive, as if going in circles. The expression "to spin a yarn" is widely used to describe telling a story, but a story that is very creative and especially a long-drawn-out or totally fanciful one. This expression has a double meaning, for both "spun fiber" and "a tale."

In medieval times, poor families relied on homespun yarn to make their own cloth and clothes. Girls and unmarried women would keep busy by spinning; hence "spinster" became synonymous with the term for an unmarried woman. Subsequent improvements with spinning wheels and then mechanical methods made hand-spinning increasingly uneconomic, but as late as the twentieth century hand-spinning remained widespread in poor countries. Interestingly, in conscious rejection of international industrialization, Gandhi was a notable spinner.

Weaving

Weaving is a process of making cloth by interlacing fibers on a loom. Looms intertwine both across (weft) and lengthwise (warp). Humans have created a host of looms, from simple back-strap looms made from tree branches, to more complex, computer-operated contraptions. Sometimes the upper crossbeams on a loom are referred to as the "beam of heaven," while the bottom represents the earth, and the living world is symbolized in the woven creation. Significance is attributed to birds weaving their nests, and spiders drawing threads from themselves to create a web.

Weaving is typically referred to in literature as part of a divine process. The mystery of life creation is encapsulated in the weaving metaphor: the child is a blending of both parents' bodily substances, woven together in the mother's womb. In North Africa, weavers recite similar blessings when they cut the last threads of a completed cloth as when cutting the umbilical cord of a newborn (ARAS 2010). Weaving has been used as a metaphor for society, as well as for death (used in shrouds and coffin linings). Derivatives of the word *faber* include forge and fabricate; these both mean to make, but also to make something with the intent to deceive.

As a metaphor, to weave is to combine (elements) into a complex whole. Weaving also refers to contriving something, as in a tale. Weaving can be used as an analog for social relationships, typically referring to procreation and regeneration, as well as the lifecycle of birth, maturation, death, and decay. Weaving provides metaphors to illustrate the mental process required to manage fragments, fog, and confusion. Deborah Howard (2006) uses quilting and weaving as metaphors for healing our communities. She calls on the Jewish concept of *tikkun olam*, healing and repairing the world, and refers to the "tattered quilt of humanity," and the "individual torn, twisted and distorted woven cloths that make up this quilt." Although Howard's primary goal is to discuss racism and how to take responsibility and action to repair it, her textile metaphors are easily applied to the individual, the person, like many of us, who is often left wounded just by the act of living life. She states that for the healing process to occur, one must first apply an entirely new fabric to the backing of the quilt. On an individual level, this could refer to our need for a major overhaul, major change. Then, the batting must be re-balanced and all dirt, paint, discoloration, and distortion removed. Individual torn pieces must be re-woven, and new thread must be used for repairs. This refers to the psychological healing of wounds. Finally, new threads must be used to reconnect the entire quilt, the backing, batting, and top fabric. This continues to repair the wounds and divisions, and creates a more natural, connected state.

Women's use of textiles for psychological reasons

Historically, textile-making was central to the role of women and happened largely in the home or a communal area. However, there is also evidence that women expanded their textile-making in order to soften, beautify, and adorn their environments and bodies. In any case, textile-making has typically been associated with utility and functionality.

With the advent of the Industrial Revolution in the mid-1800s, textile-making moved increasingly out of the home and community domains and into factories. Machinery brought about automation and mechanization, which brought about faster production and a more uniform product. Slowly over the following decades, individual textile-making declined. This was probably further exacerbated as women questioned and rejected stereotypic feminine constructs that they perceived had to do with domesticity and oppression (Turney 2009). Fiber arts were seen as uncreative, old-fashioned and ugly. They were looked on as craft, not art, and marginalized to the mundane and mediocre. There is still prejudice against handcrafters today; many refer to crafts as all that is "bad" in art and design (Turney 2009).

Despite the denigration of textile-making by early feminists, there has been a resurgence of interest since the early part of the twenty-first century. It has been labeled everything from the "craft revolution" to the "new generation of do-it-yourselfers." Many have commented on reasons for this change. It is in part due to the rejection of the dominant consumption culture (Joy 2009). It may also be due to the need for connections; handcrafters seek a common community, a collective identity to associate with that is often missing in today's urbanization (MacDonald 1988; Myzelev 2009). Celebrities have also been a factor, serving as role models and inspiration to popularize knitting, for example Julia Roberts, Cameron Diaz, and even Russell Crowe. The internet also has played a role, allowing handcrafters to share their interests, learn from one another, buy materials, and socialize both locally and internationally (e.g. MacDonald 1988). Availability of specialized products that were once unobtainable (e.g. exotic fibers) and the commercialization of equipment to make home textiles easier to use and buy (e.g. wet felting machines) have also increased accessibility. Some authors think that the image of handcrafters has changed dramatically, from stodgy old women to hip, young, fashionable women. Some writers have gone so far as to repackage textile handcraft-making with sexuality. In these scenarios, knitting is seen as decadent, self-indulgent, and subversive (Myzelev 2009). *Stitch-'n'-bitch Nation* is an example of how fun, trendy youth, in Gen X and younger, can create knit and crochet items that have relevance to the twenty-first century (e.g. iPod cases).

As the pendulum has swung back, textile handcrafters are more accepted as true artists, elevated beyond the derogatory "crafts-person" (Joy 2009). Today, the textile arts are appreciated as practices that are loosely based on the use of fiber-related materials and textile techniques and concepts (Valoma, personal communication, November 2010).

Few investigators have explored the psychological value of textile-making for women. The majority of research has involved qualitative studies with very small, localized, homogeneous samples (Johnson and Wilson 2005; Nelson, LaBat, and Williams 2002, 2005; Reynolds 1999, 2000, 2002; Schofield-Tomschin and Littrell 2001). The samples studied have typically been convenience samples (not random), and quite often the investigator, a fiber artist herself, has interviewed her friends and colleagues (e.g. Johnson and Wilson 2005; Riley 2008). Most of the published research on textile-making has not come from psychology, but the occupational therapy field, bringing a completely different framework and focus. Research on textile-making has explored reasons why women engage in the activity. Johnson and Wilson (2005) determined that textile handcraft-making gave women a sense of their place in the world, provided both tangible and intangible benefits, and connected them to their personal histories. Riley (2008) suggested textile-making brought women an enhanced sense of self and a collective identity; some women reported textile-making was an inner spiritual or psychological experience.

In the United Kingdom, Frances Reynolds has explored the role of the textile arts in women with unresolved grief (Reynolds 1999), depression (Reynolds 2000), and chronic illnesses including chronic fatigue syndrome/myalgic encephalopathy (CFS/ME) (Reynolds, Vivat, and Prior 2008), cancer (Reynolds, Lim, and Prior 2008), and mixed chronic illnesses and long-term health problems (e.g. Reynolds 2002, 2004a, 2004b). Through Reynolds' qualitative interviews, she has suggested that the textile arts allow women to cope with grief, depression, and a wide range of physical impairments to express, restore, and manage their illnesses, while simultaneously experiencing joy, confidence, and social connectivity.

I recently completed the first large-scale (n = 891) quantitative and qualitative research study with a multinational sample of textile-handcrafters (Collier 2011). I inquired about the pattern of women's textile-making, the meaning of textiles in their lives, the reasons why they made textiles, and how they used (or did not use) textiles to cope with difficult mood states.

I found that the pattern of textile-making was interesting. The more techniques that women used, the more techniques they mastered. Thus, they mastered quite a variety of fiber mediums (Collier 2011). Specifically, most women reported using at least a dozen textile techniques, and had mastery over half of these techniques. Interestingly, during the previous three years, women used only a few of these techniques. Thus, women had been using only about 25 percent of their skills at any given time during the previous three years. If you see a woman who sews, she probably has moderate to high skills in at least ten other fiber techniques (e.g. knitting, crochet, felting, spinning, lace-making, beading). As a textile art therapist, this is useful information to explore!

I found that knitting was the most commonly used textile technique in women today. This is not surprising because the popularity of knitting has increased over the past few decades (Turney 2009). In addition to knitting, sewing, weaving, quilting, and spinning were all common activities that participants had tried, felt mastery over, and had used during the past several years. Interestingly, crocheting, embroidery, and cross-stitch were techniques that participants had tried and felt mastery over, but rarely used. Although crocheting has made somewhat of a comeback in the past decade, these three crafts may still be considered too "old fashioned." Textile design and multi-media techniques all were used, but not self-rated as skillful.

Why did most women make handcrafts? Because they enjoyed it! In fact, making handcrafts for income was the least likely reason that women reported for creating with fibers. Other reasons for making handcrafts included: loving the aesthetics of textiles; the grounding quality of textile-making; psychological fulfillment; the desire to "do for others"; social fulfillment; having tangible outcomes in their lives; coping with illness/disability; cognitive coping; and not wanting "idle hands."

It is ironic that despite being labeled a "craft" and "women's work," textile-making provided an important source of cognitive coping, or intellectual stimulation, for many women. Geda (2009) at the Mayo Clinic in Minnesota suggested that people who engaged in cognitively challenging activities, such as computers or crafting (specifically knitting and quilt-making), in middle age or later life, had a decreased risk of mild cognitive impairment that protected against memory loss. Textile handcraft guild participation was also associated with better emotional and cognitive adjustment in older women (Schofield-Tomschin and Littrell 2001).

The majority of handcrafters preferred to give away or keep their products, rather than sell them. Despite their mastery at using textiles, most of the women in the study did not consider themselves to be professionals.

I also found that textile-making was an effective way to cope with difficult mood states. Women who reported using textiles to cope (textile-copers) were compared with women who did not (non-textile-copers). Slightly fewer than half of the respondents (47.1%) indicated that they used textile-making techniques to change terrible moods. Textile-copers were far more engaged and effective at changing their mood states than the textile non-copers, who used other leisure activities or hobbies to cope (e.g. exercising, reading, spending time in nature, venting, religious activities, resting). More than half of these women already knew how to apply textile-making to cope with their lives; the other half may fare even better by using their skills.

The most common techniques used by textile-copers when upset were: knitting or crocheting (37.1%); weaving (22.4%); spinning (16.7%); engaging in an activity related to textile-making (13.3%) (e.g. "plan a project," "go shopping for yarn," "go through and sort my supplies"); and sewing or quilting (7.5%). The non-textile-copers (52.9%) reported using the following leisure activities when faced with a difficult mood: exercising (especially walking) (32.2%); reading (8.7%); spending time in nature (7.9%); venting (7.1%); practicing religious activities (7.1%); resting (7.1%); relaxing (3.0%); and talking to friends (3.0%).

In a recent art therapy study, Dalebroux, Goldstein, and Winner (2008) reported that the greatest mood valence change in participants occurred after creating a drawing that depicted a positive emotion, compared with venting or a neutral control. This is contrary to the more typical approach in art therapy: to encourage clients to express negative feelings through their art-making.

Dalebroux *et al.* (2008) suggested that art-making can be most beneficial by orienting people away from distressed feelings and towards more positive feelings to create short-term mood repair. Approximately half of these textile handcrafters discovered this for themselves: the aesthetics and grounding quality of textile-making helps them to cope with negative moods. By focusing on creating something beautiful with their art, textile-copers experienced more success and rejuvenation than non-textile-copers.

Several investigators have discussed the concept of skill and "flow" in artistic and athletic endeavors (e.g. Nakamura and Csikszentmihalyi 2005; Rheinberg 2008). Flow is a mental state in which a person is fully engaged in an activity, has mastery yet feels challenged by the activity, becomes completely absorbed, feels an energized focus, and finds the activity to be intrinsically rewarding (Csikszentmihalyi 1990). My results are consistent with the flow theory. The textile-copers, who reported more success and rejuvenation with mood change, were also significantly more skilled and engaged in their handcraft-making than non-textile-copers. Skill and flow, combined with the desire to create an aesthetic and to feel grounded, are all motivations that can be accessed by textile handcrafters when faced with turbulent life events and illnesses.

One could question whether any activity, hobby, or leisure activity that involves flow would have similar results. This is very likely true. Griffiths (2008) reported that a variety of creative activities, especially if they facilitated engagement and flow, balanced skill with challenge, and gave the client control over choosing the activity, could be used as therapeutic mediums. Iwasaki, Mactavish, and Mackay (2005) found that leisure activities provided a positive diversion from stress and a context for rejuvenation and renewal across a variety of samples and settings.

Textile handcrafts may very well be an important entry point for the art therapist working with women. In my experience, most women do not consider themselves to be artists when creating textiles. Instead they typically see their work as practical, useful, possibly attractive, maybe a little bit artistic, but certainly not "professional." Yet the level of textile handcraft creativity and skill that I often see in women is frequently exquisite, with mastery that is exceptional. In both my practice as a clinical psychologist and my work as a fiber artist, I have found that a large number of these women already use their textile mediums for psychological reasons. They use textile-making to calm down, to feel centered, to have control over a small part of their lives, to have social opportunities, and, for some, just to immerse themselves in the sheer pleasure of the creative process. When a skilled clinician then suggests how to apply textile-making for even more pointed, specific, personal growth, expression, and communication, women gladly add a new, often metaphoric, dimension to their handcraft-making. Thus, for many women, textile-making is already implicitly valued and can be deepened and enhanced by adding a therapeutic perspective. Over and over again, I have found textile handcrafts to be a safe, familiar way to engage women in art-making for psychological reasons.

Chapter 3

She's Come Unraveled

MENTAL WELL-BEING IN
GIRLS AND WOMEN

What do we mean by abnormal?

Abnormal behavior is typically thought of as the opposite of mental well-being. It has been called emotional disturbance, insanity, nervous breakdown, madness, and even craziness. There are multiple ways to define psychological disturbance, and each relies on its own dogma, context, and jargon. From a layman's perspective, people who are *different* are seen as strange or even crazy. The field of abnormal psychology defines mental disorders as an "impairment in some important aspect of life (e.g. work, relationships, thinking, or personal distress), as well as culturally inappropriate behavior" (Durand and Barlow 2009). From a cross-cultural perspective, the definition of normal versus abnormal must consider how behavior varies across societies and cultures. Feminist perspectives believe that mental health diagnoses and care misrepresent, unequally treat, and unjustifiably pathologize women. In most medical contexts, physicians, especially psychiatrists, measure people with consistent diagnostic standards, often regardless of cultural diversity or context. One characteristic that almost every definition of mental well-being shares is an assumption about what the ideal life should be like. This, in turn, carries judgments about how to define proper and improper behavior.

There is also considerable debate even within the mental health field about how to describe psychopathology. Current internationally recognized clinical diagnostic schemes rely more on categorical systems to define *mental disorder* and provide standardized criteria for each diagnosis. The two most widely established systems are: 1) ICD-10, Chapter V, "Mental and Behavioural Disorders," part of the *International Classification of Diseases* produced by the World Health Organization (WHO 1992); and 2) the *Diagnostic and Statistical Manual of Mental Disorders* (DSM), produced by the American Psychiatric Association (2001). Although historically there have been significant differences between these two systems, more recently there has been convergence so that the codes are broadly comparable. In addition to DSM and the WHO classification system, there are also specific classification schemes for use in non-Western cultures (see, for example, the *Chinese Classification of Mental Disorders*), as well as manuals for alternative theoretical persuasions, for example the *Psychodynamic Diagnostic Manual.* These are not widely used in the USA and Europe.

Regardless of the classification system used, we do know that mental illness and behavioral problems are intricately tied to a person's social, environmental, and physical reality. The roots of poor mental health in women can be coupled with hunger (more than 60% are starving), work (women are typically poorly paid for labor-intensive work), and domestic violence (surveys report it as high as 60%). We know that there are established risk factors that are genetic, biological (e.g. poor prenatal care, drug and/or alcohol abuse by mother, prematurity, anoxia, low birth weight), and environmental (e.g. poor responsivity or lack of sensitivity by caretaker, low level of language or poverty). Likewise, psychological pathways include coercive parenting, physical and sexual abuse, and poor parental attachment.

Mental illness in girls

Every child that lives will have emotional and behavioral problems; most of these, however, are transient. There is no getting around it: there is stress in development and stress in the adaptation to family and societal expectations. There will always be problems in every family, in every society. The important point is that 80 percent of all children and adolescents will manage the stress of growth, development, and life effectively (Schroeder and Gordon 2002). Unfortunately, the remaining 20 percent suffer so severely that it often interferes with their daily functioning. This, in turn, leads to emotional and behavioral complications, which can set the stage for serious impairment in crucial life domains, such as academic achievement, interpersonal competencies, and independent living skills. Research suggests that the majority of mental disturbances in adults have their origins in childhood and adolescence.

Within the 20 percent of adolescents that have emotional disturbance, girls are seven times more likely than boys to be depressed, and twice as likely to attempt suicide (American Psychological Association 2007). They are three times more likely than boys to have a negative body image (often reflected in eating disorders such as anorexia and bulimia), and one in five girls in the USA between the ages of 12 and 17 drink alcohol and smoke cigarettes (American Psychological Association 2007).

Research points to several possible reasons for this gender imbalance. The biological and hormonal changes that occur during puberty in girls are likely to contribute to the sharp increase in rates of depression in adolescence. Aggravating this difference even more, puberty appears to occur earlier than in the past: the average age of either breasts or pubic hair showing up in Caucasians is now 9.7 years (instead of 11), and 8.1 years for African-Americans (instead of 10) (Aksglaede *et al.* 2009; Herman-Giddens *et al.* 1997). Regrettably, girls who develop puberty at a younger age also date earlier, have sex sooner, are subjected to more psychological stress earlier, have more behavioral problems (depression, aggression, social withdrawal, sleep problems, obsessive behavior), and are more likely to drink alcohol and smoke cigarettes (Zuckerman 2009). They also tend to have lower self-esteem, poorer coping skills, miss more days of school, and are more likely to attempt suicide.

Another reason for the gender difference in psychopathology is that girls may undergo more socio-economic hardships, such as poverty, poor education, childhood sexual abuse, and other traumas, than boys. One study reported that more than 70 percent of depressed girls experienced a difficult or stressful life event prior to experiencing a depressive episode, as compared with only 14 percent of boys (Zuckerman 2009). Research has also demonstrated that girls are more likely than boys to continue feeling bad after experiencing stressful or difficult situations or events, setting the stage for depression (Zuckerman 2009). Girls also tend to doubt themselves more, doubt their problem-solving abilities more, and view their problems as more unsolvable, than boys (Zuckerman 2009).

Recent research by the American Psychological Association Task Force suggested that the "sexualization" of girls is also contributing to their increased psychopathology (Zurbriggen *et al.* 2007). Almost every form of media and marketing today focuses on the sexualization of females, particularly young women (Zurbriggen *et al.* 2007). These messages are invariably channeled down into girls' interpersonal relationships. The American Psychological Association report linked the sexualization and objectification of girls directly to the mental health problems, especially eating disorders, low self-esteem, and depression and depressed mood. Girls who have little confidence in their own body have increased shame and anxiety. The opposite is also true; girls who perceive themselves as physically attractive have better self-esteem.

Mental illness in women

The gender differences in mental illness found for girls appear to continue into womanhood, both nationally and internationally (WHO 2011a). For example, women have higher rates of depressive disorders, anxiety disorders, post-traumatic stress disorder, somatization and dissociative disorders, eating disorders, and personality disorders, than men (WHO 2011a). Depressive disorders account for close to 41.9 percent of the disability from neuropsychiatric disorders among women compared with 29.3 percent among men. We also know that physicians are more likely to diagnose depression in women compared with men, even when they present with identical symptoms. Having a female gender actually significantly increases the likelihood that physicians will prescribe mood-altering psychotropic drugs. Gender differences also exist in the pattern of help-seeking for psychological disorder: women are more likely to seek help from and disclose their mental health problems to a primary care physician. Alternately, men are more likely to seek mental health specialist care and utilize inpatient care (WHO 2011a). Gender stereotypes also probably influence the perception that women have greater emotional problems (i.e. because they appear more affectively labile). This can then present obstacles to the accurate identification and treatment of psychological disorders.

Even when women do have similar psychiatric prevalence rates to men, there are still notable differences in the treatment course. For example, women with psychotic and bipolar disorders, which have similar prevalence rates in women and men, have a later onset of the disease and a different pattern of comorbidity and cycling than men do (Surgeon General's Workshop on Women's Mental Health 2005; WHO 2011a).

As with girls, there are a variety of factors that contribute to these gender differences. First there are the obvious *biological differences* between men and women. Research has clearly demonstrated that female hormones, such as estrogen and progesterone, influence both brain function and stress response. Over the course of a lifetime, it is known that menstruation, pregnancy, postpartum, peri-menopause, and menopause all directly increase the occurrence and intensity of depressive and anxiety symptoms (American Psychiatric Association 2009). Research has also accumulated suggesting that female-specific disorders have explicit pathogenic mechanisms which are in turn associated with detrimental outcomes (Wittchen 2010).

Violence, both at a national level and interpersonal level, plays an important role in gender-related mental health differences. Approximately 80 percent of the 50 million people affected by violent national and international conflicts, civil wars, disasters, and displacement are women and children (WHO 2011a). The lifetime prevalence rates of violence against women ranges anywhere from

16 percent to 50 percent, and at least one in five women suffers from rape or attempted rape in their lifetimes (WHO 2011b). The prevalence is probably much higher than this: women are still reluctant to disclose a history of violent victimization even when physicians directly ask about it. The complexity of violence-related health outcomes has been found to increase when victimization goes undetected. The end result is higher and more costly rates of utilization of the health and mental health care system.

Stress comes in many forms, but also accounts for the poor mental health status of women. Internationally, women take on multiple roles and experience gender discrimination, poverty, hunger, malnutrition, overwork, domestic violence, and sexual abuse more frequently than men. There is a direct and significant relationship between the frequency and the severity of these socio-economic stressors, and the frequency and the severity of mental health problems in women (WHO 2011a). Furthermore, the severe stress that these types of life events lead to is also known to cause further loss, inferiority, humiliation, and entrapment which are each, in turn, predictive of depression.

Controversies about acknowledging gender difference in mental health

Despite the documented differences between males and females (e.g. in the help seeking, assessment, diagnosis, treatment, and course of mental illness in women), acknowledging gender differences in mental illness is still weighted with controversy. There is an inherent conflict between taking an interdisciplinary, psychosocial view of mental well-being compared with relying on diagnostic classification systems such as DSM and ICD-10. Psychosocial models consider the range of lifestyle issues and social forces that impact women. In contrast, classification manuals rely more and more on neurobiological models of mental illness. There has been a great deal of discussion about adding several new diagnoses in the upcoming DSM-V. Quite a few investigators support identifying several new mental illness diagnoses for women because they think identification will lead to better mental health care and treatment. Suggested diagnoses include peri- and post-natal depression, post-traumatic stress disorder (PTSD) associated with fertility treatment and childbirth, disorders of parent-to-infant attachment, peri-natal bereavement, peri-menopausal depression, and premenstrual dysphoric disorder (PMDD).

Alternately, other professionals view these gender-specific disorders as stigmatizing to women (Wittchen 2010). Take for example PMDD, which is severe mood symptoms associated with menstruation. The actual incidence of PMDD is probably only 1.3 percent in the population (Gehlert *et al.* 2009). In contrast, an estimated 20–40 percent of all women experience mild to moderate menstrual symptoms (e.g. headaches, crankiness, irritability) before and during menarche (Gehlert *et al.* 2009). By providing gender-specific diagnoses, some investigators believe we are pathologizing *normal* female processes. This, in turn, opens women up to societal discrimination. Those in support of these diagnoses argue that gender-specific diagnoses validate the experiences of the women that do have PMDD, thereby increasing the odds for health insurance coverage and providing impetus for additional research and therapy.

An alternative model to mental illness

While identifying severe mental health concerns holds an appropriate place in clinical practice, there are other ways to conceptualize concerns and issues that women experience that are *less pathologizing*. One approach that I often use is that of *passages in a woman's life*, where life is a series of events on a long journey.

Over a century ago, Arnold Van Gennep (1960) presented a model of phases in a man's life, where he described men's growth as moving through separation to transition and then on to assimilation. Transitioning from childhood to adulthood might be marked in a Native American culture by hunting in solo. At each phase, a man separates from his status, goes through some type of ritual transition that possibly includes dangers, and then is incorporated back into his original society with a new status.

Other more recent authors (e.g. Bridges 2004) have described these "transitions" as composed of endings, neutral zones, and new beginnings. Transitions and turmoil are thus seen as a natural part of one's life journey.

Of course, many Westernized women living in the third wave of feminism truly do have the opportunity to go through life passages as described above. However, because of the necessary biological changes women go through (menarche, childbirth, etc.), as well as cross-cultural differences, it is critical to question the applicability of Gennep's and Bridges' model to all females. For starters, women typically hold a lower status in most cultures and are often not even given the opportunity to physically separate. In countries where marriages are arranged, women typically move directly from their family of origin to their husband's family home. When role transitions do occur, they are frequently more symbolic than spatial. Childbirth marks the transition of a young woman to motherhood; spatial separation just doesn't make sense!

Because of these gender differences, Lincoln (1991) termed the changes women go through as a process of *enclosure, magnification* (or *metamorphosis*), and *emergence*. Some have even likened women's passages to the metamorphosis of a butterfly, going from caterpillar to cocoon and then on to butterfly. Brenner (2007) astutely described these changes as "becoming more developed forms of their original selves" (p.13). Thus, women transition to new roles, while keeping their previous roles: daughters (i.e. maidens) to wives and on to mothers and on to spiritual warriors and then on to crones, instead of physically separating from the group, going through difficult challenges, and then re-joining the group with new perspectives, as men are more likely to do.

Another reason that the model does not apply as directly to females is that women simply do not have the same emotional, and perhaps physical, need to separate from others during times of changes and turmoil. Instead, women are much more likely to affiliate with each other. Taylor and her colleagues have explored this affiliative need in women, especially when under stress, and labeled it as a need to "tend and befriend" (Taylor *et al.* 2000). They define "tend and befriend" as the female's underlying biological need to protect her offspring (tend) and then seek out the social group for mutual defense (befriend). Their theory speculates that it would have been evolutionarily superior for females to develop a calm response to stressors instead of a "fight or flight" response. If a mother were to either fight or flee during times of danger, her offspring's chance for survival would decrease dramatically, especially if she is pregnant, smaller in stature, or compromised by caring for multiple children. Thus, the more typical female response to stress is to engage in relationships with friends and to care-take. Again, these activities are very likely biologically adaptive to protect the women and their offspring, as well as to further reduce distress.

Taylor and colleagues have found that there are indeed biobehavioral mechanisms that underlie this female behavior pattern, such as oxytocin and endogenous opioid peptides. Her recent research suggested that oxytocin may actually serve as a *social thermostat* that is responsive to the adequacy of social resources. Oxytocin would prompt affiliative behavior when social support fell below an adequate level, and then reduce biological and psychological stress response once positive social contacts were established (Taylor and Gonzaga 2007).

Passages in a woman's life

Reinterpreting the male "journey," Brenner conceptualizes the concept of "passages" in girls' and women's lives. She describes three types of passages: that of the body, that of the self, and that of loss.

According to Brenner, *passages of the body* correspond to the very real physiological changes women experience as they develop and mature. Although classically these have been referred to as the "three blood mysteries," Brenner conceives of a wider range of physical transitions including sexual initiation, conceiving and birthing, miscarriage and abortion, as well as healing from major illness and/or injury. *Passages of the self* account for the wide range of personal and interpersonal milestones that women go through, small or large. These can include coming of age, coming into

~

one's own, forging a significant life relationship, finding and re-establishing relationships, celebrating and honoring events, and acknowledging accomplishments and personal growth. *Passages of loss* may be particularly difficult for us as women, as the social connections we hold are frequently the most sacred. These passages can include the obvious (i.e. death), as well as the ending, changing, or loss of any important relationship (person, parent, child, spouse, close friend). The loss we experience will invariably be accompanied by a variety of emotions, including grief, anger, and anxiety.

For the purposes of this book, I conceptualize emotional turmoil and issues that women go through in the context of passages. How well one navigates through these passages can occur on a *continuum*, going from exceptional mastery, to normal, to problematic, to severely problematic. The ability to move through these passages with mastery and well-being will undoubtedly be influenced by one's social, environmental, and physical reality. This in no way invalidates the reality of mental illness, which in this framework would be described as severely problematic navigation. Nor does it invalidate the reality of how biological, psychological, social, and environmental conditions play a role in mental illness. Instead, it allows us to think of women holistically and contextually. Resiliency and predisposition factors will contribute to how well any of us can navigate the passages in our lives.

Please note that when a client does have severe, challenging concerns with life passage(s), or appears to have severe emotional disturbance, it is important for the therapist to encourage her to seek mental health consultation for diagnostic services and recommendations. The exploration of these passages with textiles is optimally meant for women with normal to problematic difficulties.

Chapter 4

Uncovering the Truth

ASSESSING WHERE TO START

Mental health assessment

There are many arenas within the mental health profession that do not emphasize and/or value diagnostic nomenclature. Many of the issues surrounding the appropriateness of using psychological labels were introduced in Chapter 3. As a clinical psychologist, I believe that it is still important for a provider to know where on the continuum between mental *health* and mental *illness* a client falls. If a 38-year-old female comes to me and appears sad and dysphoric, I need to be able to determine whether this is a stress-related affective response, a simple or complicated bereavement reaction, a reflection of an overall chronic dysthymic disorder, or a major depressive episode. Furthermore, as a clinician, I should have the prerequisite skills to identify and evaluate whether the client has suicidal ideation and/or is psychotic. In these more extreme situations, a referral to a different type of mental health provider may be warranted, for example psychiatrist or clinical psychologist, especially if you are concerned about suicidality and psychosis. To neglect to identify the severity of a person's psychological state and embark on textile psychotherapy without this prior knowledge could exacerbate the client's problems.

There are two screening measures I would like to recommend. The first is the simplest to administer and is called the Patient Health Questionnaire (PHQ). In the mid-1990s, Kroenke and colleagues at Columbia University developed the first generation of the PHQ, called the Primary Care Evaluation of Mental

Disorders (PRIME-MD) (Kroenke *et al.* 2010). The PRIME-MD contained 12 modules for the evaluation of mental health disorders frequently seen in the primary care setting. It was developed as a tool for medical professionals to quickly assess mental health concerns. After over a decade of research, the PHQ has proven to be valid and reliable. The newest version is shorter and can be self-administered, provider administered, or even nurse technician administered. The PHQ is particularly useful for identifying symptoms associated with depression, anxiety, alcohol abuse, eating disorders, and somatoform disorders. Various versions of the questionnaire are available on-line for no charge (see, for example, http://www.phqscreeners.com/overview.aspx). Not only is it easy to administer, but it has shown excellent accuracy, sensitivity, and specificity agreement with independent mental health professionals. Patients with PHQ diagnoses have typically indicated greater functional impairment, and use significantly more disability days and health care when compared with patients without PHQ diagnoses. The average time required to administer the PHQ is less than three minutes and it can be administered by anyone with a medical or mental health training background.

The second mental health assessment measure I would like to recommend is the Composite International Diagnosis Interview for Women (CIDI-V), developed by the World Health Organization (WHO) (Martini *et al.* 2009). The measure provides a systematic and comprehensive approach to female-specific issues in mental disorders and psychopathological research (Martini *et al.* 2009). It allows for a reliable examination of a wide range of mental disorders with embedded modular additions of women-specific conditions and factors (menstruation, pregnancy, postpartum, or menopause). The CIDI-V was originally developed for epidemiological studies. Currently, it has been widely used in clinical practice to study prevalence and incidence, maintenance, comorbidity patterns, and temporal relationships with the female reproductive cycle (Wittchen 2010). The CIDI-V also covers concerns not recognized elsewhere, such as the impact of adverse pregnancy outcomes (e.g. stillbirth) and the consequences of abdominal operations.

Textile background

Unlike other visual art fields, most women with experience in fiber arts have significant skills in a number of techniques. As I mentioned, my research suggested that women have, on average, familiarity with at least 11 different textile techniques, and mastery with approximately five of these. Given the breadth of background that may already exist, the provider may want to explicitly evaluate this training in order to decide which mediums to start with the client.

The Appendix provides my textile survey that can be used to screen experience and knowledge with various textile mediums (Collier 2011). Women are first asked to indicate which techniques they have ever tried from a list of 18 techniques: spinning fibers; dyeing fibers; knitting; crocheting; weaving; quilting; sewing; textile surface design; felting; braiding, macramé, or kumihimo; embroidery; cross-stitch; needlepoint; beading; basketry; paper-making; lace-making; and rug hooking. Women can also name additional handcrafts that they have made. By far the most common techniques that women have tried, currently use, and have mastery with are: knitting; sewing; crocheting; weaving; embroidery; cross-stitch; quilting; spinning fibers; felting; dyeing fibers; beading; and textile surface design. In contrast, it is much less common for women to use braiding, macramé, or kumihimo; needlepoint; rug hooking; basketry; paper-making; and lace-making. Women are also asked what types of objects they typically make, and whether these objects are functional or non-functional.

For each technique, the client will then rate her skill level on a five-point scale (1 = no skills and 5 = excellent), as well as the frequency with which she has used the technique to make something in the past three years (1 = never and 5 = very often). This will give the provider a sense about mediums the client is most comfortable using. You will probably find that some techniques are known to the client, but rarely used. For example, women frequently know how to needlepoint and embroider, but rarely do so. With the popularity of knitting and crocheting, a large number of women will have familiarity with these handcrafts.

Third, it is important to consider the variety of reasons why women make textile handcrafts. Asking women about these reasons can provide insight into their motivation as well as assist the clinician in understanding ways to engage the client in the future. Based on factor analysis and content coding of open-ended responses for almost 900 women, I have grouped these reasons according to the following categories:

- Aesthetic need
- Feeling grounded
- Psychological
  ◦ Brings out positive feelings
  ◦ Reduces negative feelings
  ◦ Distraction
  ◦ Reframes situation(s)
  ◦ Metaphorical
- Likes to do for others
- Social satisfaction
- Financial
- Cognitive
- Idle hands
- Physical
- Historical marker

(See Q7 in the Appendix for more on these reasons.)

Some women very conscientiously use textile-making to cope with and change difficult mood states. My research has indicated that the most common fiber art techniques used by textile-copers when upset are: knitting or crocheting (37.1%); weaving (22.4%); spinning (16.7%); getting ready to make textiles (13.3%) (such as "planning a project," "shopping for yarn," "examining and sorting my supplies"); and sewing or quilting (7.5%) (Collier 2011). In women who make textiles, the mood-enhancing effects of textile-coping was far more successful than for other types of coping. Said another way, women who knit, weave, spin, sew, and quilt, when upset, reported greater success at changing their mood states, feeling rejuvenated, and feeling engaged by the activities, than women who relied on other non-textile coping and leisure activities (e.g. going for a walk, talking to friends, reading a book). It is important to ask women specifically to indicate whether they use textiles to cope with difficult moods. If they do not, there is reason to believe doing so would be helpful. Based on my research, I have also incorporated the concepts of how rejuvenating these textile techniques are.

A small but significant and extremely passionate subset of women in the textile survey were adamant that they never created textiles when upset. They firmly believed that the making of textiles should only be done when positive energy and thoughts could be transferred to the object being made. If they were making a garment that they wanted to infuse with hope and love and spirituality, they thought coming to the handcraft-making in a negative mood would sabotage their work. Some women gave prayer shawls as an example. Although these have been made for centuries, in 1998 Janet Bristow and Victoria Galo, graduates of the 1997 Women's Leadership Institute at the Hartford Seminary in Hartford, Connecticut, started a Prayer Shawl Ministry. They combined their love of knitting and crocheting with spiritual practice and put blessings and prayers into each shawl they created. They then gave these shawls to those women in need of comfort and solace, as well as in celebration and joy. Some recipients, in kind, continued the process by in turn making a shawl and passing it on to someone in need.

This is reminiscent of *Like Water for Chocolate*, by Laura Esquivel (1989). In the book, Tita has strange magic in the kitchen. Her emotions are transferred into whatever dish she is creating and then go into whoever eats the food. Feelings of sadness and despair, or passion and adoration, turn into sickness and misery or lust and sexual fireworks in the recipient. As with *Like Water for*

Chocolate, this textile-making subgroup did not want to take their disheartened energy and "place" it into their creations.

Interestingly, the women who had the most skill and experience in fiber arts actually reported the opposite of this. They had so mastered their skills at textile-making that they knew how to put aside, neutralize, and transform any personal agitation or sadness while creating with textiles. Most of the time, they felt that textile-making offered them a creative outlet for their concerns, and for many, the act of textile-making both rejuvenated and enlivened them. The majority of the fiber artists interviewed in Chapter 10 give examples of this process.

A few other issues will be useful to assess when conducting a textile survey. First, inquire as to which handcrafts are stimulating or calming, or used to increase and/or decrease their energy or arousal level. For many women, the repetition and simplicity of fiber-making, especially spinning and knitting, is very soothing and relaxing. I have heard women say that the smell of sheep lanolin and the feeling of grease on their hands when spinning is wonderful, particularly if they are sitting in the sun on a warm spring day. Now for me, one who developed a terrible allergy to lanolin while spinning in dirty, greasy wool, it is anything but relaxing to sneeze and stop to get a tissue! In contrast, weavers and quilt-makers reported these activities as the most arousing and stimulating. When you think about it, both weaving and quilting involve complex patterning and decision-making. Careful attention to detail must be maintained throughout the entirety of the tasks. This absorption and engagement is challenging and truly requires considerable skill. Csikszentmihalyi (1990) would say that these later activities involve "flow." Although some women may always want to calm down, and others want to increase their energy, most will have different needs at different times. Possibly to sit and be calm, when nothing can be done but accept a situation; possibly cognitive distraction coupled with ego-enhancement of creating a stunning, visually beautiful, and tactile-stimulating fabric at other times. The textile survey also includes specific questions about the main activities women identify with, and whether these activities result in flow.

It is also important to understand how essential socializing is for women with regards to their handcraft-making. There are many textile arts that are done alone, such as weaving and sewing. Likewise, knitting is an activity that can be done in many different settings. Today's women also use guilds, professional groups, virtual networks, and study groups to be with others who share common enthusiasm about fiber-making. In the past, quilting circles were an important way for women to connect. There will be individual differences in the need and expectation for socializing while creating handcrafts, as well as intra-individual differences: each person may vary at any given time whether they would prefer to be alone or in a group.

Finally, the amount of intellectual focus a given technique requires is important to assess. If a client is going through chemotherapy and she rates quilting as involving a tremendous amount of intellectual focus for her, this may not be the best medium to use.

Individual differences and aesthetics

Does your client consider herself to be artistic? As having a personal sense of aesthetics? Is she attuned to the visual aspects of her environment, such as its color and organization? Is she attentive of furniture orientation and style? What type of art does she make? How does she think about her art? I would suggest asking these questions and more, of your client, both to help elucidate the type(s) of projects you can suggest, to indicate more about "who" your client is, as well as to help you understand the way that textiles are used in her life.

Research does suggest that mental illness is associated with artistic style. Ludwig (1998) examined lifetime rates of mental disorders among artists whose work was primarily formal (structural, compositional, or decorative elements) compared with artists whose work was primarily emotive (emphasizing self-expression). Emotive artists had more than three times the incidence of mental disorders than artists in the formal category (75% versus 22%). Although it is not "diagnostic," clients who make functional, formal pieces may be more grounded, psychologically, than clients who create textiles as a means of self-expression.

There is a significant body of research that indicates substantial cognitive and information processing differences reflected in preference for specific types of art. Feist and Brady (2004) examined 104 college participants (68 female) and their results suggested that more open participants preferred every form of art presented, but especially abstract art. Loomis and Saltz (1984) reported that rational and cognitive styles were associated with representational artistic styles, and irrational cognitive styles were associated with more abstract styles. They also found that extroverts tended to have greater irrational cognitive styles, where introverts tended to be more abstract. Gridley (2006) surveyed painters, collage artists, and printmakers, in a sample evenly divided between males and females. He found that artists preferred a legislative style (inventing and developing new ideas of their own) more than an executive style (preferring to implement pre-existing ideas). Gridley also indicated that artists preferred change more than maintaining the status quo. Older literature in psychology is consistent with these findings. Dudek and Marchand (1983) reported that artists with lower cognitive defenses and controls (indicated by the projective personality test, the Rorschach) painted in a loosely controlled, "painterly" manner. In contrast, individuals who were more rigid in their defensive style were more formal and linear. Rawlings and Bastian (2002) examined the role of sensation-seeking, introversion and extroversion in undergraduate student ratings of 72 paintings previously divided into two stylistic (Abstract and Traditional) and five content (Erotic, Pleasant, Neutral, Violent, Unpleasant) categories. They reported that sensation-seeking (seeking novelty and new situations) was associated with liking abstract art styles, and disliking unpleasant and violent paintings. Mastandrea, Bartoli, and Bove (2009) reported similar results, where people who prefer abstract, modern art have higher levels of the personality trait sensation-seeking, compared with people who prefer realistic art in ancient art museums.

These findings suggest that women who create textile handcrafts because of a need for the aesthetics, or to express themselves artistically, may also be people who cope well with ambiguity, people who seek change, and people who are open and curious. They may also be people who are more intense and emotionally volatile. In contrast, handcrafters who are more rational and conscientious, as well as functionally focused in what they make, may be cognitively and/or psychologically less flexible and open to change, as well as less interested in creative exploration. These latter women may be less responsive to creating art without structure, or art that is more abstract and/or theoretical. In addition, they may be less interested in exploring issues using new textile mediums, or exploring the boundaries of mediums they already use.

Color

Color is an important variable for most handcrafters. Some women will embrace the dynamics of color; others will have nothing to do with it and stay with neutral tones and/or black and white. It is important to discuss this concept with your client. What is her preference for certain schemas? What meanings do particular colors hold? Are some colors more provocative or more emotive than others?

There is widespread belief that individual colors have a psychological impact on affect. Blue is frequently reported as representing peace, tranquility, and calm; green is seen as demonstrating nature, the environment, health, and vigor; red is seen as implying danger, desire, violence, and anger. In the commercial world, personality associations and color are taken quite literally. For example, many architects and interior designers teach that certain colors increase stress and depression. Others profess that they can recommend specific colors based on demographics like age, gender, and region of the country.

Unfortunately, most of these "findings" come from marketing research and are not reported in peer-reviewed scientific journals. The two most widely known systems are the Luscher Color Diagnostik system and the Dewey Color System; these have both been around for decades. Dr. Max Luscher first developed the Luscher Color Diagnostik system in 1947. Today, the Luscher system is copyrighted and still widely circulated in Europe. There remains limited, if any, modern-day research supporting his theory (e.g. Kertzman *et al.* 2003; Picco and Dzindolet 1994). Another widely used system, the Dewey system, was developed in the 1980s. The Dewey system asks about favorite and least favorite colors, to create an astrological-like description of the individual. The Dewey system claims to be associated with individual preferences, making it helpful in vocational support. It is also patented and copyrighted. There always exists a tension between the not-for-profit academic world and the private sector. Clearly, the Luscher and Dewey systems have not been subjected to peer-reviewed journals to substantiate their claims, but have each been a market success. However, given the lack of published research findings, it is fair to seriously doubt their validity.

In my analysis, the reality is that are very few "facts" in the field of psychology to support a global theory of color and personality. Most psychologists, for good reason, view color symbolism with skepticism and think the properties of color have been overstated and embellished. People are just too complex to reduce their individual color preferences to a cook-book typology.

We do know some things about color that can be agreed on. First, people have specific, individual associations, and these associations vary depending on his or her personal and/or cultural experiences. There also may be some associations that are more universal, in an earth sense, because of the characteristics of our natural environment: green is associated with vegetation, hence with growth and life; red is associated with fire and blood, hence with drama and danger. At an individual level, however, the differences can vary substantially. Yellow might suggest happiness and excitement to one person, or cowardice, illness, and hazard to another. Cultural associations with color may also have completely opposite meanings. White is frequently used as the color of purity in the USA; however, in Japan, China, and India, it is associated with death. Green suggests safety in the USA but possibly criminality in France.

We must also recognize that even when there is consistency across cultures, there will always be both positive and negative associations to each color within a given society. While there is agreement in the USA that white signifies purity and innocence (positive), there is also agreement that it suggests sterility and coldness (negative). Green may be associated with nature and fertility (positive), but linguistically it is also used to refer to someone who is inexperienced and envious (negative). Some have described colors with temperature terms like cool and warm. The cool colors (blue, green, purple) are seen as restful, quieting, and calming, and the warm colors (red, yellow, orange) are seen as active and stimulating. Research results on this typology have also proved to be inconsistent (e.g. Ainsworth, Simpson, and Cassell 1993; Kwallek *et al.* 1996).

Part of the complexity with color and personality research is that there has been inconsistency with the systems used to describe and define colors. For example, color samples are usually not drawn from a standardized system of color notation, and many times investigators elicit individual responses to verbal labels of color instead of the actual stimuli. Luscher's and Dewey's approach relies on individual colors, but the specific hues, values, and chroma are not in the public domain.

Interestingly, when more complex color systems have been used, that is, where two or more colors are arranged in relation to each other, results are more reliable. One emerging paradigm comes from Rollins College, called the Inventory of Color Preference. In this approach, individuals are asked to rate preference for single colors and then combination colors: "achromatic" schemes that involve a combination of black, white, or gray; "keyed" schemes that are achromatic values with a single hue, such as black, white, and red; "monochromatic" schemes, which are different values (shades, tints, and tones) of the same hue (e.g. red and pink); "analogous" schemes, combining hues adjacent to each other on the color wheel (e.g. red and orange); and, finally, "complementary" schemes that combine colors opposite on the color wheel (e.g. red and green) (Earle and Harris 2007; Harris *et al.* 2009). These investigators found that people were very consistent in choosing color schemes. They also found that while people changed preferences for colors, they tended to stay within the same pattern. For example, if you liked complementary schemes, you may like yellow, then red, then blue over time. When your preference was yellow, you liked violet (complementary); when your preference changed to blue you liked blue with orange (again complementary); and when your preference changed to red, you preferred red with green.

To date, few investigators of color, mood, and personality have explored the relationship between color and individual differences. Rosenbloom (2006) found that sensation seekers preferred to create more complex images using more than one color in the experimental session, and preferred red or "hot" colors (considered to be arousing, stimulating, exciting and attractive, and at the same time irritating), compared with low-sensation seekers.

In the textile survey you will find specific questions to evaluate the client's personal meaning associated with colors. There are also questions that are based on Harris's research at Rollins College, which account for interest in particular types of color schemes. I would suggest that you explore the meaning of color and color preference individually with your client, as part of the process of getting to know her.

Insights from Rorschach

Another way to provide a context about how color use reflects internal emotional functioning, in art, comes from the Rorschach inkblot test, a projective psychological test. The recipient's perceptions of ten inkblots are recorded and then analyzed using psychological interpretation, complex scientifically derived algorithms, or both. There has been continued controversy about whether the Rorschach can accurately allow psychologists to describe personality characteristics and emotional functioning. In the late 1960s, Dr. John E. Exner developed a system referred to as the "Exner system." Exner's analyses led to standardized administration, objective, reliable coding, and a normative database. Although content was noted, the system was more concerned with the "process" of how the client saw what they did. The main components of the Exner system are as follows: form (or shape), content, popularity of content, color, movement, shading, texture, proportions, use of white space, creativity (developmental quality), and cognitive organizational quality. Each of these components is examined alone and in relationship to one another. For example, in the Exner system, research suggests that when people are more focused on details they may have poorer stress tolerance. Exner reports that perception of texture represents a trait-like tendency for affectional needs and loneliness. Low use of popular content could indicate both greater individuality yet non-conventionality.

Using the Exner system, the Rorschach is now seen as more of a reflection of response styles to novel, ambiguous situations, rather than a reflection of personality. These response styles, in turn, may be associated with psychological characteristics. In addition, the Rorschach, via the Exner system, is thought to reflect information about cognitive processing style and flexibility.

John Suler, at Rider University in New Jersey, has conceptualized that the Exner system may be a useful tool for self-awareness when used with artists. Suler suggested that the type of art made may reflect dimensions of a person's response style—which he or she is unaware of. Suler believes that our personality style is reflected in the way we create images, as well as in how we react to them: "because the things you tend to notice about [photos] tend to be the things you strive to create in your own."

Thus, the art we and others make may say something about us: it may reflect who we are and what our basic needs are. To date, no investigators have applied the Exner determinants to artists and their creations. Like Suler, in both my clinical experience and artwork, I think that the "determinants" described by Exner may, in fact, provide us with another level of insight into the artist's or handcrafter's cognitive style and flexibility, values, and psychological status.

According to Suler, in photography, the *form* is usually obvious: if you have a picture of a car, a boat, or a house, that is what it is. But consider *location*. Some people focus more on the totality of an image, in its entirety, while others pay attention to specific elements or even unusually small details. Exner suggested that a holistic view of an image is fairly typical and conventional, and probably practical and realistic. Alternately, the ability to notice details can indicate both hyper-vigilance—the ability to see the unusual—or, if this perceptual tendency becomes too extreme, it might indicate a preoccupation with trivia, obsessive thinking, and sometimes paranoia. In textiles, indeed, function often follows form and serves a practical use (Collier 2011). But might the handcrafter who is preoccupied with the fine details of an item and is exceptionally perfectionistic about uniformity be more obsessive and hyper-vigilant, in general, than a handcrafter who is more interested in the overall impact of an item?

As with Exner, Suler reports that creating *movement* in an image is seen as a sophisticated sign of mature thinking, intelligence, and creativity, when applied to humans and animals. Textile handcrafters may not create "direct" movement; nothing will be moving on its own. But like any art form, perceived motion in textiles can be observed in drape, color contrast, texture, and repeating patterns. Likewise, *color* in the Exner system suggests both vibrancy and passion, as well as emotional lability and intensity. Interestingly, a combination of both movement and color are positive indicators, suggesting both introspection and emotional stability. In contrast, a low frequency of both color and movement suggests a person is lacking in both creativity and emotional stability.

Texture is implicitly part of textile-making. The Exner system describes texture responses, for example tactile sensations that describe the surface (such as smooth, rough, grainy, sharp, furry, and bumpy), as corresponding to loneliness and a lack of contact comfort. Exner also reports that people separated from those they care about show an increase in texture responses. If texture is the main motivation for handcraft-making, we should consider whether fiber artists have intense feelings of isolation.

Shading on the Rorschach is a focus on the changes in lightness and darkness. These shading responses, as well as dwelling on the "blackness" of the inkblots, tend to be associated with stress, anxiety, or depression. In textiles, possibly the shading or blackness conveys sadness or an anxious mood.

Additional components of the Exner system involve *symmetry*, *white space*, and *orientation*. *Symmetry* is inherent in the inkblots because they were formed by splashing ink onto paper and folding the paper in half. The Exner system purports that symmetry is indicative of a self-reflective and introspective person. Possibly, people who create symmetry in their textiles have these same characteristics. Alas, that would suggest that the creation of asymmetry might be unusual, the lack of balance in design metaphorically revealing a lack of balance internally. *White space* is the area between or around what is seen. Attention to white space is seen as a very restrained and unconscious way of defying the test instructions; Exner sees these responses as indicating oppositional, passive-aggressive, or rebellious tendencies. Of course, it also might reflect an ability to notice the unusual. In textiles, concentrating on white space probably does not suggest inherent rebelliousness; the ability to see and work with negative space is likely to be crucial to good composition and an advanced skill.

Finally, *orientation* on the Rorschach refers to how the card is literally handed to the client in an upright position. It is typical for people to keep this orientation during the interview. Exner believed that changing the orientation (e.g. turning it upside down or sideways) reflects novel perspective, flexibility, and curiosity in problem solving.

The Exner system may provide a framework for exploring with the client how individual proclivity towards materials and creations reflects internal processes. It is interesting to take note that Exner's "determinants" are essentially the components of design. The large body of parallel research may suggest that these components are associated with specific thought processes. Where some perceptions are sophisticated signs of psychological complexity, taken to an extreme they can also indicate psychopathology.

Each of these elements of design are evaluated in the textile survey. As with color analysis, these characteristics do not have to predict anything specific about your client. However, understanding your client's preference for design elements may help you gain a deeper understanding for how she views the world.

Chapter 5

Interwoven Lives

CROSS-CULTURAL APPLICATIONS
OF TEXTILE ART THERAPY

Introduction

Throughout my graduate training I was taught to be sensitive and aware of the role of culture, diversity, and individual differences in psychotherapy. This wasn't much of a problem to me because I thought of myself as a liberal, open-minded White person who was willing to accept anyone who came my way. Yet it seemed as if the message from my professors and colleagues was to avoid working with clients from different cultures, including lesbian, gay, bisexual, and transgender (LGBT) clients, because there were perfectly qualified therapists available that "understood" those issues better than I ever would. And if I did find myself in a position where I was working with people who weren't the "same" as me, I was taught a cookbook-style list of dos and don'ts in psychotherapy. For example, don't worry if your African-American clients won't look you in the eye, and don't try so hard to look directly at them. Do try to be authoritative and directive with your Asian clients because they expect you to have authority and knowledge, even if you are a female. Don't be concerned if your Hispanic clients are intensely emotional; that is normal.

I imagine this training is fairly typical. I think I interpreted "diversity" in the 1980s as meaning someone who was different from me. I had no clue about White privilege, or how being White had influenced the very fabric of whom I had become. Instead, I thought cultural sensitivity meant that no two people were ever alike, and I accepted that some differences were greater than others. Even though my class-mates were from a variety of ethnic and international backgrounds, I diligently took notes so that I would know how to be appropriate when I encountered "real" diversity in psychotherapy. I didn't worry about it much anyway because I was living in a big city and there were lots of therapists from diverse ethnicities available to refer to. And, as an agnostic young woman from a Jewish background who grew up in Los Angeles during the 1960s and 1970s, I was definitely not that different from my average client. I had confidence I would know how to handle "diversity" when I encountered it because of my training.

That said, nothing prepared me for how to handle my new role as a Chief Clinical Psychologist in the tiny island country of the Republic of Palau, except for life itself and thankfully a few key Palauan co-workers. And the words of an elder, sage, and psychiatrist named Dr. Dale. Before I get to Dr. Dale, let me tell you a brief story about diversity in the "real" global world. My husband (who was a newly graduated psychiatrist at the time) and I were the only graduate-level trained mental health workers in Palau. We had been there one week, still smitten by the beauty of living in a tropical diving paradise for two years. We were casually referred a client on the medical ward (around the corner from the Behavioral Health ward), a ten-year-old victim of sexual abuse. We were asked to see her and to tell no one about why she was on the medical ward. We were also warned that if we did (tell anyone), we would suffer the wrath of her family, who were a violent clan, and we would be in grave physical danger.

Now what are two Western-trained highly educated mental health providers to do? Call in the child specialists of course, and get this child out of there! No; too dangerous for her and for us. That was just the beginning of it, of the clash between what we thought was right (based on a Western perspective), and what we were empowered to do (based on being a professional in a different country and culture).

Dr. Dale was long known as a consultant in Palau, as he first "discovered" that there were exceptionally high rates of schizophrenia while he was sailing around the Pacific. Although he worked at the University of Hawaii's School of Medicine, Dr. Dale came back and forth to Palau every year, for almost 25 years, providing mental health consultation, treatment, and research. As our main predecessor, he thankfully had sincere and positive relationships with the late Minister of Health and health care providers, as well as many of the consumers. Dr. Dale met my husband and me in Hawaii, at his home, on the final leg of our journey to begin working in Palau. He had long since retired and was helping Palau's then Minister of Health prepare us for the two-year job ahead. After a three-hour tour around the big island of Hawaii and lunch, this is pretty much all he told us for our cultural training: "Be quiet and watch. Don't try to do too much too quickly; wait at least one year before you try to make any changes. Spend more time watching and listening respectfully, than talking." We both left that meeting thinking Dr. Dale was somewhat demented and definitely eccentric and certainly old. Was that all he had to say to us?

Ironically, when all is said and done 16 years later, I have to say his words have had more relevance in the course of my cross-cultural work than anything else I have ever learned. Despite whatever research I review in this chapter, my best advice to you is similar to the definitely not demented, certainly eccentric, *and* sage Dr. Dale: Be quiet and watch. Listen respectfully more than you talk; build relationships, and go slowly. Find people from the culture you are working with who you respect and allow them to serve as cultural brokers. And, as with my initial UCLA training, empower the cultural brokers to do the lion's share of the work. It is still true that being more alike than different helps in psychotherapy (Snowden and Cheung 1990; Zhang, Snowden, and Sue 1998).

Multicultural competence

In the US population there has been an increased need for multicultural competence because there has been an increase in cultural diversity. The US Census Bureau (2006) reported that one-third of the US population includes people of ethnic minority backgrounds (not Caucasian), and that number is rising. The same is true in the UK: Britain's ethnic minority population is expected to increase from 8 percent to 20 percent of the population over the next 40 years (Dayspring 2010). According to Professor Philip Rees of the University of Leeds, "The ethnic makeup of the UK's population is evolving significantly. Groups outside the White British majority are increasing in size and share, not just in the areas of initial migration, but throughout the country, and our projections suggest that this trend is set to continue through to 2051."

Immigrants constitute 12 percent of the US population and that number is also increasing: between 1990 and 2000 immigrants increased by 57 percent. Almost 20 percent of US residents speak languages other than English (US Census Bureau 2003). There are also long-standing studies indicating that ethnic minorities underutilize clinical services when compared with Caucasians. In addition, ethnic minorities are given more severe psychiatric diagnoses and are typically perceived as being in greater distress than Caucasians when they do present for services (Whaley and Davis 2007).

In August 2002, the American Psychological Association published guidelines on multiculturalism (American Psychological Association 2003). The multicultural guidelines had a long series of predecessors that began in the 1970s. It was more than a means to address multiculturalism and diversity in therapy; it addressed multiculturalism and diversity in psychologist education, training, research, practice, and organizational change. The predominant focus was with US ethnic and racial minority groups, as well as individuals, children, and families from biracial, multiethnic, and multiracial backgrounds.

The document also provided definitions for several words, namely culture, race, ethnicity, multiculturalism, and diversity. *Culture* was defined as "the belief systems and value orientations that influence customs, norms, practices, and social institutions including psychological processes (language, care taking practices, media, and educational systems) and organizations" (American Psychological Association 2003). Culture was equated with "worldview," beliefs, values, and practices, especially religious and spiritual traditions. *Race* was emphatically defined as a socially constructed concept, not a biologically determined fact. Race was something that "others" (i.e. non-psychologists) might assign individuals to, based on their physical characteristics. *Ethnicity* was much murkier to define and took on the definition of culture (e.g. "one's culture of origin and concomitant sense of belonging"). The terms *multiculturalism* and *diversity* recognized the scope of race, ethnicity, language, sexual orientation, gender, age, disability, class status, education, religious/spiritual orientation, and other cultural dimensions, on the individual's personal identity.

The guidelines were a landmark in the field of psychology, but did not truly specify what it meant to be *culturally competent*. Sue (1998) originally defined cultural competence to mean the possession of the knowledge and skills of a particular culture so that the delivery of services to that population was effective. More recently, Sue and Torino (2005) expanded this definition to mean awareness, knowledge, and skills that allow the counselor to communicate, interact, negotiate, and intervene on behalf of clients from different backgrounds. Other authors define it more broadly, such as the ability to recognize the importance of culture and incorporating that perspective into practice (Whaley and Davis 2007).

It is more and more obvious that any definition of cultural competence must also take into account the role of the *psychologist's own culture, beliefs, and values* in the therapeutic interaction. In addition, it is unrealistic for a therapist to have a complex understanding of *every* culture. Fields (2010) argues, instead, that an ongoing cultural exchange is essential between client and clinician about culture, cultural assumptions, and cultural interactions. The therapist must be open to exploring the discrepancy between his or her own culture and the client's, that is, is willing to look at it. This is more important than knowing about the beliefs and values of any given culture. Clinicians can easily make Type I errors (Chu 2007), where there is an assumption that a clinical issue is cultural when it is not, and Type II errors, assuming an issue is not cultural when it is.

White privilege and racism

If you are Caucasian, there are two important concepts that should be understood in order to be a culturally competent therapist: White privilege and racism. *White privilege* can be defined as "unearned advantages of being White in a racially stratified society" (Neville, Worthington, and Spanierman 2001). The corollary to White privilege is the disadvantage that a person of color experiences. *Racism* is defined by the American Psychological Association as discrimination against people based on their skin color or ethnic heritage. However, some people believe that a definition of racism is not complete without adding concepts of privilege and power. As such, racism would be defined as culturally sanctioned strategies that defend the advantages of power, privilege, and prestige. Both concepts are largely unacknowledged by most White people, and, when acknowledged, meet with strong negative reactions (Pinterits, Poteat, and Spanierman 2009). These reactions are come by honestly. In some, the acknowledgment of White privilege and racism is associated with the loss of benefits, materially and interpersonally. Individual acknowledgment may be difficult because it could be met with rejection from one's peers and social groups. Others feel guilt and shame because, once aware of White privilege and racism, it is normal to feel terrible that it occurs and that, as a White person, you have been unconsciously part of it. In others, there is outright anger, both anger to bring up the topic because it reminds one of the injustice, and anger stemming from denial and defensiveness at insinuating that White privilege exists.

Research does show that being "color-blind" (where clinicians believe that they perceive everyone as equal) is actually associated with lower cultural competence (see Muszynski 2009). Some clinical organizations go so far as to say that an effective therapist must be aware of how racism and White privilege are part of the therapist's personal and professional life (de Silva 2007). Once explored, this awareness should be used to ameliorate its influence on every part of work and home life. Thus, it is seen as the clinician's responsibility to promote change in an organization and society. This is the same type of responsibility we hold to recognize and intervene with child abuse. In the USA, if we were to observe child abuse in a public setting, even amongst strangers, we are morally and ethically obligated to intervene and/or report the situation.

While a complete exploration of these issues is not possible within the confines of this book, I do believe that open discussion must occur within, at the least, your collegial group, in order to honestly attend to issues of culture, diversity, race, and racism.

The nuts and bolts: What can you do to be culturally competent?

In the *Diagnostic and Statistical Manual of Mental Disorders*, Fourth Edition, Text Revision (DSM-IV-TR; American Psychiatric Association 2001), culture is defined as the "values, beliefs, and practices that represent a given ethno cultural group." Cultural attitudes and beliefs influence how mental illness is accepted and understood in a given individual, coping strategies that are adopted, inclinations to access and utilize services, and responses to treatment. Identifying and "defining" culture does lead to blanket generalizations about people that are frequently inaccurate and superficial. But not to do so would lead to overlooking cultural variations that are critical to consider. Clinicians need to look at both general processes and culture-specific processes.

At best, this definition of culture is fraught with difficulties. According to López and Guarnaccia (2000), culture is not just *within* the individual, nor is it a psychological phenomenon. Both the client's social and physical worlds produce his or her culture. And, culture is not static; it is really a *process* more than an entity. The training I received in the early 1980s, which attempted to freeze culture into a set of generalized value orientations or behaviors, misrepresents what culture actually is.

Even in Palau, the culture of the current generation is different from that of the previous generation. There are also differences within the generations based on schooling, both within the country and abroad. The older generations that lived under

Japanese occupation during the first half of the twentieth century were heavily influenced by Japanese worldviews. The younger generations, raised under American occupation until 1994, were exposed to American values and education; they were extremely Westernized by comparison. Thus people influence their culture by changing it, adding to it, or even rejecting it.

Migration, immigration, trauma, ethnic-racial identity confusion, and even PTSD are other ways that people can influence their culture of origin. After the Vietnam War, en route to migrate from Laos to the USA, many Hmong people were essentially trapped in refugee camps for several decades. The refugee camps further traumatized people who had already experienced the terror of the war. This led to more cultural changes for the Hmong before they ever arrived in the USA. Once in the USA, some Hmong moved to the mid-west (Minnesota and Wisconsin), some remained in California. Each group has since adapted to very different American cultures even within the USA, as there are broad-based cultural differences between American White Midwestern and West-coast people.

DSM-IV-TR suggests considering the following perspectives when integrating a cultural perspective. First, note the person's ethnic or cultural reference group. Don't assume that a mixed-race person has allegiance to one ethnicity over the other. This is especially true for immigrants and ethnic minorities. You must explore the degree of involvement with the person's culture of origin and the host culture, as well as the person's language abilities and use preferences.

Second, be aware if there are cultural explanations for psychopathology that you observe. Are distress and the need for social support communicated through somatic complaints (e.g. nerves, headaches, possessing spirits)? How "abnormal" are the individual's symptoms relative to his or her cultural reference group? Are there specific local illness categories used by the person's family and community to identify the condition? Are there perceived causes or explanatory models that the person and his/her reference group uses to explain the illness? Finally, does the person have preferences for specific types of care?

Third, you will need to consider the person's psychosocial environment and how he/she functions in that environment. You will want to note culturally relevant interpretations of social stressors, available social supports, and level of functioning and disability. Look at religion and kin networks.

Fourth, as mentioned at the beginning of the chapter, you must consider how cultural elements will interplay between the therapist and the client. This goes beyond just identifying if a behavior is normal or pathological. There may be differences in background, notwithstanding culture, that include social status, language, communication of symptoms, understanding of symptoms, symptoms of cultural significance, how relationships are negotiated, and the level of intimacy one is comfortable with. All of these elements will have a major impact on diagnosis and treatment.

Fifth, some professionals believe that case formulation must include the recognition of culture-bound syndromes. However, others believe that culture-bound syndromes in diagnostic manuals exoticize the role of culture. Furthermore, why do cultural considerations only apply to "minority" groups? In fact, during the creation of DSM-V, disorders that afflicted mostly Western and European countries were not seen as culture-bound syndromes. For example, why are anorexia nervosa and chronic fatigue syndrome considered culture-bound syndromes?

Mental health concerns nationally and internationally

The WHO reports that there are actually higher rates of mental health problems in specific groups of people internationally, especially people from Africa, Latin America, Asia, and the Pacific. Desjarlais *et al.* (1995) compiled research across the world to identify the range of mental health and behavioral problems (e.g. mental disorders, violence, suicide). Mental illness and related problems exacted a significant toll on health and well-being of people worldwide, producing a greater burden based on a "disability-adjusted life years" index than from that of TB, cancer, and heart disease. Depressive disorders produced the fifth greatest burden for women and the seventh greatest burden for men, even across all physical and mental illnesses. And, as discussed in Chapter 3, we also know that mental illness and behavioral problems are complexly tied to social roots.

The Office of the Surgeon General, the Center for Mental Health Services, and the National Institute of Mental Health (2001) indicated that as many as 21 percent of adults and children in the USA suffer from mental disorder. While the rates of mental illness may be similar across cultures, service provision and utilization is not. There are barriers to treatment, and these include the general lack of available services, mistrust of providers, and fear of racism, discrimination, and simply barriers to language and communication. Research indicates that, in the USA today, minorities receive poorer mental health care and have less representation in mental health research. In addition, fewer minorities recover after mental illness because of poorer quality of care.

Culture and art

Intuitively, it seems obvious that culture will influence the type of visual images and textiles that women have had experience with as well as preferences for. As Masuda *et al.* (2008) suggest, visual images are not just mere copies of the real world, but instead, two-dimensional representations of the three-dimensional world. Thus styles are strongly influenced by the culture in which they are produced. Nisbett and colleagues (Nisbett 2003; Nisbett *et al.* 2001) have suggested that the strong value placed on social harmony has prompted east Asians to attend more to cues in the social world. In contrast, the heavy emphasis placed on autonomy in Westerners drives them to pay attention to objects that they can control by exercise of will. These same differences are also in religions: Eastern religions look at interrelationship of all in the world; Western religions tend to emphasize how to control discrete objects by paying close attention to their attributes and the categories to which they belong.

Recent studies by Masuda and associates have indeed confirmed that culture influences a person's aesthetic interpretation. Masuda *et al.* (2009) reported that there are marked differences in cognitive activity, including categorization, causal explanation, and logical versus dialectical inference, in Asian versus Western perceptions of art. Specifically, they found that Asian people attended more to the contextual information in an artwork, and Westerners focused most on salient objects and their properties. Participants were presented with prominent images of cartoon figures with smaller, less salient figures placed in the background. Japanese undergraduate students were more likely than Americans to be influenced by the background figures' facial expressions when making judgments of the target figure's emotion; smiling target figures were seen as less happy when background figures were frowning than when smiling. They explained these differences as reflecting social practices in east Asia, where there is more of an importance placed on and sensitivity to the social and contextual cues in interpersonal interactions.

Cultural experiences are also associated with artistic style (Masuda *et al.* 2009). In an analysis of artwork, a floating perspective is more typical in Asian-style art and a linear perspective is more dominant in European-style art. Masuda and colleagues suggested that this reflects the east Asian holistic pattern of attention and inclusiveness, compared with the Western analytic pattern of attention to salient objects.

I suggest that you spend some time and examine the client's worldview. What are the client's values, beliefs, and assumptions about the world? These are based on a person's cultural, social, religious/spiritual, and/or ethnic/racial background.

One scale clinicians might be interested in is called the "Worldview Analysis Scale" (WAS) (Obasi, Flores, and Lindaal 2009). The WAS is a 45-item questionnaire that assesses seven dimensions of worldview—the philosophical assumptions which determine the way in which people perceive, think, feel, and experience the world. Obasi reported that there are seven reliable, valid factors including: materialistic universe, tangible realism, communalism, indigenous values, knowledge of self, spiritual immortality, and spiritualism. This may be a useful tool for exploring concepts of culture, in addition to a comprehensive clinical interview.

Chapter 6

Theoretical Underpinnings of Textile Art Therapy

Metaphors and archetypes

How do we perceive "reality"? To oversimplify, reality comes to us through our senses. Our ears, eyes, nose, mouth, and skin perceive the world and then send complex, patterned signals to our brains. As a young baby, these stimuli do not make much sense. Over time, as our brains mature, we create "frames" of reality, essentially mental structures that provide us with quick ways to process the perceived information. Eventually, these mental frames can come to *symbolically* represent objects, such that a single word or symbol can evoke a variety of different meanings. Symbols are one way we create analogies to understand the physical world, or reality, and metaphors are another. A *metaphor* is a comparison between two things that have a similarity; they give name to something that belongs to a completely different object. Metaphors typically apply something that is concrete or conceivable to something that is intangible or conceptual (e.g. Tom really boils me when he gets to ranting) (Lakoff and Johnson 1980). Similes are just more explicit metaphors; they are overt comparisons using the words "like" or "seems" (e.g. Tom makes me feel like boiling [water] when he gets to ranting). Both similes and metaphors use phrases, instead of single words, as symbols do. Symbols and metaphors are both patterned after the original item in reality, and both serve as mental frames for reality. Symbols and metaphors become so common to us that we typically do not need extensive knowledge of the original element to appreciate the meaning or intent.

Jung has suggested that when symbols and metaphors are used frequently across cultures, they can be thought of as *archetypes*. Archetypes are repeating patterns of thought and action that have occurred throughout the ages, across people, across countries, and across continents (Jung 1964). Archetypes are the main concept I will draw on from Jung; Jungians usually couch the concept of archetypes in a "collective unconscious." The collective unconscious is also called the *universal mind* that all of humanity shares and has access to. To me, belief in the universal mind is not necessary to explore the use of symbols, metaphors, and archetypes in therapy.

In this chapter I review how symbols, metaphors, and archetypes can be used in conjunction with psychotherapy, especially by engaging personal narratives, guided imagery, and textile art-making. It is natural for clients to generate metaphoric images when describing their problems and telling their stories and these typically reflect their own idiosyncratic perceptions of reality. Once identified, a therapist can focus on these symbols to explore both the sensory aspects and the feelings associated with the issue at hand. These three methods can then codify a new, revised metaphorical understanding of problems and solutions. They can provide both literal and figurative vehicles for internal narrative reconstruction. The textile-making provides the added benefit that most fiber mediums are filled with their own metaphors (e.g. felting).

Metaphors

Metaphors carry meaning in a symbolic form, often a form that the person is unaware of. Lakoff and Johnson (1980) suggested that metaphors deeply reflect embedded values in our culture. They described two types of metaphor: *conventional metaphors* and *new metaphors*. We typically rely on conventional metaphors in our daily lives; these reflect the structure and nuances of the culture we live in. They are different from new metaphors, or metaphors that are fresh, creative ways of making sense of experience. New metaphors allow us to gain an unsullied point of view on our circumstances.

There are many ways that metaphors are useful in art therapy. Moon (2007) described therapeutic art as the practice of making personal metaphors concrete and tangible. Then, through the process of exploration, the client can gain new perspective (and hence new metaphors) in order to reframe past and current experiences. Thus, the therapist acts as a guide who encourages the client to make her individual metaphors real, allowing the treatment to occur more non-verbally and experientially.

Ultimately, an individual's metaphoric language can be seen as a direct expression of his or her structure of reality (Burns 2007). Burns suggested that therapeutic metaphors fall into one of four categories: *client-generated, therapist-generated, collaborative,* and *experiential.* Therapists who utilize a metaphoric approach often listen for and reflect on *client-generated metaphors* as they make their initial assessment about the client's problem.

Therapist-generated metaphors, alternately, are stories that the therapist creates or finds that reflect his or her professional understanding of the client's situation. Therapists use this approach by drawing on world myths, legends, folklore, fairy tales, or made-up stories that are relevant, then talking through, creating art, or inducing hypnosis and guided imagery for exploration. For example, fairies frequently behave in a healing capacity in mythology, or act as agents between the material world of humans and the invisible forces of nature. Likewise, mythological beings are seen as possessing powers that can help mortals achieve non-human tasks.

Collaborative metaphors combine the first two: the therapist actively works with the client's personal stories and metaphors to collaboratively transform them into a healthier re-conceptualization of the problem. The goal is to encourage the client to move forward with a new understanding and ultimately better resolution of the problem. Silverman (2004) has the client work collaboratively with the therapist to select a myth or fairy tale character which evokes a personal sense of relevance. He suggested that the client does not need to fully understand why the story resonates with his or her critical psychological issues. Using the performing art medium of drama therapy, the client is then guided in an in-depth exploration of the chosen myth or story. Called "The Story Within" approach, the client is encouraged to develop a deep relationship with the main character. The therapist's role is to set up a safe structure that will guide the client through this process.

Finally, *experiential metaphors* in therapy take the process one step further: they involve the client in real-world experiential activities that have a metaphoric intent. These activities serve to embody the therapeutic message in a novel experience, hence generalizing the learning. Barker (1985) chooses a story and then has the client use the tale to explore her issues in order to better understand inner conflicts. These explorations encourage the translation of the process into a visual art medium. Barker views the symbolic processes encountered in fairy tales and stories as "opening up" options and solutions to the client, possibly solutions that had not previously occurred to them. Thus, Barker suggests that by applying metaphors to art, the experiential symbol produced gives the motif visual dimension.

One therapist has applied metaphor therapy to guided imagery, which he calls *guided metaphor imagery* (Battino 2007). At the onset of psychotherapy, Battino introduces the client to the idea of having her own *life story*, the story she tells herself and others about how she got to the present time. This is the story that he or she believes to be true. As with all stories, there is a beginning, middle, and end, as well as themes and key episodes. Next, he asks the client to relate this life story as if it were a one-page summary, followed by a single sentence, followed by a word or phrase. Condensing the story into a sentence or phrase forces her to find the central theme of what she believes. Clients are then asked how they would change their life story, even if that involved evoking a miracle. They envision, in detail, how creating a new "past" would change their present and future lives. After this step, the therapist uses the guided metaphor imagery session to consolidate the process, having the client "re-tell" her life story and new life. As will be described later, this is done after a brief relaxation period, finding a mental vision of safety, and then delivering the image with affirmations that the healing/change will take place and continue. Battino, an Ericksonian-trained therapist, makes sure to keep the story-telling vague to allow the client to discover and fill in the details.

Archetypes

As reviewed earlier, Jung defined archetypes as universally recognized symbols and metaphors that appear in folklore, sagas, fairy tales, legends, literature, mythology, religion, music themes, and even prehistoric art. From Jung's perspective, archetypes are the foundation for our personality; they are what motivate us and influence our beliefs, thoughts, and actions (e.g. Adler and Hull 1970). Jung actually identified very few archetypes: the Shadow; Wise Old Man; Child; Mother (Earth); Anima (Female Pattern); and Animus (Male Pattern). While Jung acknowledged that there were probably many more archetypes, he believed that most archetypes were linked to these core figures and ultimately represented specific aspects of these. Thus these archetypes were seen as building blocks for "character" archetypes that had unique thoughts, values, abilities, emotions, voices, energies, and physical characteristics.

The Shadow, although called an archetype, can be looked at as the flip side of each archetype, the weaknesses and shortcomings that go with each characteristic. Thus the Shadow is the dark side of our inner mind, the unexpressed, unrealized, and at times rejected aspects of who we are. As with any of our negative characteristics, it is imperative that we face and accept the shortcomings. If we deny them and are unaware of our shadow(s), we leave ourselves open to being blind-sighted by them. From a Jungian perspective, we need to neutralize the shadow by acknowledging it and dealing with it. Our shadow(s) can also provide us with strength and be an asset in the appropriate circumstance; it can also be an adaptive, although a pathological, survival mechanism.

Since Jung's death in the early 1960s, many authors, psychologists, and philosophers have expanded on this list of archetypes. Supplementary archetypes have included *family* categories, such as the father as stern, powerful, and controlling; the mother as feeding, nurturing, and soothing; and the child as birth, beginnings, innocence, and salvation. Some have included *story* archetypes, such as the hero (as rescuer and champion); the wise old person (or mentor as knowledge and guidance); the magician (as mysterious and powerful); the earth mother (as nature); the witch or sorceress (as dangerous); and the trickster (as deceiving and hidden). Another category can be called *animal* archetypes, such as the faithful dog (unquestioning loyalty), the enduring horse (never gives up), and the devious cat (self-serving).

From my perspective, archetypes are useful metaphors that can be selected to explore important client issues. The issue of how many archetypes there are is less important than how archetypes non verbally capture different emanations of the person and her issue(s). When you can identify an archetypal pattern to associate with potential problems and dilemmas, it is useful for the therapist to bring this to the client's attention, as is done when using therapist or collaborative metaphors. In Chapter 8, I will provide a list of archetypes and symbols that I think readily associate with specific life stages, issues, and transitions.

Rites of passage

As discussed in Chapter 3, many cultures recognize the importance of life transitions, especially those that occur at birth, the onset of puberty, marriage, life-threatening illness or injury, and finally death. In North America, school graduation, divorce, and retirement are important, as well as baptisms, bar mitzvahs, and confirmations. Every culture has unique passages, and they can be intentionally ritualized with ceremonies in order to help both the individuals and their relatives and friends cope with the changes.

All too often, rites of passage do not happen in our Western society today. Instead, they are replaced by governmental determination of status, such as in the USA getting a driver's license at age 16, voting at age 18, and drinking alcohol at age 21. By leaving all other transitions unmarked, a person may feel unrecognized and incomplete. It may be important for you to look for ways to mark these passages with women. This does more than move a woman from one status to another, it allows for a shift in consciousness (Brenner 2007). Identifying an unmarked passage may be a critical step in a woman's re-conceptualization of her life. This can be done either through the actual attention to the phase(s) of the ritual during expressive writing, guided imagery, and textile-making, or through embracing specific symbols and archetypes to create a ritual.

It is important to consider which elements of ritual to use. Typically, rituals include: purification to make one ready for a new status (washing hands and feet, smudging, smoke burning sage to cleanse, oil anointing); calling on spirits to state the intention for the ritual actions to follow (prayer, invoke divine for help, seek blessing of ancestors, dance, sing); calling in light to mark or sanctify the event (candles, build fires); making sacrifice to indicate the testing of strength endurance, resolve, or resiliency (sensory deprivation, keep vigil, fast, period of silence, meditate); gathering in community as a reflection of women's inclusiveness, compassion, and social needs (give or exchange gifts, feast, share food, join hands); worshiping (prayer, making offerings, creating altars with items of individual significance including power objects); communing (express oneself through music, song, dance, symbolic gestures); exorcizing (rid oneself of something unwanted or deemed to be of negative value; symbolized by cutting cord, rip piece of fabric or article of clothing, burning, burying, scattering); symbolically dying (cross thresholds, move in or out of a circle, create act that implies spatial movement); and rebirthing (creation, wearing, exchange of masks, dressing oneself in symbolic clothing) (Brenner 2007). Not every feature of a ritual needs to be included, only the relevant aspects.

There are some important facets when creating rituals that must be considered (e.g. Grimes 1995). First, where will it be held? Will it be indoors or outdoors? What type of space is needed? If it is outdoors, will you need to build a space, and if so, what type of materials will be required? You need to consider what kinds of preparations are necessary for the space. Second, objects will need to be made or gathered for the ritual. Third, time for the ritual needs to be considered. If the passage will be seasonal, the timing is set and there will be a limited window of opportunity to perform it. Finally, sound, language, and action are important considerations. For example, will there be live music or singing and dancing? Alternately, one could use gestures and prayers.

Techniques for exploring archetypes (in addition to textile art therapy)

Guided imagery

I refer to guided imagery, mental imagery, and visualization as one and the same in this book. None of these are "new" techniques. Imagery and visualization are well established in many indigenous practices, religions (e.g. Hinduism, Judaism), and traditional medicines (e.g. Chinese medicine). During a state of physical relaxation, the person is directed to visualize scenes, scenes that can be story-based, metaphorical, and even dream-like. In many ways, guided imagery is a waking dream. Guided imagery is often thought of as a way to access the images of one's unconscious mind, or "inner self," in order to resolve problems, promote insights, and bring about change. Trained guides usually work interactively with images that arise out of the person's imagination, teaching them how to access and use these insights and solutions. Guided imagery frequently allows for empowering images that can help a person to cope and to change.

I do not use hypnosis in this book. While guided imagery and hypnosis both appear to be very similar and often overlap, they are not the same. In both, the person achieves an initial state of relaxation. But in hypnosis, an individual's relaxation is enhanced through hypnotic deepening techniques and the person becomes highly susceptible to suggestions which are given by the counselor. It is thought that changes occur through these direct suggestions. Not all hypnosis involves guided imagery, and guided imagery does not necessarily result in a hypnotized state. If a person has had little success using hypnosis, he/she may still be quite effective at using guided imagery.

During guided imagery, the client is first placed in a calm, receptive state with verbal guidance. The relaxing state can be achieved through a variety of methods, including deep muscle relaxation, focused breathing, and imagining white light calming their body. The choice of which specific relaxation technique to use is typically influenced by both the provider and the client; it is usually something that both the provider and the client are comfortable with. Next, the provider will elicit places (e.g. in the mountains, at the lake or beach, at a family cabin) where the client has felt very comfortable and secure in the past and then use these images. Thus, once in a truly deep state of relaxation, the person is encouraged to imagine this (or these) secure place(s). Sometimes people will imagine loved ones in the scene. Other clients have discovered a bustling place filled with strangers (a bench in New York's Central Park on a Saturday afternoon in summer). Any of these are fine; the key is for the person to feel as emotionally secure as possible.

Then the imagery adventure begins. The practitioner may present a story-line to the person, a new metaphor (as with Battino 2007), or a mythic, folklore image, then allow the person's imagination to take over. Following several successful sessions with a practitioner, the person will hopefully be able to use the techniques on her own in expressive writing and textile-making.

Scientists are not sure exactly how guided imagery works, but it appears to be quite useful in reducing stress by lowering blood pressure and slowing heart rate, and treating insomnia, obesity, and anxiety disorders, such as phobias. Guided imagery has also been used for problem solving and to increase creativity and imagination, as well as to assist in sports training and rehabilitative medicine. It has multiple applications in medicine, including respiratory disorders, cancer, and chronic diseases. For example, researchers at Ohio State University in Columbus found that people with cancer who used imagery during chemotherapy felt more relaxed, better prepared for their treatment, and more positive about their care. They also coped better with the side-effects of chemotherapy than those who didn't use the techniques. Researchers at Massachusetts General Hospital in Boston found that visualization decreased menstrual distress and changed the length of menstrual cycles in women aged 21 to 40. Investigators at the University of New Mexico, Albuquerque, found that visualization was associated with an increase of breast milk production in mothers of infants at a neonatal intensive care unit.

While there are many books on the subject, the most effective images are the ones that have personal meaning to the person. When battling tumors, people sometimes imagine that their healthy cells are plump, juicy berries and the cancerous cells are dried, shriveled pieces of fruit. They might picture their immune cells as strong, powerful sharks that eat and carry away the cancer cells. Another image for healing is that the immune cells are silver bullets coming in and annihilating the tumor cells.

Some experts recommend actually personifying a condition and "reasoning" with it. This way the person has a chance to learn from his/her condition. If a person is plagued by headaches, for example, he/she might imagine the headache as a gremlin, tightening a rope across their temples. Then the person will ask the gremlin why he's there and what they can do to make him loosen his grip. The gremlin might "tell" the person that they have had too little sleep, too much junk food, or not enough rest and time away from work.

Expressive writing

The therapeutic use of writing has a long history. In puritanical days, women were encouraged to write as a means of self-discipline, and it was probably a way to control them. Jung had clients write in diaries to record dreams and fantasies of recurrent figures, images, and symbols. Ira Progoff brought forward Jung's diary recording as a form of "continuing confrontation with oneself in the midst of life." Three-ring binders were used with sections for recording daily life, work, events, body, society, and the figure of inner wisdom. Hinz (1975) introduced the concept of diary writing that synthesized psychology with literature.

Early research (Adams 1990) suggested that journaling, in conjunction with a program of psychotherapy, moved clients through issues more quickly and integrated new learning more readily. Adams described this as drawing on one's "higher self": recognizing the symbology of your life; developing your intuition; exploring your creativity (write a poem, add music, sing a song, doodle, paint a picture); and tracking the cycles, patterns, and trends in your life.

In the late 1980s, Pennebaker and his colleagues reported that disclosing information, thoughts, and feelings about personal and meaningful topics (called experimental disclosure) was associated with positive health and psychological consequences (e.g. Pennebaker and Beall 1986). They had college students write for 15 minutes on four consecutive days about "the most traumatic or upsetting experiences" of their entire lives. Controls wrote about superficial topics (such as their room or their shoes). Results indicated that writing about deepest thoughts and feelings was significantly associated with better self-reported physical health four months later, with less frequent visits to the health center and a trend towards fewer days out of role owing to illness.

By 2006, there were about 150 randomized studies of experimental disclosure. Frattaroli (2006) examined the results of random effects analyses, reporting that experimental disclosure was effective, with a positive and significant average r-effect size of .075. There have been inconsistent results about possible moderators (e.g. personality, age, gender, temperament) of the expressive writing paradigm (Baikie 2008), but subsequent reviews (e.g. Sexton and Pennebaker 2009) continue to provide a solid body of evidence suggesting it has a positive influences. It is important to keep in mind that the immediate impact of expressive writing is frequently distressing, with short-term increases in distress, negative mood, and physical symptoms, and decreases in positive mood, compared with controls. However, at longer-term follow-up, results suggest that both objective (e.g. blood pressure, immune functioning) and subjective (e.g. visits to doctor) health benefits occur, in conjunction with self-reported emotional state (e.g. mood, depression, well-being, intrusive thoughts). For example, Weinman *et al.* (2008) found that participants who wrote about traumatic events had significantly smaller wounds 14 and 21 days after biopsy, compared with those who wrote about time management.

It appears that expressive writing, as used in these laboratory settings, is most beneficial for trauma survivors (Pennebaker and Beall 1986). Limited benefits have been found for male psychiatric prison inmates (Richards *et al.* 2000), victims of natural disaster (Smyth *et al.* 2002), and individuals who have experienced a recent relationship breakup (Lepore *et al.* 2002). However, research indicates that expressive writing is no more helpful than in a control condition in people with body image issues (Earnhardt *et al.* 2002), children of alcoholics (Gallant and Lafreniere 2003), caregivers of children with chronic illness (Schwartz and Drotar 2004), students screened for suicidality (Kovac and Range 2002), and individuals who have experienced a bereavement (O'Connor *et al.* 2003; Range, Kovac, and Marion 2000). In addition, expressive, intensive writing has been found to be detrimental for adult survivors of childhood abuse (Batten *et al.* 2002).

HOW DOES IT WORK?

Venting, or emotional catharsis, does not seem to be the mechanism associated with positive outcomes. In fact, writing only about emotions linked to trauma has been found to be not as helpful as writing about both the event and the emotions (Pennebaker and Beall 1986). Furthermore, expressive writing health benefits were unrelated to the reported negative emotion expressed or reported just after writing (Smyth 1998). Instead, Pennebaker, Francis, and Booth (2001) suggested that expressive writing worked by developing a coherent narrative. Over the course of writing, participants with the greatest health improvement used more positive-emotion words, a moderate number of negative-emotion words, and an increased number of "cognitive mechanism" words (the latter include insight words such as *understand* and *realize* and causal words such as *because* and *reason*) (Pennebaker 1997).

One critical element in expressive writing is the structure. Danoff-Burg *et al.* (2010) reported that when writing about stressful life events, participants who had structured instructions produced superior psychological health benefits than did those participants who received standard expressive writing instructions (i.e. that did not specify the essay's structure). For example, instructions would look like this:

> *For the next 4 days, I would like you to write your very deepest thoughts and feelings about the most traumatic experience of your entire life or an extremely important emotional issue that has affected you and your life. In your writing, I'd like you to really let go and explore your deepest emotions and thoughts. You might tie your topic to your relationships with others, including parents, lovers, friends or relatives; to your past, your present or your future; or to who you have been, who you would like to be or who you are now. You may write about the same general issues or experiences on all days of writing or about different topics each day. All of your writing will be completely confidential. Don't worry about spelling, grammar or sentence structure. The only rule is that once you begin writing, you continue until the time is up. (Baikie and Wilhelm 2005)*

Summary

In summary, there are many ways to explore metaphorical material with your client: asking the client, providing them for the client, or working together collaboratively with the client. Sometimes, creating rituals will be very important activities to validate life changes. Guided imagery and expressive writing have each been shown to be successful techniques in and of themselves. By identifying metaphors, the therapist can help the client work experientially, through textile-making, guided imagery, and structured writing, to heal and re-design these metaphors.

Chapter 7

Pulling in the Warp Threads You Will Weave With

Issues, Metaphors, and Project Suggestions

The following issues may be important topics to consider and discuss with your client before starting the therapeutic textile-making experience.

Threads to consider

Functional vs. non-functional art

Is it fair to say that most textile handcraft pieces created by women are functional, and most pieces created by professional fiber artists non-functional? This difference is something I have observed over the years, but especially when interviewing professional artists for this book. The artists did not care if their work was functional. Several of them purposefully made non-functional pieces as a way to emphasize that they were creating art that had meaning (not practical, craft items). In contrast, most of the women that I have encountered in workshops, therapy, and my research make textiles that are functional. The average handcrafter is simply not comfortable making something that is impractical. Remember, functionality is at the heart of why women have historically created textiles: it was a necessity. Even in today's world, producing functional handcraft items justifies that a woman is not spending her time idly when creating. Certainly, most professional artists draw a line between themselves and the handcrafter around this very issue.

Conscious or unconscious metaphors?

Another way the artist creations were different from handcrafter creations was when it came to metaphors. Almost every textile artist that I spoke with had an artist statement, and that statement typically described how their work metaphorically or symbolically reflected their concerns and values (see Chapter 10). In contrast, it is a rarity to find handcrafters (not self-defined as professional) who consciously create symbolic pieces with fibers. I say "consciously" because there probably is an unrecognized translation of mood and issues into the style, color, form, and texture of a project. But this may not be something the handcrafter is directly aware of or makes a conscious choice about.

Before my children I had a miscarriage during my first pregnancy. This came after four years of infertility. Because we were living outside of the USA in an undeveloped country, we returned to family in Indiana for both support and medical care. During that month, I became preoccupied with making a wool coat from hand-woven fabric purchased by a relative in Scotland. Despite being an avid seamstress, I helplessly insisted that my mother-in-law participate at every step. The colors were dark and intense; the coat was huge and extremely fuzzy and textured. Looking back, I think I was obviously sad and angry. But to cope, I passed the time by creating self-comfort by way of a cocoon. I was also trying to relate to my baby's world (what it must feel like to be embraced in darkness and warmth), as well as re-enacting how much I wanted to keep him safe and sound. My desperation about making the coat "just right" reflected my lack of control over making the baby "just right"; if only I could figure out how to make the coat the right way, the baby would be (have been) safe. I still have the coat but can't bear to wear it. It symbolizes all of my grief and loss, all of my pain and sadness, all of my inability to create my baby boy. At that time, and for years afterwards, I would have told you that it was just a coat. Now, I can recognize (and embrace!) how much more it reflects.

Creativity vs. structure

Many women make textiles within the confines of a structure. They follow patterns made by others, such as for needlepoint and quilting and sewing. They also rely on traditional images that were handed down to them within their family, ethnicity, and culture. Many authors say this is how we can differentiate the crafts-person from the artist (Turney 2004): the crafts-person makes prescribed items, following a precise pattern. The artist takes the medium to new extremes, experiments with what is made, and creates something that is unique. I see it as a continuum that is more fluid for some women and rigid for others. Often, once greater mastery is achieved with a technique, handcrafters will leave the world of patterns to create more novel items. Once I understood the logistics of how to knit and crochet, as well as the structure of a knit or crocheted garment, I began to create my own designs. This was a natural progression for me. In contrast, I am still a relative novice at kumihimo and rarely make anything without a pattern. I know women who follow patterns for every type of handcraft, and others who will never follow a pattern for any handcrafts. Consider what Pamela Hastings (2003) has said: each person is born with a unique capacity for creativity, and "anything we make with creative intention is Art." Hastings also emphasized that art-making, in this type of context, should be used for the self, only, and for transformation. The focus should be on the process, the execution, and the contemplation involved. The object is to play with the colors, the textures, the objects, and the rhythm.

These are loaded issues and I suggest you explore them with your clients before embarking on a therapeutic textile experience. What meaning would it hold to create something that is non-functional? Can she allow herself to engage in this type of a project? What would it mean to her, and what would she fear others would think of her? Explore her insecurities in moving beyond traditional work and that of her predecessors. Could she tolerate or consider herself as an artist instead of a crafts-person? This may fundamentally reveal her confidence level; to leave the confines of a pattern, of a set story-line, and embark on her own journey, might be the greatest challenge that lies ahead.

Fundamentally, the issue is whether to create her own path, or to follow what others have laid out for her. You also will need to explore how she may have used textiles in the past to indirectly express issues and concerns (as in my coat). She may need a great deal of validation and encouragement to make this transition, and will need help "elevating" her self-concept to that of a creator, by following her own path and trusting her own creative instincts.

After you

Women are taught to think of themselves *after* others, and, adaptively, this makes sense. Postpone their needs: they can eat after their children have been fed; they can have new shoes after their family has been clothed; they can rest after others are comfortable. They also enjoy allowing the needs of those they cherish to come first. It is a way to show respect, to show caring. Is it surprising, then, to find that most women make textiles for other people, not themselves? It is much less common, and possibly seen as "selfish," to handcraft for one's self. My research has indicated that more textile handcrafters give their handwork away than keep it. When you begin a textile therapy project with your client, you must discuss how the client feels about making something for herself. If she is not comfortable doing so, it will be important to integrate who the project is for with the issue that is being explored, instead of polarizing with her around this issue.

Recycling and repurposing

Consider having the client re-use, repurpose, and recycle natural fibers whenever possible (Workman 2010). You can find many items at garage sales, donation centers, thrift stores, and even in your family's closet. Here are some ideas. Used wool sweaters can be felted and used as fabric; even sweaters with holes will be fine when felted. You can cut woven wool from pants and blazers into strips for rugs and weaving. Patterned fabric like plaids and houndstooth offer excellent color and texture choices that can be hand-dyed. Sweaters, especially those with a chunky knit, can be unraveled to re-harvest the yarn. You can also use leather and suede from old skirts, purses, and pants, or denim from old jeans, to create quilt squares and strips for weaving or a rag rug. All of the fabric from old cotton quilts can be integrated into new projects, even the batting.

You can also find "new" art supplies in the old. Old vinyl LP records can be re-used as bangles, bowls, and jewelry. You can turn broken pieces of crayons into crayon cakes. Of special value to me is finding cotton crocheted doilies, hand-embroidered tablecloths and handkerchiefs, and unfinished needlepoint. These are then integrated into my textile projects as a way of respecting the unnamed women who created before me. Have women collect plastic packaging from food and personal items to melt (between parchment paper with an iron), then sew, as a collage.

Making something new out of something old is a way for all of us to lessen our impact on the earth. It connects us to the past and puts value on handwork (Soule 2009). As women, we are well positioned for this task. Amanda Wills reported that 70 percent of households make recycling a priority, and more than two-thirds of these residents identify the woman of the home as the "recycling enforcer" (Wills 2009).

It also appears that older women recycle more than those who are younger (i.e. more than half of the 65-plus age group voted the recycling bin as an essential item in the house, compared with one-third of 25–44-year-olds). "It is about responsibility to the planet and the next generation which comes with being a mother" (Le Var, cited in Gray 2010).

Americans are pledging to lead greener lives in 2010, according to a recent study by Schomer (2009). Of the 1000 adults polled, 53 percent said they would make a green New Year's resolution—

and women were leading the way. Women are more likely than men to experience "green guilt," as the poll calls it—41 percent versus just 27 percent of men. As a result, women are more focused on following through with their green resolutions (52% will "very likely" adopt green habits in 2010, as opposed to 33% of men). Another reason is that women in developing countries bear the brunt of climate change—if there's a poor harvest, it's still their responsibility to ensure their family has enough food—making it interesting that American women, though for very different reasons, share that heightened concern (Schomer 2009).

Van Eyk McCain (2010), emphasizing that human beings must live more lightly and cooperatively with the earth, believes that the elderwoman is a critical and inspirational role model. Similarly, the Grandmothers (2011) ask us to imagine a world of perfect balance, peace, and progress for ourselves, our planet, and future generations.

Finally, making something new from something used and discarded is metaphorically rich, especially as we age. Artist Nancy Rakoczy makes nontraditional garments from discarded materials—garbage bags and newspaper plastic encasements. Rakoczy stated that "discarded plastic is just like us, invisible. You can be all dressed up and if you are an elderly woman, you are invisible. When you take discarded material and knit with it, it becomes something else, something special" (Rakoczy, personal communication, 2010).

Make multiple pieces on the same theme

Many artists will work on a series for a show. I know one woman in Indiana who has been creating the same type of hand-made paper Kachina Doll forms, albeit with slight variations, for almost 30 years. Doing multiple pieces on the same theme can reveal new levels of meaning and understanding for psychological issues (Hastings 2003). Hastings likens this to "peeling an onion," where with each fresh layer, more complexity is revealed, with miniscule changes. Just as in psychotherapy, people will continue to explore psychological issues around a central theme for years; one metaphor re-vamped over and over through textile art, writing, and imagery can provide ongoing and rich material for exploration.

Enjoy yourself!

As Hastings stated, "unravel the negative and re-knit the positive" (Hastings 2003). Making fiber art is enjoyable; many think it is the bee's knees, if you will. I can think of little more pleasurable than playing with colors that I adore, fibers that are amazing to touch (such as merino, bamboo, angora, and alpaca), yarn that is textured and chunky, and then creating these gorgeous materials into something that is unique, that I can complete, that I have to hold. It is fun, it is intellectually challenging and stimulating, it is soothing, it is exhilarating, and it is healing. It doesn't have to be serious. The direct meaning may not be revealed until several pieces are done, or ever, but the process can be a journey to embrace.

Metaphors of myth, material, and object

In the next chapter, I have provided examples of how I have linked psychological themes with metaphors, symbols, or archetypes, objects, textiles, as well as possible elements of ritual and design that are germane. In addition, there is some suggested reading for inspiration and additional concepts.

Every attempt was made to use metaphor archetypes that likely occur across different cultural traditions. However, individual ethnic and cultural customs vary and thus should be explored with your client. Ask your client about whether there are folklores, tales, and symbols that encapsulate the issues at hand and use that terminology. An example is with the earth mother image. This is a metaphor archetype that has been used historically across a variety of cultures and societies (Myss 2002). In Western traditions Mother Earth and Mother Nature are used in association with fertility, fecundity, and agricultural bounty. The earth mother is seen as the life-giving and nurturing features of nature that embody the mother. Algonquin legend refers to the earth mother as Nokomis, the Grandmother; Nokomis lives beneath the clouds and provides water to feed the plants, animals, and people. South American groups living in the Andean mountain ranges, which stretch from Ecuador to Chile, use mother earth mythology stemming from the Incas. Pachamama, translated as Mother Universe, is a fertility goddess who oversees planting and harvesting.

You can inquire about folktales and stories from your client's culture of origin. You can also rely on folktales and mythology from geographical regions they are comfortable with; Africa, the Americas, Asia, Europe, the Middle East, and Oceania have especially rich traditions. You can also look for stories that present religious allegories that the client relates to. Mary is an icon that many Catholic women relate to. You can explore The Hero's Journey, or an everyday hero known for her achievements and noble qualities, an ordinary person who shows great courage. I have also found that the younger generations have grown up with so much cinema, movies, music, and television that they can easily relate to archetypal symbols in media characters.

Suggested framework and techniques for textile therapy

As described in Chapter 4, the best place to start is with a comprehensive assessment. This will allow you to fully understand the depth and breadth of psychological concerns the person has. You will also want to evaluate her textile-making history, aesthetic style, associations with color, use of form, function, movement, texture, white space, symmetry, and orientation. Finally, you will want to evaluate the client's cultural background and values (Chapter 5).

Introduce the value of exploring archetypes, symbols, and metaphors

Based on the client's background, you need to determine how the client will relate (or not) to the concept of the archetype, symbols, metaphors, and goddesses. Make sure that these concepts are congruent with her religious and/or spiritual beliefs. If they do not align, determine if it would be acceptable for her to explore issues this way. See whether there are historical figures that she relates to. For example, if you want to have her explore her fighting spirit, the warrior woman archetype is found in the Greek Goddess Athena, the television characters Xena and Buffy the Vampire Slayer, and even Tara and Quanyin, the Tibetan and Chinese bodhisattvas of compassion.

Explore the artisan archetype

Myss (2002) describes the artisan archetype as a musician, an author, an actor, a crafts-person, a sculptor, and even a weaver. The artisan archetype personifies the passionate emotional and physical need one has for expression of life's extraordinariness with any medium of art. Myss described the shadow of the artist as possibly the madness that accompanies the genius, or the martyrdom of the starving artist.

Determine how the client relates to the artisan archetype. As expressed earlier, she may not even identify herself as an artist or a crafts-person. If not, why? If so, what are the strengths and weaknesses associated with this self-conceptualization? How might her creativity and generativity be limited because of this conceptualization, or lack thereof?

Determine which door to enter for therapy

There are always many different ways to begin to explore developmental issues with textile therapy.

YOU CHOOSE

As described with metaphor therapy, you can choose the metaphors for your client after determining which passages have been problematic. As you assess what brings the client to therapy, think about which passages are most pertinent to your client. If there are several unresolved issues that pertain to a variety of passages, try to help her create a hierarchy that these issues stem from. For example, current relationship difficulty issues may stem from unresolved issues surrounding sexual abuse in childhood, which led to poor integration of sexuality in her life during the young adult stage. Difficulties in her relationships may result in conflicts about what her own "perfect" union would be like. Prioritize these issues and join with her in where to start. With this type of "door," you can suggest images and metaphors for her to work with, and begin a discussion that is followed with journal writing, guided imagery, and then textile exploration.

THE CLIENT CHOOSES

Alternately, you can have the client choose which archetypes, goddesses, or angels to explore; have her find images that strike an internal chord. I typically work collaboratively and individually with each person to determine what is appealing to her. This may also guide you towards the issues that are pressing.

There are quite a few images created by artists that you can use to guide this approach. Susan Seddon Boulet has created a set called *Goddess Knowledge Cards* that include 48 cards depicting goddesses from cultures around the world containing the Middle Eastern, Chinese, Scandinavian, and Egyptian, as well as Greek and Roman, pantheon. A completely different style is that of Thalia Took's *Goddess Oracles*, a set of 81 cards that depict feminine deities from all over the globe. Her style is artistic, strong, and distinct, not "cutesy." Another set, also called *Goddess Oracles*, was produced by Amy Sophia Marashinsky and Hrana Janto. This deck combines pictures of goddesses from cultures around the world, but also includes goddess poetry, ritual, and mythology for guidance and insight. Deborah Koff-Chapin (Center for Touch Drawing), an artist and therapist, has produced two sets of cards, *SoulCard 1* and *SoulCard 2*, each with distinctive and deeply resonating spiritual images. Myss uses an intellectual approach, having her clients read through almost 100 archetypes to determine the 12 that form the central part of her personality make-up. She also has cards (*Archetype Cards*) for the more visually inclined. If your client is even less oriented to the archetype theme, you can use *Goddess on the Go* by Amy Sophia Marashinsky and Melissa Harris. These cards depict 33 paintings of active women and each is lined with a heart-centered affirmative phrase. Finally, the *Angel Oracle Therapy Cards*, by Doreen Virtue, is a set of divination cards that explore guardian angels and archangels.

LET THE MATERIALS AND OBJECTS BE THE GUIDE

After your textile assessment, you may want to think about both the textile materials and objects that are important to your client. Begin by asking her to explore the attraction to these mediums, physically, psychologically, and spiritually. As described in Chapter 4, why would a person emphasize texture over form? How does the need for precision and to be exacting in her replication of reality reflect her issues? Have her take the textile medium she is most engaged with (or the type of object) and encourage her to push it into a different direction. If she usually only works with vessels made of felt, encourage her to start creating other objects with felt, or trying to use different kinds of felting techniques (e.g. nuno felt, needle felt). If and when resistance occurs, reflect on this process, and try to encourage her to try something new. As you will see in the sample exercises that follow, objects in-and-of-themselves hold a great deal of symbolic value. At an intuitive level, your client may already be working through her issues with the persistence of creating specific objects. Do you have a quilter who only makes wall hangings? You could explore the meaning of making wall hangings instead of bed coverings or window shades, especially if you think the client would benefit from moving on to a different form.

INCORPORATE TEXTILE HANDCRAFTS INTO HER RITUALS

Finally, you can enter the client's world by determining the type of ritual elements needed. As described in Chapter 6, most life passages are not dealt with ceremoniously. Creating a ritual can validate the client's passage in a remarkable way. Although all of the components of ritual were listed, not all need to be used. For example, if dealing with physical and sexual trauma, you could incorporate the elements of purification, calling in the light, gathering in community, and exorcizing. The client can make a textile amulet as a form of protection in the future, something she can calm herself with when she is fearful. The creation of the amulet gives her control and mastery, and a way to process how unprotected she felt as a child. Through this formalized ritual, she will be able to focus on the light (or the positive, or the powers that be) to help her when she has difficulty coping, she will have acknowledgment from a support network that she was harmed, and she will be able to exorcize or purge the experience from her current self. The purification can be used as a way to start anew, and integrate the past harm into a new, stronger self.

Guided imagery structure

With that said, you should always be flexible. If you think a different metaphor archetype will work better for your client, by all means change it. As a therapist, you might not think a specific imagery exercise is appropriate for someone for a number of reasons, for example her mental health history, her culture of origin, or her abuse history. You can look for other archetypes and metaphors in this book, or skip the imagery altogether. If your client spontaneously changes the imagery on her own during the session, go with that vision (unless, of course, it is too disturbing).

If you are new to using guided imagery, you might not be aware that there will be quite a bit of variability in how people imagine scenes. Some will see vivid colors and images, some may only hear sounds, some will be attentive to texture and physical sensations, some may perceive only general impressions of an image. Make sure that you explore with the client which sensory modality they are attuned to, both before you begin using the imagery and after each imagery session. Start out by incorporating a variety of sights, sounds, and feelings into your descriptions, and then determine what works best.

It is always best to prepare people for imagery by spending several sessions teaching them how to use general physical relaxation techniques and deep breathing. When you begin the actual imagery, it is important to first tell the person what you will be doing, especially if you do not have a full clinical history. For example, someone might be terrified of water; thus you would not want to use ocean or lake imagery. Give the person permission to come out of the imagery at any time, as well as permission to tell you if they have unexpected disturbing feelings.

Guided imagery is not very difficult for most people to use. Just like learning to play a musical instrument or play a sport, it takes persistence and patience. Most people suggest practicing relaxation and then imagery for 15 to 20 minutes a day initially to ensure that they are learning it properly. As they become more skilled and comfortable with the technique they will be able to use it over shorter time periods throughout the day.

For clients who seem new to the imagery process or are emotionally fragile, physical relaxation is usually the best place to start. Guided imagery is not usually recommended for psychotic clients who cannot distinguish the difference between suggested images and reality. In addition, it is not recommended for clients who are emotionally fragile or unstable.

Some clients, particularly those with anxiety disorders, will experience a sense of panic or even a panic attack when relaxation procedures are started. Called relaxation induced anxiety (RIA), this is not uncommon. If this happens, allow the client to come out of the imagery (although she will probably do this on her own). You can reassure her that this is not abnormal, and that you can assist her in de-conditioning herself to the relaxation imagery. However, this may take a much slower approach than time may allow, going in small steps. The reader is referred to Schwartz, Schwartz, and Monastra (2003) for how to handle RIA clinically.

Make sure the atmosphere is right for imagery. Try to prevent unexpected noises and distractions, as much as possible, and that the room is comfortable: not too cool and not too hot. If it is impossible to avoid distractions, then incorporate the distractions into the guided imagery. For example, if you have the sound of cars driving by, you can point out how "as you notice the sounds of the traffic, you might be surprised to find that they relax you more and more."

When you conduct the imagery, make sure that you pace yourself. That means talk slowly (but not so slowly that it is annoying!). You can start at your normal pace, but slow it down as the relaxation progresses. Use your voice as a tool: calming and relaxing. I have noticed when recording audiotapes that my voice becomes slower and deeper than my regular "talking" voice as the imagery continues. Sound editors find this somewhat annoying because they invariably need to change the sound range. Thus, I always begin with my normal speaking voice, which has a rather high-pitched and child-like quality. As the imagery progresses, I deepen and lower it, using a melodic tone and emphasizing words for impact that probably would not be emphasized during normal speech patterns. I often put in comments that encourage the client to notice changes, allowing room for their own internal dialog.

Pay attention to the participant; does the person look alert? Does the person look tense and uncomfortable with the experience? If tense, you could spend additional time in the relaxation phase. Or, you could incorporate suggestions that acknowledge this tension and give the person permission to be critical and uncertain, while at the same time relaxing. For example, I might say: "As you continue to allow your body to relax more and more, it is okay to allow part of your mind to watch and observe, wondering if the relaxation and imagery will happen at all. That is fine, as while you watch, and are aware of what is happening, part of you allows your body to continue to relax, more and more."

Is she awake or falling asleep? If the person falls asleep, you can either gently remind her with words or a soft touch that she is learning how to relax now, and needs to come back to awareness, not sleep (so wake up!). Alternately, you can allow her to take the much-needed sleep and after a few minutes wake her gently.

At the end of the imagery, start having the participant transition to the present by re-focusing on the surroundings (e.g. noises in the room previously tuned out) and her body (e.g. stretch legs). If needed, repeat these instructions so that the person is encouraged to be refreshed and alert. Here is an example of what I usually say: "Bring your attention back to this room, and the sounds and smells around you. I am going to count back from 5 to 1, and with each number, you will feel more and more alert, bringing back with you a deep sense of relaxation. By the time I reach 1, you will be completely refreshed, relaxed, and alert. 5...picture the room around you; 4...begin to wiggle your toes; 3...begin to slowly stretch and move your body; 2...more and more alert; 1...your eyes opening now, feeling relaxed, peaceful, and alert."

When the person is fully alert again, it is important to "process the experience." Find out what worked and what didn't work. Find out if she is relaxed, or self-conscious. Comment on any process you observed (such as "You looked tense at first, then much later, you relaxed when I presented the forest imagery"). You may need to normalize experiences (e.g. people are often uncomfortable at first, and feel as if they are watching themselves and not relaxing).

REVIEW OF GUIDED IMAGERY SESSIONS
Each of the guided imagery exercises should have a similar structure:

1. *Relaxation.* Make sure the client has had 2–3 practice sessions to learn physical relaxation before starting guided imagery. At the beginning of each guided imagery session, always have your client spend 5–8 minutes physically relaxing.

2. *Special place.* During the first 2–3 practice sessions, help the client identify a special and safe place in her mind's eye that she can always return to. This process will also develop more ease in mental visualization. After the physical relaxation, have the client "go" to this special place and await, in readiness, the imagery experience.

3. *The guided imagery "experience."* Most guided imagery sessions will involve an "adventure," exploring an archetype, myth, or symbol that is particularly pertinent. Many examples of metaphors and archetypes are suggested in Chapter 8.

4. *Awakening.* Bring the client gradually out of the imagery, back to awareness in the room.

Examples of basic physical relaxation exercises

METHOD 1: TENSE AND RELEASE

Have the client tense and relax each muscle group, giving suggestions to mentally release tension after each group. You can have the person move "down" from her head all the way to her toes, or, if you like, from her toes up to her head. The person is instructed to tighten each muscle of the specific body part, and then let go of all the tension. Have the client "feel the relaxation spread" throughout her body; she relaxes. Usually, I include both sides of the body part at once (e.g. both the right and the left foot). However, you might choose to go slower and alternate between the right side and the left side of the body (e.g. for feet, you would first have them tense the right foot, then the left foot). Here is an example of what I would say: "I want you to tighten all of the muscles in your feet. Feel the toes ball together towards the bottom of your foot. Feel the tension as your feet strain; to know relaxation you must first know tension…tighter, tighter, hold it, hold it, now release. [*Your voice now slows down and is lower.*] Let go of all the tension. Release the tension and notice the relaxation flowing in. Feel the comfortable warmth of relaxation spread throughout your toes and feet, as they feel so relaxed. Now I would like you to tense the muscles in your calves…" Continue from the legs, to the knees, thighs, hips, buttocks, abdominal area, hands, arms, face, jaw, cheeks, and scalp.

METHOD 2: PROGRESSIVE RELAXATION

Start with the person's head, and slowly move down each part of the body, suggesting that the person feels more and more relaxed as you continue. Thus instead of focusing on the difference between tension and relaxation, I use a visual image such as like light coming down from the sky. "Imagine a beam of light coming from the sky, possibly like a helicopter shining its light on you. You can see any color really, white, blue, purple; any color. I want you to notice that as the light slowly and effortlessly moves down into your body, it smoothes out and dissolves any tension, leaving a sense of relaxation, more and more relaxed. So, as the beam of light swirls throughout your face, you feel more and more relaxed, more and more comfortable."

METHOD 3: DEEP BREATHING

"We will begin by learning how to take very deep, full breaths. To the count of 4, take in a full deep breath and fill up the lower part of your lungs with fresh, relaxing air. Notice how your abdomen raises up when it is full. Now hold the air to the count of 1...2...3...4. Now, let the air out to the count of 1...2...3...4. Notice how your abdomen squeezes in to allow all of the air to be released, letting go of all of your tension. This time, take another deep breath and go beyond the lower part of your lungs; also fill up the mid and upper portion of your lungs. Hold...2...3...4. As you let the air out, be aware of the natural rhythm so that the air is released from the upper portion of your lungs, the middle portion of your lungs, and the bottom portion. At the same time, these portions push in so as to expel all of the air in your lungs. Repeat, breathing in 1–2–3–4, and out 1–2–3–4." Because so many of these clients are visually stimulated, I give the suggestion that the air is colored, in a healing, comfortable, relaxing color.

Examples of guided imagery

Here are some examples of the guided imagery I use. Note how much more structure is provided in Example 1 than Example 2. I usually start guided imagery with more structure and provide less over time. Also, notice that in Example 1, I use the archetypal image I associated with the psychological issue. Alternately (or additionally), I could have used the basket and vessel metaphor with no archetype image. In Example 2, I use the material and object metaphor (beads). I could have used the Jester archetype or Goddess of Mirth instead or at a different time. You get to be creative and intuitive here!

EXAMPLE 1: THE MOTHER ARCHETYPE (GUAN-
YIN) IN GUIDED IMAGERY FOR FERTILITY ISSUES

When you find yourself in your comfortable, special place, you can begin walking along a path until you see a beautiful, calm pool of water. The water has a silver glistening quality to it, as if it is sparkling like millions of tiny little diamonds. It is so serene and full of life and energy, yet very, very still. It looks refreshing; you may even want to dip your hands or feet into the water and revitalize yourself; it is very unusual water. It is exceptional because the water comes from the flowing springs above, in the gentle hills. The hills that hold a cave and a meadow, the place you will find her, the one you will ask for compassion. You begin to walk along until you see a gentle flowing stream that feeds into the pool. Gradually, very slowly, you follow the stream uphill. Every now and then you hear a faint musical sound; not quite loud enough that you can tell where it is coming from. As you keep walking, it sounds closer, although when you stop, it stops with you, so soft and evasive. You begin to feel some excitement, as this place is different from any place you have ever been to before. You see that the waterfalls are directly ahead. The falls where the water cascades down in a complicated array of cliffs, it flows over many 1- to 3-meter steps, down to a picturesque valley for about 800 meters, before plunging over another steep 40-meter cliff. Then it falls into a breathtaking gorge surrounded by dense forest. Down and further down, the water rushes past you. It sprays a gentle mist, like an atmosphere of fog, cooling you on a warm, sunny day. You may notice that the water is crystal clear. The lyrical sound is more distant now, because the sound of the waterfalls has muffled all of the other sounds of the forest. You know you must walk up, slowly, up each tier, one by one, staying to the side so that you don't slip. There are little carved-out places on each stone that help you to step, as if somehow you are being invited to continue. Keep going up, slowly, carefully, but calmly, knowing you will arrive soon at your destination. [*Silence.*]

Now, alas, you can begin to see an opening on the other side of the waterfalls, a clearing that is filled with lush grass and moss and wild flowers. Flowers that smell more fragrant than any smell you have ever noticed before, filling your nose with the sweet, delicious smell of plumeria, or maybe it is like nectar, or maybe it is like honeysuckle, or maybe even like jasmine. A unique aroma that has a lovely scent.

And just like that, you see her. She is sitting just outside of the cave, cloaked in white robes. White. You know that, for her, white is the color of purity. Her gowns are long and flowing, and she seems to have a golden aura surrounding her veiled but transparent hair. You notice that she sits in the Lotus yoga pose, with a radiant, beautiful, welcoming smile on her face. She sits on a cushion, yet it appears to also be a flower. It must be a lotus flower because she is actually sitting afloat in a shallow pool of water. She holds a vase and silently beckons you to come closer, for she has a message. And just like that, you are sitting on a similar lotus flower, yet it is a cushion, yet it is a flower. It is so comfortable, your body cradles into the cushion; you may even feel like you are suspended in time. Without ever opening your mouth, you ask her to help you, to help your body, to bring peace to your body and allow your body to be receptive to the life force. Part of you may want to cry. And part of you may feel perfectly content. Anything you feel is acceptable, for she smiles knowingly at you.

[*Quiet.*] She looks so familiar, yet so different. She is not surprised that you have come to ask for her help. Many before you have come seeking compassion. She stands. She gently walks over to you, and takes the vase in her hand, and suddenly you realize it is filled with the most exceptionally beautiful pink-gold light that you have ever seen. It is light, yet it is color, it is transparent and yet it is liquid, all at the same time. She stands next to you, and slowly begins pouring into you the most glorious sensation of love and adoration you may have ever experienced. You see that the vase contains all of the colors of compassion and love; and she fills you up with this compassion and love, and your sadness and anticipation seem less and less and become fainter and fainter, swept downstream into the waterfalls and purified by the river. You are at once reminded that you are valuable and loved, that the golden, rose color sign of hope and compassion surrounds you. You know that there is life force inside of you; regardless if it materializes into a being, it is part of you. You contain this feeling inside and you feel peace.

Then she hands you a willow branch. The branch is about as long as your arm, and has a soft brown color. It feels soft, very pliant, but also very tough. The branch is slender yet long. There is tenacity to this branch, it is so alive. You notice the branch can bend, but it does not break. It can adapt, it can flex. You smell the willow branch. It has an astringent, sharp smell, but also a slightly fruity smell. You are curious, and gently scratch the bark, and suddenly, you feel your pain eased. Your body and your psyche feel so alive. With her eyes showing you the way, you see the willow tree and begin to walk towards it. If you are comfortable, walk over and find a place to sit, a nook by the roots of the tree. [*Silence.*] You can hear that gentle sound once again, as if there is a song played on a gamelan, yet it comes from the willow tree, as it gently sways in the breeze. It gently sways in the breeze.

She comes to you and offers you one last gift. This gift, she says, will calm you when you need to be filled with the rose and golden glow of peace, when you feel the emptiness of your own womb. Let this gift pour hope and confidence in you that everything will turn out right. That you can be well, that you are well, no matter how it all turns out. This third gift can be used when you make your own vessel, the one to show you are full no matter what happens. Full of love and lightness and compassion, compassion for yourself, you almost float down with the water.

Allow yourself to take the willow branch, the lovely glow of healing rose-gold light, and your third, special gift with you as you prepare to return to your outer world and your body. You thank her for these gifts; you feel more at peace than you ever thought possible. More peaceful than you could ever have imagined.

You walk down slowly, following the same footsteps etched in the stone, and begin to return to your own, very, very special place. Taking with you all of these gifts, knowing that you can find this calmness again, just by recalling the experience of being in the presence of the compassionate one.

EXAMPLE 2: MILAGROS BEADS FOR HEALING

The day is glorious. You are sitting in your special place, awaiting the adventure that your inner self will take you on. The warmth of the sunshine spreads generously onto your skin and fills your body with magnificent pulsations of light, each pulse radiating throughout your being, bringing you a sense of peace and inner reverence.

As you sit calmly, enjoying the warmth and stillness, something catches your attention on the ground; it looks like a tiny, baby rose. It is a miniature rose that is perfectly round and balanced, just like a perfect bead. The petals are velveteen and it has a primordial perfume.

As you look up, you may be surprised to find that you now are in a secluded rose garden, a quiet cloister protected by the flowers. All around you are roses, roses of every possible color, more colors than you have ever seen. Some roses are growing neatly in orderly bushes. Some have spread wildly, growing tenaciously on benches and lattice. Some roses are in neat, small pots; some have spread along the moss like wild flowers. The garden is exquisite, a celestial garden, and a place for meditation and prayer, if you like. This is a place to bloom, a place you have earned and can flourish in. You see garland after garland of flowers. *Mala* in Hindi language. And there you are, in the center of a sacred circle, a circle of flowers. You are reminded of the never-ending circle of life.

You are protected in this circle. Only healing and wellness can enter. You feel whole in this circle. Aware of the cyclic flow of nature, of the seasons of birth, life, death, and even rebirth. There is mystical protection here. You marvel at the repetitive symbols of the circle, all the way down to the molecular level. Here within a circle of flowers, in a sacred circle within a circle, is the circle of life; you have come full circle. Your cells are the very essence of this circle. They are the same, they are you. And in this garden, this circlet of roses, you are protected and you are healed. You are whole again and you are well. Allow yourself to take in this wholeness, and breathe in the sweet smell of health and continuity to each cell in your body.

As you await and splendor in the quietness, you notice a very small bag. It is the bag of healing. Notice the specific colors and patterns on the bag; they are very unusual and significant. You know that it is right for you to open this bag, and you find that it is filled with roots and leaves and small charms. These charms are sacred, and they are for you and for your healing. There may be one, there may be several. Take several moments to examine these Milagros, or tiny "miracles." They may represent body parts, or they may be beautiful circular beads, representing the circle of life. The objects could be symbolic, for you alone. Words cannot say what they are, but you have an inner sense of knowing about what they are. [*Silence.*]

Look deeper into your tiny medicine bag. You might find some crystals or gemstones, stones that hold significance to your inner self because of the power these stones radiate. You can rub the stone or stones against your skin; if you do, notice how good your skin feels. The light of the sun seems to energize and cleanse the stone, and this energy is transferred to your body. The stones can be held in your hand, against your arm, even on your feet. Allow yourself to feel comforted as you move the gemstone on your body, letting in the energy and light to balance your cells.

And now, as you look up again, each of these rose bushes becomes a bead, a rosary of sorts when taken as a whole. You recognize how fulfilling it would feel to make your own beads, beads that can represent the healing power of this circle within you. Allow yourself to bask in this sacred place, knowing that you can return at any time. And until you do, you can manifest your desire for healing and for peace by envisioning this untroubled, unfettered place of well-being through your hands, in your beads.

And when you are ready, you can begin to leave this special place, knowing that, at any time, you can return... [*Proceed to the exit suggestions.*]

Expressive writing

You may want to begin the therapeutic process by having the client create a journal as a textile art experience (see section 12 in

Chapter 8). This would set the stage for the creative processes to come. Any type of book can be used, from blank books to spiral notebooks to three-ring binders to an artist oversized sketch pad. I frequently shop "dollar" stores for basic journals to give to clients to change and make their own. Have the client identify special writing instruments, such as colored pencils and pens, markers, and even highlighters. Ask the person what feels good to write with.

You will want to take time with the client to explore the rationale for journal writing. Ask her what would be her own personal reason or motivation. If she is uncertain, you could suggest getting to know herself more, learning how to use the journal for problem solving, just taking the time for herself, recording her personal history, processing a relationship, having fun, and becoming her own friend or sounding board.

Authors of journaling books frequently suggest some basic guidelines for journaling. First, forget the requirements and restrictions you have been taught about writing (Rainer 2004); you can write about everything and anything. There are no mistakes; no spelling, grammar, or punctuation rules; your journal can be messy. Second, if you don't like how it feels to write about something, don't. Third, you don't have to write every day. It also does not need to be a lifetime commitment. The client can stop writing when she feels it isn't helpful, or just wants to stop for the day. Fourth, *the client decides who reads the journal*; it is not a given that the therapist reads it. The client should be encouraged to protect her own privacy by keeping the journal safe: put away or with her. Fifth, the client can say anything she wants about anyone. She is even allowed to whine, swear, complain, or get angry!

Like the guided imagery, it is helpful to have the client take a few minutes to center herself and quiet her mind at the beginning of journal writing. You may want to suggest a brief physical relaxation exercise such as slow, even breathing. Some type of ritual is helpful that involves getting ready to write, for example going to a quiet room, making sure there is time available, and having special coffee or tea. It is also helpful to encourage the client to do something pleasant when finished, such as taking a bath or walk, or asking for a hug.

Clients often wonder about what to write. Most authors suggest starting with short, structured assignments, moving eventually to loose, open-ended, unstructured assignments. Rainer (2004) talks about four ways to use expressive writing: description, to convey information perceived by the senses—sight, touch, smell, taste, and hearing; free-intuitive writing, to allow for the language of intuition; catharsis, to release and express emotions; and reflection, to contemplate and use one's intellect. The eventual goal of expressive writing in textile art therapy will be catharsis and reflection, so as to have the client explore metaphor archetypes and symbols outside of the session. However, in the beginning, you will probably want to start with descriptive writing and free-intuitive writing. Encourage clients to "write fast, write everything, include everything, write from your feelings, write from your body, and accept whatever comes" (Rainer 2004). The client can be encouraged to do this by describing her day; making lists about a specific topic; writing about what she has recently made with textiles; creating a self-portrait in words or images; and drawing a map of where she has lived and/or parts of herself and how they are connected.

To specifically explore metaphoric archetypes, here are some questions you can ask (adapted from Myss 2002):

1. How long has this archetypal pattern been a part of my life?

2. How has this archetypal pattern been associated with this issue?

3. What role has this archetype played for me in relationship to this issue?

4. What relationship does this archetype have to my unresolved issues, and how might this archetype now help me in understanding those situations?

5. What myths, fairy tales, or spiritual stories do I associate with this archetype?

6. Has this archetype appeared in my dreams? Describe.

7. Does thinking about this archetype make me feel empowered or disempowered?

8. Has this archetype played a role in my physical, emotional, and/or spiritual life?

9. What can I learn about my own shadow aspect of this archetype?

10. Has the shadow of this archetype caused me to block or forgo changes that needed to happen?

11. What guidance might this archetype have to offer me in the present moment?

Chapter 8

Unveiling the Textile Techniques

Physical passages

The textile techniques for physical passages are outlined in Table 8.1 and explored in more detail below.

1. Coming of age: Tribal belly dancing skirt and choli
PSYCHOLOGICAL ISSUES

Some young women experience very painful menstrual periods and some have prolonged periods. Some started their periods late, some very early. Having early periods has been associated with a host of self-esteem issues in girls, largely because sexual attention based on how they look is incongruent with their as-yet developed self-concepts. As described in Chapter 3, pre-menstrual symptoms are normal but can be extremely uncomfortable and disruptive for some girls and women, requiring psychopharmacological intervention. These issues aside, we typically do little to acknowledge the amazing transition from childhood to child bearing, yet the meanings of the ensuing physical and emotional changes are profound. Most of what follows in this section is not as relevant to pathology. Instead, it is focused on how to create a positive community that recognizes and witnesses the young girl's changes.

Table 8.1 Textile techniques for physical passages

Psychological issue	Archetype, metaphor, myth, or symbol	Object to make	Textile materials	Relevance of object and textile	Elements of ritual that could be emphasized	Design elements to emphasize
1. Coming of age	Persephone Wild Genie Virgin archetype Maiden archetype	Tribal belly dancing skirt and choli	Silk fabric Needlepoint (choli)	Belly dancing Dancing skirt Color Needlepoint Sewing	Purification Calling in light Gathering in community	Color Movement
2. Sensuality and sexuality	Freya Lover archetype	Boudoir covering	Any, but texture and sensuality are important	Skin Covering Texture Boudoir	Purification Calling on spirit Calling in light Communing	Texture
3. Motherhood	Mother archetype Amazon Medial Hetaira	Mother's apron	Sewing	Apron	Any or all	Form Movement
4. Fertility issues	Guan-yin (or Kuan Yin) and Ix-chel: Mother archetype	The womb vessel	Felt Basketry	Basket Vessel Uterus or womb	Purification Calling on spirit Making sacrifice	Form
5. Menopause	Crone archetype Spiritual Warrior	The Crone (or Spiritual Warrior) birth doll	Various methods, including knit, crochet, felt, sew	Birthing the crone Dolls Figural sculptures Fabric	Gather in community Communing Exorcizing Symbolically dying Rebirthing	Form Color
6. Physical and/or sexual trauma	Artemis Wounded Child archetype Heroine	Amulet forget-me-nots	Up-cycled and re-cycled materials such as lace, needlepoint, etc.	Amulet Lace Needlepoint Up-cycled material	Purification Calling in light Gather in community Exorcizing	Texture Shading
7. Death and bereavement	Inanna Phoenix bird Destroyer archetype Creator archetype Nephthys	Dyeing kite alive	Dyeing yardage Kite-making	Kite Dyeing	Symbolically dying Communing Worshiping Calling in light	Form Movement

RELEVANCE OF SYMBOLS, OBJECT, TEXTILE, AND FORM

There are quite a few symbols relevant to coming of age and first menstruation. The most obvious psychological archetypes are that of the *Maiden* and the *Virgin*. At her best, the Maiden represents the purity and innocence of childhood, where hopes, dreams, and magic still prevail. The shadow of the Maiden is that of a very self-centered, selfish person, where dreams and energy are focused on achieving her own personal needs. The Virgin is another useful archetype, emphasizing more the desire to remain pure and uncorrupted. Taken to an extreme, the Virgin isolates herself from others and never transitions into a full, sexual being.

There are many good ideas in the popular literature about how to create a ceremony for entrance into menarche. One approach I like is to have the client create items of clothing associated with belly dancing, especially a dancing skirt. The symbol of the dancing skirt can mark the entrance of a girl into a community of women who will be there to support her and appreciate her. It can also be a healing experience for women who associate puberty changes with shame and embarrassment.

Until the past two decades, belly dancing has been associated with female erotic dancers. Belly dancers as such typically provided a sexualized, staged cabaret-style dance and were clothed in lingerie-like wear. In recent years, more modern belly dancing groups have essentially restructured and resurfaced the activity in a way that counters common stereotypes. There are multiple formats, such as the US Tribal; these offer a fusion of dancing moves and costumes from a variety of cultures including Turkish, Egyptian, North African, Persian, and Middle Eastern. New-age belly dancing introduces aspects of popular culture, such as Goth; others even bring in disciplines like yoga.

The majority of new-age belly dancing styles are evolving practices. But whatever their formats, there are multiple commonalities. Most emphasize feminine empowerment. Belly dancing is typically done collectively in a group, where women celebrate their sense of community. There are also complicated forms of non-verbal communication that occur through cues and formations while dancing. These quiet communications allow women an opportunity for intimacy. In most contemporary belly dancing, women are not dancing for an audience, but for themselves and for each other. While dancing, women "witness" one another as a symbolic way to acknowledge their sensuality and life-creating and sustaining capacities. Furthermore, most belly dancing movements are essential to the development and maintenance of the abdominal core: expressive movement of hips, abdomen, and torso muscles are critical for child-bearing and for satisfying sexuality. Belly dancing also encourages body self-esteem; all body types are celebrated, even those outside of the Western norm (e.g. overweight).

Clothing for belly dancing varies but usually includes a dancing skirt, a choli (midriff shirt), and veils, scarves, head wraps, and belts. The dancing skirt is often made from as many as 25 yards of fabric in order to create a beautiful twirling, riveting motion when dancing, as if the dancer is flying. Although there is no one meaning for any color, red is suggested because it is associated with blood and life. Some people associate red with passion and rage. Have your client explore what color(s) symbolize this coming of age, but encourage the use of vibrant colors. A variety of textiles can be used for the skirt. I usually prefer hand-dyed silk or hand-woven shibori fabrics because of their texture, flow, and transparency. Needlepoint has often been used in cultures to signify a young woman moving into the maiden and then mother phase of life. The choli can be made with needlepoint as a symbolic transition into womanhood. Veils are discussed more in section 8 of this chapter.

SUGGESTED READING

One interesting book worth reading is called *The Wild Genie: The Healing Power of Menstruation* (Pope 2001). In the book, Pope encourages women to accept their cyclical nature and encourages them to develop positive rituals for girls who enter menarche. Pope challenges the reader to reframe seeing menstrual blood as the escape of the "wicked genie" each month, a genie that must be kept hidden and silent and then bottled up again. Instead, menarche is viewed across cultures as allowing women to come into their own power, sometimes even supernatural power, such as that of the shaman or healer. Not only do these roles become apparent when menarche begins, but the exquisite sensitivity and emotions that occur allow women to deepen their connection with life itself.

2. Sensuality and sexuality: Boudoir covering

PSYCHOLOGICAL ISSUES

There are many different issues women experience in reference to sexuality, and these change over time. Initial sexual experiences might have been traumatic; ongoing intimate relationships may be unsatisfactory. There could be confusion about gender identity, difficulties in finding sexual satisfaction while living with a new or ongoing disability, or even concerns about changes that come with aging. All of these variables contribute to sexual pleasure and dissatisfaction.

RELEVANCE OF SYMBOLS, OBJECT, TEXTILE, AND FORM

There are a number of archetypes that can depict sexual concerns. The most "pure" form of the sexual archetype is the *Lover*. The Lover represents passion and selfless devotion to another person. Taken to an extreme, the Lover's shadow is obsessive and fanatical, compulsively taking over. Another sexual archetype includes the *Femme Fatale*, also known as the seductress or enchantress, who manipulates sex for status, money, or power. Typically the Femme Fatale has little emotional involvement with her targets; they serve a purpose for her and are disposable. The opposite of the Femme Fatale is the Virgin archetype, where the sexual image is associated with purity and lack of corruption. The shadow of the Virgin archetype is the woman who resists her sexuality; this could occur because of fear and revulsion, prior history of sexual abuse, or the feared loss of innocence.

I like to use Freya, the Norse goddess of love and beauty, as a positive image for sexuality. Freya is actually known for her sensuality. Sensuality can be seen as an important part of sexuality, a part that one needs to be comfortable with and appreciate. The type of object I usually use to explore issues of sensuality and sexuality is a boudoir "covering" for the bed or body. Boudoir literally means "sulking" room, but more typically refers to a woman's private dressing room or bedroom. In recent days, the term has had more of a romantic quality and offers a sense of privacy, intimacy, and sensuality. There are now boudoir models and boudoir photographers; any woman can have boudoir photography taken. Boudoir photography is generally lingerie-based, nude, or has an implied glamour in a romantic setting. The look can be fresh and natural or dramatic and sensual with or without having to fully expose the body. Boudoir photography is typically soft and has a vintage, nature-inspired look. It is aimed at empowering women and showing their true beauty.

Texture and sensuality are essential for the boudoir cover. I suggest having the client conceptualize making the boudoir cover as a second "skin," one that is purely for pleasure. As described in Chapter 2, skin is how we receive tactile stimulation, and it is both a boundary between ourselves and others ("outside" of us). Our skin is waterproof, elastic, permeable, and washable. It communicates touch, pressure, temperature, and pain. Touch is one of the first sensations to develop in the fetus and one of the last sensations to recede in the elderly or dying. Spend time exploring the concept and meaning of "skin" with your client, and how cloth coverings of actual skin illuminate this metaphor.

It will be important to explore the meaning of bed and bedding. Functionally, bedding keeps a person warm and safe, and adds comfort while sleeping. It can also be used to shut out what is feared, as in "hiding under the covers." The bedroom is personal and intimate and usually suggests rest and sleep. The bedroom is typically a haven, far from daily life and closer to one's true self. It can symbolize recuperation as well as love-making. From a negative perspective, it can also be associated with fear and frightening dreams. Some people have experienced incest and rape in the bedroom, or sickness and death. The silence of the bedroom can magnify anxiety and worrisome thoughts (ARAS 2010). Explore these meanings and help the client to re-channel any negative associations into beautiful, second-skin coverings.

3. Motherhood: Mother's apron

> The strings were tied, it was freshly washed, and maybe even
>   pressed.
> For Grandma, it was everyday to choose one when she dressed.
> The simple apron that it was, you would never think about;
> the things she used it for, that made it look worn out.
>
> She may have used it to hold some wildflowers that she'd found.
> Or to hide a crying child's face when a stranger came around.
> Imagine all the little tears that were wiped with just that cloth.
> Or it became a potholder to serve some chicken broth.
>
> She probably carried kindling to stoke the kitchen fire.
> To hold a load of laundry, or to wipe the clothesline wire.
> When canning all her vegetables, it was used to wipe her brow.
> You never know, she might have used it to shoo flies from the
>   cow.
>
> She might have carried eggs in from the chicken coop outside.
> Whatever chore she used it for, she did them all with pride.
> When Grandma went to heaven, God said she now could rest.
> I'm sure the apron that she chose, was her Sunday best.
>
> *(Trivett 2007)*

PSYCHOLOGICAL ISSUES

Motherhood can be one of the most joyous experiences a woman will ever experience. And it can also be one of the most stressful. The stress typically starts the moment a woman brings her baby home, when she truly grasps that the infant will be completely dependent on her from now on. The anxiety, uncertainty, and insecurity can be overpowering. This is true regardless of whether a woman is a first-time mother or expecting an additional child. As many as 85 percent of all women will experience symptoms of post-partum depression shortly after giving birth. This is probably because of the biological changes that occur, including lower levels of serotonin, after childbirth. However, in 10–15 percent of women, a more disabling and persistent form of depression will develop (Kessler *et al.* 2007).

Authors have described different phases of mothering, but they usually include early, middle, and late (e.g. Barnard and Solchany 2002; Francis-Connolly 2000). During the early stage, birth to 12 years of age, nurturance is key. Mothering requires a great deal of endurance and flexibility. She must provide for all needs, including nutrition and toileting, safety and early socialization. Mothers are always "on call" and on the go, with little "downtime" as they are faced with helping with homework, keeping up with team sports, and embracing the psychosocial needs of their children. Try juggling this with building their own careers; the result is often guilt for either wanting to be home with their children or guilt for not wanting to be there at all.

During the middle stage (children between the ages of 13 and 17), the road map changes again; motherhood is characterized by finding the balance between rules and limits. The mother must provide direction and structure, yet promote autonomy. This stage can be psychologically difficult for the mother while she tries to stay grounded in the midst of her children's hormonal turmoil, and sometimes her own peri-menopausal symptoms.

Then, when the late stage occurs, at 18 years of age or older, the mother needs to step back even further, allowing the children to assimilate into early adulthood. Classically called the "empty nest," the mother still "serves" her children as they cope with college, relationships, and finding new meaning if in a long-term relationship.

Add to any of these phases financial hardship, lack of support from partner/spouse, or single parenting, it is not surprising that many women will not pay attention to their own needs. Everything from lack of sleep, exercise, and proper diet, to lack of time to socialize and groom, mothers often find themselves in an overwhelming rollercoaster of highs and lows, working 24×7 as nurturers, providers, counselors, nurses, and especially teachers. Be on the lookout for identity issues, loneliness, career issues, and a sense of inadequacy.

RELEVANCE OF SYMBOLS, OBJECT, TEXTILE, AND FORM

The *Mother* archetype is fundamental to all cultures. At her best, she can be seen as a life-giver, the source of nurturance, patience, and love. The good Mother archetype is a provider for her children and family and typically puts her children's needs before her own. She is responsible for and fiercely protective of her children. The shadow Mother is one who is abusive and abandons; she can also be expressed as one who devours. The shadow Mother does not encourage healthy development and autonomy; instead, she imparts guilt about separation and independence. The shadow Mother may be socially depicted as today's career mother, who puts her own needs before that of her children.

Wolff (1985) described women as having four main archetypes that are central to her nature: the *Amazon*, the *Mother*, the *Medial*, and the *Hetaira*. According to Wolff, each female has one or two of these dimensions that are more prominent. The Amazon sees herself as an equal to men and functions well in the patriarchal world. Her focus is on achievement and making her mark. She is energized by competition and readily criticizes herself (and others). The Amazon woman holds high expectations for everyone and is intimidating to most, especially men. The classic Mother archetype represents the soothing, care-taking female. She is described as cherishing and nursing, helping and charitable, teaching and protective. The Mother archetype is satisfied by the process of offering fulfillment and support to others and wants nothing in return. The Medial archetype is described as the symbol-forming function. This is the classic intuitive, inner, wise self. The Medial woman listens to her body signals and symptoms, her dreams and life's synchronicities, and accepts the guidance of her inner voice. Finally, Wolff defines the Hetaira archetype as the feminine symbol of intimacy. Hetaira is the ultimate companion, even of herself. She is comfortable with any situation, physically, emotionally, or spiritually, and surrenders submissively.

Each of these characteristics will contribute to a woman's expression of the Mother archetype. If she has been predominantly an Amazon woman prior to motherhood, how will the adjustment to the classic Mother role work for her? Or, does she express too much of both the Mother and Hetaira archetypes, rendering her a care-taker of everyone's needs but her own? Wolff's conceptualization is not meant to label people, but to provide a shared vocabulary for exploring issues of motherhood.

One object I suggest having the client make for exploring motherhood is an apron. Aprons hold complex historical meanings for the twenty-first-century woman. The word is derived from Latin, *mappa,* and French, *naperon.* In Middle English, *napron* meant napkin, cloth, or covering. There are indicators of apron use all the way back to the Upper Paleolithic period in Europe (ARAS 2010). It is thought that the apron may have been the first piece of clothing worn by humans.

Aprons cover the abdominal, pelvic, and genital areas. This can be important for different professions, such as cooks, artists, and metal smiths; they are hygienic and protective wear. Covering the abdominal area with an apron would also shield an unborn child, possibly reflecting the mother's natural maternal instincts. In the 1960s, aprons became stereotypic metaphors of the repressed, unliberated female, the homemaker's uniform. They epitomized the symbol of enforced domesticity and women dominated by the chores of housewifery. Interestingly, in recent years, the apron has become fashionable again. Some think this is because the third wave feminists have rediscovered the domestic arts; they experience little shame in cooking, or in taking care of their children and homes. "An apron doesn't define you; an apron celebrates what you do for the people you love" (Lynch 2011).

Vicky Jo Bogart, an avid apron collector, began collecting aprons after her Czechoslovakian grandmother died. She loved aprons because they triggered memories from her youth and her heritage. Her collection, now at almost 300, reflects the individuality of the women who wore them. "They would express themselves on this little piece of fabric" (Richards 2011).

Have your client explore what aprons have meant to her. What type of aprons is she attracted to, and from what era? Is she intrigued or appalled by the 1950s/1960s style? What are her stereotypes about aprons, and her fantasies? Does an apron seem appropriate to her lifestyle? Indulgent? A necessity? What would she want to communicate to other people if she was seen wearing an apron?

To make an apron, have your client use unusual materials that she enjoys working with. This could mean that she creates special hand-woven cloth to sew with, or she creates a fabric collage with quilting techniques. Clients can find fabric from old, used aprons in thrift stores and re-work it into something quite un-apron-like, something that reflects what they really value in motherhood. Fabric from her old clothing stash could be recycled into an apron. If she is an avid outdoors woman, jeans or denim pants could be up-cycled into an apron to symbolically reflect important values. The concept of an apron can be reworked into a sculpture, similar to how Kathleen Holmes uses old crochet doilies on an armature (see Chapter 10). Aprons don't have to be objects of beauty; they can be frightening images as well. What if your client were to fashion pretty, floral fabric from an apron into a strait-jacket (restraint garment)? Encourage your client to use the concept of an apron as a springboard for fully exploring the meaning of the Mother archetype.

4. Fertility issues: The womb vessel

PSYCHOLOGICAL ISSUES

According to the Centers for Disease Control and Prevention (CDC 2011) approximately 10 percent of women (6.1 million) in the United States aged 15–44 have difficulty getting pregnant or staying pregnant. The International Council on Infertility Information Dissemination (INCIID) considers a couple to be infertile if they have not conceived after six months of unprotected intercourse, or after 12 months if the woman is over 35 years of age, or if there is incapability to carry a pregnancy to term. There are many problems associated with infertility, including smoking, excess alcohol use, stress, poor diet, overweight and underweight, sexually transmitted infections, and health problems. One additional cause is maternal age: approximately 20 percent of women wait until their 30s and 40s to have children, and, of those, one in three will experience fertility problems.

Infertility is one of the most distressing life crises that a couple can face. It is associated with feelings of loss and depression, anger, guilt, and blame. Blame is frequently channeled towards oneself, that is, at the person's body for being "inadequate," at the partner, at the doctor, even at God (punishment for something they did in their life). Infertility is also associated with sexual intimacy problems, as the goal of having a baby becomes the purpose of sex. The closeness and pleasure associated with sexuality is typically put aside or forgotten. Critical negotiations must be made between partners in order to determine how they will approach different treatment options, when to set limits on treatment, when to stop treatment, and whether other options such as adoption or surrogacy are acceptable.

RELEVANCE OF SYMBOLS, OBJECT, TEXTILE, AND FORM

Specific examples of the Mother archetype that embody symbols of fertility are Guan-yin (or Kuan Yin) and Ix-chel. Guan-yin is a Buddhist bodhisattva (or prophet) to whom childless couples turn to for help. In many ways, she is the Buddhist parallel for the Virgin Mary. Variants of Guan-yin are found in China, Korea, Japan, and even Malaysia. Guan-yin is known as the Goddess of Compassion, especially for women and children in need. Ix-chel was a Mayan goddess and called the weaver of the lifecycle and the "Lady of the Rainbow." She was known for sending rain to nourish crops, whereby she would ensure fertility by overturning her sacred womb jar so that the waters would flow.

As seen with Guan-yin, the classic object associated with female fertility is a vessel, as it is obviously shaped like a uterus or a womb. Containers, vessels, bags, and baskets have traditionally been used to hold items. Vessels can also be ampoules for feelings and personal memories. They are also dialectic: they can be filled and they can be emptied, they can hold and they can let go, they can protect and they can restrict, all at the same time. Likewise, the uterus is an empty vessel waiting to be filled with growing life. Thus it is not surprising that pots, vases, and other containers are often seen as metaphors for the female body. One group in north-eastern Nigeria creates Ga'anda shrine vessels to represent the female figure. The upper parts of these vessels have long necks, sometimes with an odd elongated face ending in a large, circular opening. The lower parts typically have designs that signify the ritual scarification marks that Ga'anda girls receive starting at age five. The marks on the shrine vessels reflect the social and cultural significance of the scarification.

Although quite a literal interpretation, vessels are the suggested object to make for fertility issues because they symbolically represent the melding process, the interwoven cycles of life. The uterus form is essentially an inverted triangle, with branches that go outwards toward fallopian tubes and then narrow at the bottom to the cervix (which becomes the birth canal, and is the vagina). Some have suggested that the womb holds the original, undifferentiated self; not only the creator of life, but the abyss before life comes to be.

There are quite a few fiber materials that can be used to create vessels. The most obvious is using basketry techniques. Basket artists like Deborah Valoma (2010) and Judy Mulford (2011) have taken traditional basket-making techniques and created quite unusual forms. Because my preferred medium is felt, I suggest using wool. Batting can be shaped around a "resist," and then hard-felted until a very firm consistency is achieved. Wool cords can be attached during the felting process to add dimension and more texture. Another medium for vessel-making includes creating a ceramic bowl or vase, or finding an interesting-shaped gourd, then drilling holes around the edges in order to incorporate pine needles, cane, or other fiber to add additional texture and form. Coiled baskets can also be created by wrapping fabric strips around a rope core and then hand or machine stitching them into place. Basically, any fiber medium can be used to sew, felt, or tack into the shape of a vessel. Encourage thinking "out of the box," or "out of the bowl," while exploring associations with the vessel metaphor and the mediums.

SUGGESTED READING

There is a very unusual and not commonly known book, *Ex Utero*, by Laurie Foos (1995). In the book, Foos plays with metaphors associated with the uterus to an absurd level. The fantasy story is about 31-year-old Rita who realizes that she has recklessly lost her uterus at the shopping mall while shopping for shoes. As she searches for the lost uterus, she gains national attention. The ultimate irony, that women are valued as mothers and devalued when infertile or childless, is brought to light. I found the humor in this book to be personally helpful while struggling with my own infertility. I have also found Foos' play on words quite helpful when framing guided imagery and using expressive writing.

5. Menopause: The Crone (or Spiritual Warrior) birth doll

PSYCHOLOGICAL ISSUES

Aging takes on new dimensions in our society today. Where once the stage of menopause signified the later part of life, we now are living longer and have many more options besides "winding down." Despite this optimism, it is still difficult to wake up and realize you have probably lived more than half of your life.

Women frequently talk about being shocked by the physical changes that occur as they age: the extra weight gain, eye puffiness, reduced energy, and physical deterioration in vision and stamina. In a society preoccupied with youth and beauty, it is hard to come to terms with a declining body. Some feel that entering this phase truly means it is too late for their dreams, that there is no way to change their health or redesign their bodies or lifestyles. Add to this the emotional rollercoaster of, and sometimes cognitive changes associated with, peri-menopause and menopause. Still, many elder women remind us that the wisdom of age ultimately brings increased emotional stability, perspective, and a grounding of values. This phase of life often results in a deep inner knowledge about what is and what is not important.

RELEVANCE OF SYMBOLS, OBJECT, TEXTILE, AND FORM

The *Crone* is a fairly typical older character in fairy tales and folklore and is a good metaphor for menopause. She is often characterized as the wise old woman, a respected elder who is at the heart of the family, someone who others turn to for wisdom and the sharing of life experience. Positive images of the Crone are associated with compassion, transformation, and healing. Often the Crone is imbued with magical qualities: the gift of understanding how to transform situations, how to influence people, and how to make visions a reality. In contrast, the archetypal shadow of the Crone is depicted as the angry, bitter old lady who has not learned from her life. She is seen as isolated and fearful, even portrayed as a witch or sorceress who uses wisdom wrongfully, in a negative and destructive way.

Alternately, the contemporary peri- and post-menopausal woman between 50 and 70 years of age can be called a *Spiritual Warrior* instead of a Crone (Quigly 2010). Quigly described the Spiritual Warrior as a woman who is not afraid to stand up to the tyranny of war and evil, or to stand united for peace and prosperity. She encourages women to look inward and see themselves as having traveled the road of life. With a lifetime of experience and wisdom, the Spiritual Warrior's job is to actively share and advocate for the younger generations. Women in the Spiritual Warrior phase have the energy to be active players in life, to fight for what they believe in.

Once your client determines whether she relates more to the Spiritual Warrior or to the Crone, I suggest having her explore making sculptural dolls. Dolls have their own history of transformation, from anthropomorphic spirits that mediate between this and other worlds, to goddesses that instill values via instruction and ritual. African and Caribbean Voodoo dolls are used to materialize visual images (Hastings 2003). Just as with children, the uncensored and uninhibited playing and making of dolls gives us a safe place to try on, modify, and discard "forbidden" roles. Your client can create a series of dolls that reflect and embrace who she has been, who she is now, and who she wants to become.

Are dolls actually sculptures? Non-textile artisans would probably say no. Textile handcrafters would argue that they are: figural sculptures and doll-making can be seen as one and the same. Figural sculptures involve design, ornamentation, and textiles; found objects, story-telling, and folklore can be incorporated. There are as many ways to make a doll as there are textiles. Doll-making can include knitting, crocheting, felting, and sewing. They can be made from paper, molded from clay, and dressed.

A very well-known feminist artist, Helen Redman, created a series of paintings titled "Birthing the Crone." Redman stated: "My art becomes pregnant with self. The end of personal fertility opens a whole new generative realm. As I labor, the images that emerge are alternately funny and painful; yet I continue to bring forth what arises within me. I like the idea that a time arrives for women to replace the biology of the womb with the creativity of the psyche" (Redman 2011). I like Redman's attitude, that the Crone or the Spiritual Warrior is birthed, and that the generative spirit can be imbued metaphorically into this new phase of life.

SUGGESTED READING

There are many books on doll-making, but few to none on the psychology of doll-making. I would suggest reading *Doll Making as a Transformative Process*, by Pamela Hastings (2003). After reviewing the history of doll-making, Hastings presents over 20 examples of how women have used doll-making to explore personal issues. Many of these women are truly artists in their own right. Hastings also has exercises to use as well as images of different mediums that people use. It is a must if you want to explore doll-making with your client.

Another interesting book to read is *Once Upon a Midlife: Classic Stories and Mythic Tales to Illuminate the Middle Years* (Chinen 2003). Most fairy tales only consider youth and possibilities. Chinen has collected stories from around the world that pick up where the Prince and Princess marry and live happily ever after. What happens after that describes the more realistic journey of twists and turns. There may be archetypes that your client may relate to, and the tales examine common crises, role reversals, settling down, reconciliation, and renewal.

6. Physical and/or sexual trauma: Amulet forget-me-nots

PSYCHOLOGICAL ISSUES

It is not surprising that women who reported abuse as children experience more physical problems and have higher scores for depression, anxiety, somatization, and interpersonal sensitivity (low self-esteem); are more likely to abuse drugs and have a history of alcohol abuse; are more likely to have attempted suicide; and are more likely to have had a psychiatric admission. And, when you combine childhood abuse with adult abuse, women who reported both have even higher levels of psychological problems and physical symptoms than those who reported childhood or adult abuse alone (McCauley *et al.* 1997). In addition, sexual abuse has been associated with the expression of hypersexualized behaviors (Friedrich *et al.* 2001), and increased aggression, depression, anxiety, and anger (Johnson *et al.* 2002). Some victims of abuse have an increased tendency towards self-harm (Santa Mina and Gallop 1998).

RELEVANCE OF SYMBOLS, OBJECT, TEXTILE, AND FORM

The classic archetype for abuse is that of the *Wounded Child*. The Wounded Child holds the memories of the abuse, neglect, and traumas from childhood. The positive side of this archetype is that it typically awakens a deep compassion and the desire to help others who have been wounded. The shadow of the Wounded Child can lead one towards self-pity and blaming of others for one's problems. The shadow also prevents the person from moving on into forgiveness. The Wounded Child is a critical archetype to explore in a person who has knowingly been abused in order to fully understand the ramifications in self-concept and the impact on her future choices.

A different approach would be to explore the archetype for protection, the *Heroine*. The Heroine awakens an inner strength and power so that the woman can overcome great obstacles. She is brave, not just for herself but for her family or group. *Artemis* is a goddess of the Greek pantheon, known to be a protector of women. She is a feminist who takes care of the underdog, the victimized, and the powerless, especially young girls. Artemis provides a healthy image for someone with a history of abuse; she is the personification of protection and strength. A less known Haitian female goddess is Erzulie Dantor, often portrayed as the Black Madonna, or the Roman Catholic "Saint Barbara Africana." Dantor, also a protector, has tribal scars on her cheek and will fiercely defend women experiencing domestic violence.

Keeping these images in mind, a powerful object to make is a protective amulet that signifies personal power. An amulet is chosen as the object because it is meant to shield the wearer from trouble and bring good luck and/or protection. Most religions have references to the protective and healing power of amulets or blessed objects. They can be carried or worn on the body, hung upon or above the bed of a sick person, or used as medicine. The image of a strong, protective female as part of this amulet further helps the client come from a position of strength and power. The hidden wounds of the child will not be forgotten.

As described in Chapter 2, up-cycled, discarded, and recycled materials hold layers upon layers of meaning. I like to have the client integrate used, cast-off, or recycled material for the amulet to add extra depth. The client can look for hand-made lace, handkerchiefs, knit/crocheted afghans, and needlepoint at thrift shops. These objects were made by unknown women, women who continue to be silent and invisible, not unlike the Wounded Child. Incorporating these materials into the amulet can have powerful symbolic meaning by acknowledging the unknown and possibly silenced sisters. The amulet can be embellished and sewn into a small bag or pouch to be worn around the neck.

Texture and shading are important elements of design to incorporate. These characteristics allow for the metaphoric expression of sadness, loneliness, and depression. Women who have undergone abuse also do well to incorporate elements of ritual after their objects have been made, such as purification, calling in the light, gathering in community, and exorcizing. The ritual allows for more symbolic re-enactment of the event, but this time with protection.

7. Death and bereavement: Dyeing kite alive
PSYCHOLOGICAL ISSUES

There are many ways to conceptualize death, bereavement, and grief, whether it is about oneself or a close friend or family member. The same feelings can be triggered by any significant personal loss (e.g. of a job, relationship, one's own health, anticipating one's own death), as well as the death of a loved one or at the end of a relationship.

Elisabeth Kübler-Ross, in her book titled *On Death and Dying* (1969), is well known for describing five grief stages: shock, denial, anger, bargaining, grieving or mourning, and acceptance or recovery. Although her theory still plays a significant role in most literature on death, dying, and bereavement, her approach has been criticized for being too simplistic. For example, by describing these emotional states as *stages*, Kübler-Ross implies that people go through the process in an orderly manner—which they don't. They can experience a few reactions, such as shock and anger, then skip to acceptance, then return to grieving. Many agree that it is more accurate to refer to the grief stages with the term *phases*. These phases do not all have to occur in each person, and many of them may reoccur. Additional phases commonly experienced include shock or disbelief, guilt, and hope. Grief symptoms can be physical, social, cultural, or religious in nature. Physical symptoms range from mild sleep or appetite problems to stress-induced heart attack. Social isolation from other loved ones and difficulty functioning are also typical.

For children, the death or loss of a loved one will be consistent with where they are developmentally. In very young children with no language, loss can be seen behaviorally, such as crying and irritability. Preschool children (e.g. three to five years old) will remember the person who has died, but consistent with their developmental perspective do not understand the permanence of death. They frequently believe that death is a temporary state and the person will magically reappear, such as going to sleep and waking up years later (e.g. Sleeping Beauty). Elementary-aged children view death as more permanent and final, but it is not unusual for them to personify death as a person or ghost that carries off people. Tweens and teens can have reactions similar to adults but may be less willing to talk about their feelings. Death seems very distant to the adolescent; they typically experience disbelief because, to them, death happens to the elderly and should be a long way off. It is common in all people, children, adolescents, and adults, to experience emotional regression in the face of grief—they behave in former, typically less mature ways of thinking, behaving, and coping. Recognize this behavior as an expression of emotional pain, and have confidence that the person will return to her normal ways as the bereavement is processed.

When symptoms of grief become more complicated, the person will experience intense emotion and longings for the deceased, have profoundly intrusive thoughts about the lost loved one, undergo extreme feelings of isolation and emptiness, avoid doing things that bring back memories of the loss, and experience worsened sleeping problems and anhedonia. When depression becomes extreme, medical intervention may be needed.

RELEVANCE OF SYMBOLS, OBJECT, TEXTILE, AND FORM

The ultimate archetype for death and loss embodies both the *Destroyer* and the *Creator*. The cyclic nature of life is personified in these two constructs: for new life to be born, systems and structures must be dismantled (Myss 2002).

Inanna, known as the Sumerian goddess of death and rebirth, captures this theme, which is prominent in ancient Middle Eastern religions. According to legend, Inanna descended to the underworld, traveling through seven gates in order to confront her dark sister Eriskegal. At each gate, she was forced to remove an item of clothing and jewelry until she was finally naked before her sister. Eriskegal then killed Inanna and hung her, where she remained for three days and nights before being resurrected by her husband's love. Another well-known myth about death and resurrection is that of the Phoenix bird. The rise of the phoenix exists in Chinese, Japanese, Russian, Egyptian, and even Native American lore. The mythical bird never truly dies. Although on earth it can live for as many as 12,000 years, at the end of its physical life, it sets up a pyre of aromatic branches and is consumed by the flames. After three days the young phoenix arises from the midst of the flames anew. Either of these images can be used in guided imagery to encourage the client to reflect on death and renewal.

The kite was chosen as an object to make for several reasons. Historically, the word *kite* is associated with the story of Nephthys, or the "Friend of Death" in the Egyptian language. Nephthys, associated with funeral rituals, was seen as one who gave guidance to the newly deceased and comfort to the deceased's living relatives. She is often depicted as a bird of prey, like the Egyptian hawk. Pictures typically show Nephthys as a woman with falcon wings that are outstretched, possibly as a symbol of protection. She has a piercing, mournful cry that probably reminded the ancients of the lamentations usually offered for the dead by wailing women.

The word *kite* actually comes from the English *kyte* and the Old English *cȳta*, meaning kite, bittern; akin to the German *Kauz*, meaning owl. The word is also used to refer to several small birds of the hawk family. Kites have been reported in many eastern cultures such as China, Indonesia, and the South Sea Islands, for thousands of years. Kites are typically made of natural fibers, including bamboo, vine, braided fibers, leaves, reeds, woven cloth, and later paper. The basic parts of a kite are the spine (supports the length of kite); the spar (curved or bowed, supports the spine); the frame (internal frame for the shell); the cover (outer shell made from cloth, plastic, or paper); the bridle (controls movement); the flying line (held by the person); the tail (for balance); and the reel (winds the flying line around).

Kite-making can be part of a ritual the person creates, for new life and for the symbolic release of life. The symbol of the kite pairs well with the phoenix bird imagery as well as Nephthys. As described in Chapter 2, dyeing fabric also carries its own metaphor. I would have the client work on a series of kites as she works through the loss and the release. There is also a gaiety and joy that comes with kite flying, which allows the person to revel in being alive. The kite creation and/or flying can become a yearly ritual in memory of the deceased or loss.

Personal passages

The textile techniques for personal passages are outlined in Table 8.2 and explored in more detail below.

8. Invisibility of self: The veil reveal

PSYCHOLOGICAL ISSUES

There are many ways that women experience invisibility. Some women have talked about their diminishing sexual appeal and beauty to men (or women), noting that the attention they enjoyed when younger eventually stopped. Others have worried about their invisibility in relationships, especially with long-term partners and children. Familiarity and care-taking both appear to contribute to this type of invisibility, where wives and mothers seemingly become hands without faces. Some women have noted their invisibility in the workplace: women in almost every profession have not reached the same levels as their male counterparts with regards to senior management and compensation. Nicole Johnson (2005), in her book *The Invisible Woman*, described that the very nature of putting others before oneself leads to invisibility.

Table 8.2 Textile techniques for personal passages

Psychological issue	Archetype, metaphor, myth, or symbol	Object to make	Textile materials	Relevance of object and textile	Elements of ritual that could be emphasized	Design elements to emphasize
8. Invisibility of self	Hestia Servant archetype Rescuer archetype	The veil reveal	Lace-making (or collecting) Weaving	Veil Net Lace	Calling on spirit Calling in light Exorcizing Rebirthing	Shading Texture White space
9. Mental health	Beiwe Healer archetype	Wreath of well-being	Wool and felt Basket materials	Wreath Circle	Purification Calling on spirit Make sacrifice Gather in spirit	Form Movement Texture
10. Seeking the ultimate union	Lover archetype	Purse first	Knitting/crocheting Using incongruous or unusual materials together	Purse Incongruous material	All	Form Movement Texture
11. Where is home?	Oshun Home	Creating a personal altar	Mixed	Shrine Altar	Calling in light Worshiping Communing	Form Color
12. Chronicling your life	Mnemosyne Kali Calendar	Redefine your narrative in a special journal	Bookmaking	Calendars Narrative Journal	Calling on spirit	Form Color
13. Body image	Gaia Mother	Body quilt	Quilt Hand-dyed fabric Embroidery Beadwork Fusible appliqué	Sewing Body image	Calling in light Making sacrifice Exorcizing	Form Color
14. World weary women	Ixcacao Amazon Medial Hetaira Mother archetype	Playing with temari balls	Embroidery Needlepoint Temari ball Embellishments	Spinning wheel Temari ball Chocolate	Making sacrifice Worshiping	Form Color Texture

RELEVANCE OF SYMBOLS, OBJECT, TEXTILE, AND FORM

Hestia is considered the Greek goddess of hearth and home. Interestingly, Hestia is a "forgotten" goddess; she has no real story, she just "is." Although once filled with grace and beauty, Hestia was more known for her attributes that included serenity, dignity, calmness, stability, and hospitality. Hestia's main function in life was to be of service to others, especially her family and community. She never left home, always staying at Mount Olympus to welcome visitors and partake in homecomings.

Hestia embodies the ultimate invisible woman, always in service to others, never recognized for her true individuality. She represents the archetype of the *Servant* and the *Rescuer*. The Servant performs the menial work of others, and has no sense of power. The Servant becomes a slave to the social system, which Hestia became. The Rescuer provides strength and support to people, especially in crisis. Although she seemingly has no expectations of reward, the Rescuer actually really does, keeping the rescued person needy so that she always has a job to do.

If a client has invisibility as a critical issue that needs exploring, it will be important to have her think about how she may have contributed to this role. To move beyond these issues, she must make conscious decisions about how she wants to be seen, and if she wants to be seen for whom she truly is.

The object for this exercise is the veil, a textile that is meant to physically hide and protect the face. There are multiple symbolic meanings associated with the veil. Psychologically, it can be used for the same reasons as the physical: to protect that which is overwhelming, to separate one from others, and to offer a disguise from one's true nature (ARAS 2010). Thus, the veil is similar to unconscious and conscious processes: hidden, unknown meanings can be revealed or "unveiled." By literally creating different types of veils, the client can explore how she has contributed to her invisibility and come to understand ways to remove the barrier.

There are a number of methods that can be used to construct a veil (e.g. woven fabric or lace-making). The client should experiment with various textile techniques, making sure to create a net-like material that is transparent (see *Veil* by Bo Breda in

Chapter 10). Breda uses steel mesh wire, telephone wire, and rhinestone embellishments. Nets are very strong, yet have a loose weave. Historically, nets were associated with entrapment and entanglement, which also touches on psychological metaphors of invisibility. Nets also represent interconnectedness and social connections, such as in the words "*net*work" and "inter*net*." It is interesting that nets contain very little tangible material and have a great deal of empty space (or white space) (ARAS 2010). White space elements in design may represent aggression. Having the client create white space on purpose may give her an outlet for her anger and frustration. The veil can be an article of clothing, can be used to surround a mask, or, like Breda's, can be free-standing.

9. Mental health: Wreath of well-being

PSYCHOLOGICAL ISSUES

Contributions to and descriptions of mental health and illness were discussed extensively in Chapter 3. What was not discussed, however, was the impact of having mental illness on the person, her family, and her friends. Coming to terms with having any form of psychiatric disorder is difficult at best, but often takes years, sometimes decades, for people to accept and then manage effectively. The initial transition from being fully functional and psychologically healthy to suffering severe psychiatric impairment can be sudden and terrifying. There is also societal stigma about having a mental illness, grief about the change this causes in the person's life, as well as sadness associated with the adjustment. Family members' and friends' reactions are influenced by the personal impact of the mental illness (such as care-taking); they often become exhausted, anxious, and burned-out from the experience.

Then there are the children of people with severe mental disorders. They are the ones who suffer the most collateral damage. These children will have a higher risk of developing mental illness themselves, both because of genetic factors as well as the inconsistency and unpredictability of their family situations. Their relationships with their parent(s) can be severely compromised, which will also potentially lead to harm, both physically and psychologically.

RELEVANCE OF SYMBOLS, OBJECT, TEXTILE, AND FORM

For the person living with a mental illness, the child forced to grow up too soon because of a parent with mental illness, or the family member enlisted to cope with a relative who has mental illness, an important archetype to explore is that of the *Healer*. The inherent challenge is to acknowledge the need for healing and to see the wound(s) associated with the mental illness.

There are very few folklore traditions that invoke the spirit of mental wellness. One of the few that I have found is that of *Beiwe*, the Goddess of Spring and Mental Clarity, of the Sami people of Finland. According to the legend, Beiwe holds the power of the sun (she is also known as the Sun Goddess), which enables plants to grow and hence provides food and sustenance for womankind. According to the Sami folklore tradition, Beiwe travels through the sky on a sled-like contraption made from reindeer antlers each spring, together with her daughter, Beiwe-Neida. Their coming marks the beginning of light and green in the Arctic region filled with harsh winters. Beiwe is also said to restore the sanity of those who have lost themselves in the darkness of the winter season. She is one of the rare deities that are invoked for the relief of mental illness. Because of this, some consider her a patron of those of us who work with the mentally ill.

Beiwe brings well-being in her wake. Have the client focus on the meaning of overall well-being. Beyond mental well-being, it can include physical, social, spiritual, and economic well-being. It could also mean competence (having the intellectual ability needed to deal with life demands), autonomy (the ability to resist environmental influences), aspiration (motivation to establish and work toward meeting goals), and integrated functioning (the ability to balance different life demands) (Pesta, McDaniel, and Bertsch 2009). Help the person understand herself in a fuller context; well-being occurs in multiple arenas and doesn't have to be defined solely on the basis of mental or emotional well-being.

There are a variety of ways to symbolically represent Beiwe in textiles. I suggest having the client create circular objects, especially a wreath headdress. Beiwe typically wears a ring or circlet of flowers on her head and is also placed in the middle of a sun, which is round, on an antler sled which curves up into a circle. The word *wreath* is derived from the Old English word meaning "to twist." Wreaths typically intertwine continuous loops of flowers, leaves, tree branches, herbs, and berries (ARAS 2010). Historically, wreaths were made of materials associated with specific gods, such as the olive leaf and Zeus. Wreaths "crown" the head, suggesting honor and authority, sometimes even the divine. In modern society, wreaths are associated with the solstice holidays, weddings, athletic victories, funerals, and even births. Their circular form suggests the continuity of life, celebrating the cycles of nature where all that withers becomes anew again. The creation of wreaths can symbolically honor your client's mental well-being, both by conjuring up Beiwe's image as a mental health healer and bringer of light, as well as by acknowledging that life's difficulties occur in cyclic patterns; happiness will eventually return.

Wreaths can be made from any type of fibrous material that is used in basketry. They can also be made from wool, felt, or fabric that is hardened. Alternately, Beiwe images can be personalized and then needle felted as a picture, or sewn into art quilts. Beiwe doll icons can be created for the client's personal altar, as a constant reminder that mental wellness is their right and within their reach.

10. Seeking the ultimate union: Purse first
PSYCHOLOGICAL ISSUES

Most men and women want to find someone extraordinary who they can spend their life with. Riela and associates (2010) described 12 precursors to falling in love—reciprocal liking, appearance, personality, similarity, familiarity, social influence, filling needs, arousal, readiness, specific cues, isolation, and mysteriousness—with respect to culture, ethnicity, gender, and speed (of falling in love). Riela *et al.* found surprisingly few differences across cultures;

most people were looking for the same things in their partners. We also know that getting married later and remaining married has been a trend since the mid-1960s. Divorce rates have decreased in both the USA and England, from 50 percent to about 40 percent. The age of first marriage is now at an all-time high, 27.5 years for men and 25.6 years for women. Sociologist Paul Amato of Pennsylvania State University suggested that marrying when older (e.g. 30s vs. 20s) is a good thing; it improves the average marital quality, results in more cohesive relationships, and results in lower divorce rates. Factors contributing to later marriage include more of an emphasis on personal self-development, completing education, and beginning careers (United Nations 2000).

So the good news is that people may be behaving more cautiously to make their choice and settle down. The bad news is that people may be looking for more unrealistic characteristics in a partner. One of the most significant variables in how we perceive sexual and romantic relationships today is a result of the television we watch. Investigators have reported that the more a person watches television, the more likely she is to develop unrealistic expectations about relationships that are potentially harmful, such as "there's such a thing as 'love at first sight'" and "the right mate 'completes you'—filling your needs and making your dreams come true" (Galician 2004; Segrin and Nabi 2002). Holmes (2004) found that the more romance-television people watched, the more they idealized relationships, the stronger their belief was that mind-reading is the norm, that fighting is destructive, and that fate brings soul-mates together.

To meet the man of her dreams, increasing numbers of women are seeking the help of modern technology—online dating. Kim *et al.* (2009) surveyed 3345 people in the USA about internet dating practices and found that internet dating was much more common than even a decade ago. That increases the dating "pool," which means overwhelming numbers of men to sort through when looking for the "ideal" mate.

RELEVANCE OF SYMBOLS, OBJECT, TEXTILE, AND FORM

The archetype of the *Lover* is a very fitting archetype for the search for a life partner. Griffin (2006) looked to the media and literature for modern examples of love images. She identified what she called romantic love change agents (Cupid, Knight in Shining Armor, Venus) and relationship story lines (Beauty and the Beast, Cinderella, Rapunzel, Romeo and Juliet, Sleeping Beauty). Griffin found three patterns of love relationship progression: Seeker, Fairy Tale, and Mature. Where seekers were looking for "true love" or enjoying the sexual infatuation of early relationships, fairy tale couples had found each other, overcome difficulties, and were committed to their love. Lastly, mature couples were long-term companions and comfortable in their relationship. She further reduced these to the Romantic ideal (i.e. relationships are based on emotional and/or physical responses to the other) and the Companionate ideal (love is built on long-term friendship and empathic closeness). These modern archetypes are important to explore. Help your client to identify which characters she relates to; try to determine if she can combine the Romantic and Companionate ideals to create a richer image of a relationship ideal.

One key way to create a realistic environment for finding a caring, loving, and positive relationship is to honestly and earnestly take stock of your life, especially past relationship patterns. I suggest having the client start with what she has enjoyed in past relationships. What were the qualities, exchanges, and interactions that worked for her? Was it the excitement of the chase, or the comfort and the affection? What was important that was shared? Was it humor, time spent in activities, or talking? Then, have her focus on what she didn't like. What were the negative, hurtful feelings and experiences, the harsh words? Were these interactions reminiscent of people in her past, such as parental or sibling relationships? Have her try to gain insight into repeating negative and positive patterns.

The next step, which is probably the most important of all, is to reflect on what she contributes to the situation. What is she insecure about? Is it the way she looks? Are there historical events that are embarrassing (such as a divorce)? What does she not like about her role in relationships? Then, have her think about what she would say if she heard a very close friend focus on these faults. Can she find ways to support herself and build herself up? It is very important to find ways for your client to love and accept herself. If not, these insecurities and self-doubts will likely be projected onto others. She will expect others to "fill" her up where she feels empty. These problems are her responsibility; if she can't love herself first, no one else can love her enough to make a difference.

Have your client think about what goes into her purse: the inside and the outside. It is also known as a bag, a clutch, a handbag, a change purse, a pocket book. The word *purse* comes from the Old English *pusa* (bag) and Latin *bursa*. It is used for carrying all kinds of items, including keys, driver's license, credit cards, photographs, cosmetics, and pens. Symbolically, such as in dreams, the purse is associated with identity and the circumstances of the purse reflects key psychological states. Thus if a purse is messy, open, or closed, it will echo her mental state. The purse becomes a metaphor for all that she carries, that weighs her down, that is positive. It has an outside "look" to it, just as each woman does, and inside baggage. Metaphorically, have your client think about how to lighten her load and fill her needs without carrying all the "stuff" in her purse.

Lisa Klakulak creates handbags to reflect symbols of "safe receptacles," strength, and durability. Some of the titles of her pieces are "Fenced," "Fortification," "Stretched," "Cautionary Containment," and "Locked" (Klakulak 2008a, 2008b).

If the client were to create her own identity metaphor with a purse, how would the purse look? Purses can be created from a variety of materials, including hand-made felt, knitting or crocheting, embroidery, sewing, and needlepoint. The exterior (and the interior) can be decorated with symbolic images. I like having the client combine incongruous or unusual material when purse-making. For example, plastic grocery bags can be cut into thin strips and then spun with linen or even wool. The end result is unexpected and represents how the coming together of people can work in surprising ways.

11. Where is home? Creating a personal altar

PSYCHOLOGICAL ISSUES

More and more, adult children live at home into their twenties and thirties. This is true in Europe, the USA, Canada, and even India. In Italy they call them bamboccioni—big babies. In the UK, they're called KIPPERS—"kids in their parents' pockets." It is a far cry from the past, when at 18 or 19, children in most Western societies moved out on their own. There are obvious economic reasons for the change: jobs are more difficult to find and the cost of living is higher. The number of young people who attend university has increased over the past four decades, which has contributed to an increase in financial dependence. There are fewer expectations in society that men and women should marry and have children early. When adult children do move out, there is frequently a "revolving door," where they come and they go.

In spite of this change, for many, returning home as an adult can have difficult psychological repercussions (Firestone 2010). Being home can trigger negative, implicit memories, memories associated with difficult feelings. When these feelings are triggered, the experience does not come with a road map indicating "wait, this is something that you felt in the past, not now." According to Siegel (2007), people can experience all of the perceptual, emotional, somatosensory, and behavioral responses from the past, without any awareness that these are actually related to experiences when we were younger. I often talk about this as if being at home "pushes your buttons." Before you know it, when the parent asks them to do something, the person behaves in childish ways, instead of their usual adult behavior. Sometimes, these child-like behaviors get carried over to other close relationships; the closer and more intimate the relationship, the more likely a person is to behave and re-enact immature responses that are not truly relevant to the present. This is another example of transference (described in Chapter 9).

There are also people who leave their childhood home but have difficulty establishing their own sense of home as an adult. They may have traveled the world, moved because of jobs, or chosen to live in a different locale. The home they grew up in may not have been a kind, loving, thoughtful place. Some "third culture kids," children who grew up with expatriate parents in a foreign country (or multiple countries), never truly have a "geographic" place to call home. Helping clients identify what they want in a home is crucial for resolving these issues. Although "home" will have multiple meanings for each person, it is critical to define what a good space feels like and to recognize how to create it in order to feel truly grounded and centered in the world.

RELEVANCE OF SYMBOLS, OBJECT, TEXTILE, AND FORM

There is actually no specific archetype for *home*. Inspiration can be found from an African goddess known as *Oshun* of the Yoruba people in Nigeria. Oshun is known for her fresh and sweet water; her name actually comes from the river that she supposedly died in. There are similar goddesses of water and love in Brazil and Cuba (Oxum), as well as in Haiti (Erzulie or Ezili). The Nigerian Oshun has several identities, but most are associated with creativity in the decoration of self, home, and temple. She is known to bless beautiful spaces, and is also regarded as a healer of emotional life. Some of Oshun's thematic symbols include mirrors, jewelry, honey, golden silks, feather fans, the number five, and the colors yellow, amber, gold, and bronze. Offerings to Oshun include sweet foods such as honey, white wine, oranges, sweets, or pumpkins, and perfume.

In addition to exploring textiles that are associated with Oshun, the shrine or altar is an object that can be explored. The word *shrine* is actually derived from the Latin word *scrinium*, which means case or chest for books or papers. To most people, shrines are considered holy or sacred places, dedicated to a venerated or worshiped figure. Many of the world's religions use shrines, including Christianity, Islam, Hinduism, Buddhism, Wicca, Chinese folk religion, and Shinto; each culture and religion has its own traditions, rituals, and rules about how to create and use them. Whereas Buddhist households require shrines to be on a shelf above the head, Chinese shrines must stand directly on the floor.

Shrines can also occur at prominent or sacred sites, even places of so-called miraculous occurrences. Shrines can be extremely large, especially if they are in places of worship, or small enough to place in a pocket. Some consider shrines to be a miniature stage, upon which a collection of symbolically important objects are placed, things that are meaningful to the person and frequently represent a higher power. Traditionally, altars include incense, candles, fire, water, oil, ash, statues, icons, spiritual books, and natural elements (Khalsa 2007).

The concept of an altar or shrine may seem unusual, especially if the ritual is not part of a person's religious or spiritual tradition. However, there are many ways to conceptualize this exercise. I would have the client explore her own sense of place in the world. Have her consider how her current living environment reflects and supports who she is, and whether this matches with her ideal living environment. In a sense, a person's entire home could be considered her altar. In smaller ways, creating a special place within the home to anchor and find peace, vitality, and comfort makes sense.

An altar does not have to have any specific format; it can change and evolve as the person changes. According to Khalsa, altars can invoke ideals, passions, interests, goals, and dreams, and can be composed of any type of objects, elements, sounds, scents, and imagery that are personally meaningful. Have the client think about visual images that make her feel at peace, such as landscapes, photographs, or personal pictures. Because I am a textile-maker, I typically have clients fashion a shrine out of fabric and decorate wood or cardboard with multiple textiles. Some clients have made the shrine with padding; others have used extremely elaborate beading. The altar can also have a series of hand-made personal objects (e.g. the Crone birth doll, temari balls) that signify home and peace.

SUGGESTED READING

See *Altar Your Space: A Guide to the Restorative Home* (Khalsa 2007). Khalsa presents a guide to creating a peaceful living space "that truly reflects and expresses who you are." He guides readers in turning their homes into personal, holistic sanctuaries. The reader is given tools to explore her personal and spiritual needs, so that she can manifest these into smaller altars within her home, or at best, making her entire home an altar.

12. Chronicling your life: Redefine your narrative in a special journal

PSYCHOLOGICAL ISSUES

In Chapter 7, the importance of journaling and expressive writing was reviewed. Expressive writing will be one component of textile therapy for most women. For others, journaling may be the single most important activity they need, and should remain the focus of their personal explorations. I usually start all textile therapy with journal-making. If the activity captivates the client, then I have her continue with it for as long as is needed.

RELEVANCE OF SYMBOLS, OBJECT, TEXTILE, AND FORM

Mnemosyne was considered the Titan goddess of memory and remembrance, the inventor of language and words. She was also considered to be the mother of the nine Muses. Her goddess role was linked to the creation of time; without our ability to remember, time would cease to even be a concept. The image of Mnemosyne conjures mental clarity and the ability to express oneself creatively and openly. The image of Mnemosyne can be used to help reclaim memories, place events in the past, present, and future, and inspire creativity. Another goddess associated with time is *Kali*, a Hindu goddess. Kali is also associated with death; some believe that the death association occurs only in the ignorant (i.e. more enlightened people are less attached to life and hence unafraid of death).

Time, as measured in increments and by calendar, has an interesting history. It allows us to know what happened in the past and what will happen in the future. It is the way we can determine how long it has been since something important transpired and when something significant will occur again. Early calendars were strongly influenced by geography. Locations that had seasonal fluctuations and cycles based their calendar on the tropical year. Geographical places that had less pronounced seasons included climate events such as heavy rains and floods, but lunar calendars measured the month. It was not until the mid-1700s that the Gregorian calendar, our current system, was adopted. Some countries, such as Turkey and Russia, were slow to join the trend and did not adopt it until the early 1900s; there is still criticism about the weaknesses of the Gregorian calendar, but no viable alternative has ever been found.

For this exercise, start with asking your client what her own unique calendar would look like. What are the significant events, positive and negative, that she orients her life around? How do these events affect her each year? As she tells her personal narrative, have the client begin to determine the distinctive ways she measures time; these may or may not have anything to do with traditional religious events. Time could be measured from the birth of her child or the death of a parent. Time could be marked by a natural catastrophe or a traumatic incident. It could be observed by a time she was abandoned, or even raped. Consider whether time is linear to her, or whether it is cyclic. Another possibility is that time didn't really "start" for her until after a special event. Maybe she remembers little of her life before being adopted by a loving step-parent. As she reviews her life, have your client explore what the main anchor points have been, for better or worse.

The activity for creating a personal narrative begins with creating a journal, or several journals. The journal-making is the art, not just the writing. It can be as simple as embellishing a plain, pre-purchased hard-bound book of paper, to creating unique pages from felt or hand-made paper. Journals can be made from copier paper that is stapled and folded down the middle, or hand-stitched books with customized binding and paper. The journal can be focused around a theme or topic; the art can serve as the non-verbal expression. Themes could include a travel journal, an exercise or diet diary, a dream journal, or a place where you jot down your goals or to-do lists. The journal can be embellished and then gesso applied, to support paint and heavy ornaments, collage, the gel medium, or embroidery.

Have the client consider the size of the journal pages: they could be very small, which is less intimidating for some people, or large to over-size. Will the pages be bulky? Some people may want to do more than write; they might want to scrap-book materials onto their journal pages. If so, have the client think about how she would want to accommodate bulk. How much room will she need for her journal? Will 20 pages be sufficient, or will she need a few hundred? The smaller books can encourage her to continue evolving her journal-making style.

13. Body image: Body quilt

PSYCHOLOGICAL ISSUES

In the Western world, obesity is endemic and most people are not happy about this. In the USA, 80 percent of all American women sampled were displeased with their appearance (Smolak 1996). On any given day, 45 percent of those women were on a diet (Smolak 1996). Eating disorders also occurred most frequently in people who had a history of dieting (Shisslak, Crago, and Estes 1995). In the United States there are reportedly 10 million females and 1 million males who have anorexia or bulimia; millions more struggle with binge eating disorder (Crowther, Wolf, and Sherwood 1992; Fairburn, Hay, and Welch 1993; Hoek 1995; Shisslak *et al.* 1995). The overall rates of eating disorders continue to increase; for example, the incidence of bulimia in females aged 10 years to 39 years tripled between 1988 and 1993 (Hoek and van Hoeken 2003). Investigators have begun to recognize that the incidence of eating disorders is much higher than they originally thought in older women (over 50). Although this may reflect new cases, it is most likely the result of lack of treatment. Unfortunately, the rate of actual mental health treatment is extremely low in all types of eating disorders.

RELEVANCE OF SYMBOLS, OBJECT, TEXTILE, AND FORM

Body image can be defined as how you see yourself when you look in the mirror or at pictures of yourself, or when you picture yourself in your mind. It has to do with our perception, imagination, emotions, and physical sensations of and about our bodies. Just as with all of our cognitions, body image is influenced by our upbringing, our families, and, most importantly, the culture that we grow up in. With a healthy body image, a woman has a true perception of her actual size and shape. She is comfortable in her skin and has affirming feelings about herself. In contrast, with a negative body image, a woman has an inaccurate and distorted perception of her shape and size, adversely compares her body with others, and feels shame and anxiety about her own body. Poor body image leads to and is associated with emotional distress, low self-esteem, unhealthy dieting habits, anxiety, depression, and, ultimately, eating disorders. In Western and European cultures, women tend to be preoccupied with their weight, which leads alternately to starvation and then gorging, and sometimes purging and then obsessing.

One of the major treatment goals for anyone with psychopathology around eating is to develop a positive body image. This can be explored through developing *healthy lifestyles* that encourage good diet and exercise. The client must learn to pay attention to her body, or listen to and respond to internal cues (i.e. hunger, satiety, fatigue); appreciate her body, recognizing the pleasures her body can provide; and accept her body: accept what her body is like, instead of longing for what it is not (Freeman 2002).

The *Mother* archetype has been suggested for a variety of psychological issues, and is applicable to eating disorders as well. *Gaia* is the symbol for the mother of all life, and her figure celebrates existence. Have your client revel in the image of Gaia provided, and explore if she can feel beautiful within herself. This is one topic you will definitely want to use journaling and guided imagery with.

Your client can either make small fabric cameos or large wall-sized quilts. Some ideas include using fabric collage with transferred images, hand-dyed fabrics, embroidery stitches, fusible appliqué, beadwork, and free-motion machine quilting. Elaine Quehl (see Chapter 10) celebrates women of all shapes, sizes, and colors in her quilts. More inspiration about how to apply body image to quilting can be found in the work of Susan Schrott (2011). Schrott uses her own hand-dyed and surface-designed textiles, threads, and mixed-media to create images of women who are courageous, joyful, and inspirational. There are quite a few excellent books on creative cloth-making that can serve as inspiration.

In addition to exploring body image through quilting, your client will benefit from the relaxation incurred while sewing. Unpublished research by Robert H. Reiner suggested that women who sewed a simple project experienced greater decreases in heart rate, blood pressure, and perspiration rate when compared with women who participated in other leisure-time activities (card games, painting, reading a newspaper, playing a hand-held video game). These other leisure activities were chosen because they required similar eye–hand movements. "The study appears to indicate that sewing is the most relaxing of the five activities reviewed due to the statistically significant drops observed in heart rate, blood pressure and perspiration rate after women sewed," says Dr. Reiner. "While sewing was the most relaxing activity, we were quite surprised to discover that heart rate actually increased for all participants while they were engaged in the other four activities, including reading the newspaper" (JAMA 1995). Anxiety and depression are highly associated with eating disorders. The act of sewing may provide direct relief from these symptoms.

14. World weary women: Playing with temari balls

PSYCHOLOGICAL ISSUES

For many who grew up during the second and third waves of feminism, the shift to becoming an active participant in the workforce was the norm. Playing on the same field as men was seen as an expectation, possibly a necessity, but certainly a right. And yet for many women, the traditional roles of mothering, home-making, and care-taking have not lessened. As such, professional women today are faced with the inordinate burden of juggling multiple roles. Some have managed complete reversals with their partners where their stay-at-home husbands replace the stereotypic female role. Others have postponed or denied relationships, even declined to have children, in lieu of their jobs. But for most women, nothing gives; they do it all, which can lead to their slow, withering demise.

There is not one way that women have dealt with these issues, nor is there one explanation for why and how some women have found or have never found the right balance between work and personal life, between raising a family and having utter and complete financial success. Barker (2001), a Jungian analyst, described one conceptualization of this dilemma. She calls it the "World Weary Woman." By Barker's account, women take on too much because that is how they learned to cope with their lives. She suggested that the intense work ethic develops more strongly in women who faced loss as a child, especially the loss of a parental figure. To survive the real life demands that continued, despite extreme personal pain and suffering, the World Weary Woman developed protective behaviors, for example excessive ambition, focus on external success, and do-it-all mentality, that in essence cut her off from her own body and emotional wisdom. These protective behaviors intruded into every part of her life as she tried to control the world around her and prevent future loss. But in essence, World Weary Woman's focus on attainment only serves to compound her alienation and allow for more layers of new loss and suffering. From the outside, the World Weary Woman may look like the epitome of success. As a doer, she has adventures and accolades. But beyond these exterior accomplishments, she is not satisfied because her pursuits still do not fill her inner void. She is vulnerable, even fragile, internally. To obtain psychological health, Barker believes a transition is needed to bring the World Weary Woman into a simpler, internally focused life. The internal path would allow her to recognize and be responsive to her physical needs, her intuition, and her inner wisdom. What follows is one approach to helping the World Weary Woman re-connect with herself, her inner child, and her creativity.

~

RELEVANCE OF SYMBOLS, OBJECT, TEXTILE, AND FORM

The World Weary Woman is the classic *Amazon* out of balance; she needs to incorporate more of the *Medial* and *Hetaira*, as well as the *Mother*. *Ixcacao* is the Mayan goddess of the cacao tree, also known as the Cocoa Woman, and provides a starting point for this transition. Ixcacao was an ancient fertility and earth goddess in a matriarchal society that valued females gathering crops, banishing hunger and providing for the safety and security of the people. Ixcacao is also known to provide people with energy by uplifting them, empowering them, and providing stress release. Ixacacao reminds us that we should rejoice in things that give us pleasure, small or large, even chocolate, which contains many physical and psychological health benefits. Dark chocolate contains a large number of antioxidants (more than eight times those found in strawberries) and flavonoids, which help to reduce blood pressure and balance hormones. Chocolate also stimulates endorphin production, providing a feeling of pleasure and acting as an anti-depressant and stimulant. The act of eating small amounts of chocolate could be seen as an indulgence, also once again taking time to appreciate the small things in life.

The textile activity I recommend for the World Weary Woman is to create temari and kimekomi balls. Temari balls are made from layers of thread. Kimekomi, also known as quilt balls, are similar but fabric is used and wrapped around a hard smooth core, such as wood.

Temari are Japanese handcrafts that can be given as tokens of good luck; they are frequently displayed as works of art. Historically, they were Japanese symbols of perfection and sometimes called a "mother's love ball." More recently, temari balls have been made into toys for young children, similar to the "Hacky Sack," which is made for tossing and kicking. Temari balls were initially made from the fibers of recycled, discarded clothing or woven household items. In the seventeenth-century Imperial Court, women competed with one another about whose ball was the most intricate, opulent, brightest made, or the one with most subtle use of color. Ball patterns developed and were embellished with embroidery thread, silk floss, and metallic threads. Some had realistic figures and gardens, others had traditional geometric patterns.

Temari balls are not difficult to make and can be decorated with a number of needlepoint techniques and fabrics. They can be manipulated to represent playfulness and the child within; they can symbolize both art and a mother's love. Temari balls can also be a source of stress release when used as a stress ball—to relieve tension in the muscles of the hands and arms. These balls can also induce relaxation by allowing for rhythmic tossing.

SUGGESTED READING

World Weary Woman: Her Wound and Transformation, by Cara Barker (2001), has a dense but interesting and useful analysis of issues pertinent to contemporary women. A Jungian analyst, Barker's book describes the exhausting and achievement orientation of females, and provides more in-depth analysis of the psychological dilemmas of the Amazon woman. Barker also provides suggestions for how to lead the World Weary Woman to a more balanced and satisfying life.

Passages of loss

The textile techniques for passages of loss are outlined in Table 8.3 and explored in more detail below.

15. Layers upon layers of emotional scars: Emotional healing shawls

PSYCHOLOGICAL ISSUES

Some people are fortunate to live a life unharmed from emotional pain, a life of well-being, by growing up and living in the context of validation, love, and support. Others are not as fortunate. They experience psychological pain, i.e. mental and non-physical suffering, that can impact mood, relationships, and personal and professional lives. Emotional pain comes about from childhood (as we have discussed, due to a variety of factors including neglect,

Table 8.3 Textile techniques for passages of loss

Psychological issue	Archetype, metaphor, myth, or symbol	Object to make	Textile materials	Relevance of object and textile	Elements of ritual that could be emphasized	Design elements to emphasize
15. Layers upon layers of emotional scars	Akeso (Aceso) Healer archetype	Emotional healing shawls	Nuno felt (laminate) Knitting, crochet	Prayer shawls Scar tissue		Texture Shading
16. Healing	Goddess of Mirth Uzume Baubo Jester or Fool archetype	Milagros bead pouch	Fabric beads Beads Milagros	Milagros Beads Medicine pouch	Purification Making sacrifice Exorcizing	Form Color Texture
17. Physical disability and deterioration	Symbols of the sacred including labyrinth, spirals Celtic knot	Don't pull the rug out	Any type of rug-making	Carpet Labyrinth Spirals Celtic knot		Form White space Color
18. Cancer	Medusa	Wigging out	Spinning	Hair Snakes Baldness Wigs		Form Texture

abuse, abandonment, or loss of parent). And emotional pain can come about during adulthood due to the end of a relationship, divorce, loss of a loved one, being a victim of crime, substance abuse, or retrenchment or loss of employment. People experience psychological pain in many forms, including recurring nightmares and mental images, the inability to stop dwelling on past hurts and disappointments, or the re-creation of negative and unhealthy relationships.

Yet we all must make a choice about how to deal with emotional pain. We can run from it and numb it with denial and brain-altering substances, or we can engage it and grow from it. To acknowledge the emotional pain does not mean to accept it as justifiable, but it is the first step in figuring out how to transform it into something healthier. Just as physical pain is usually a signal that something is wrong with the body, so too is psychological pain a signal that our psyche or soul needs repair.

RELEVANCE OF SYMBOLS, OBJECT, TEXTILE, AND FORM

The *Healer* archetype is a wonderful metaphor for these issues. The Healer archetype has passion to serve others by repairing the body, mind, and spirit. The transformation process often involves a rewiring to channel the energy needed to generate physical or emotional changes. *Akeso* (also called *Aceso*) is thought to be the Greek goddess for healing pain and wounds. She is known for the *process* of healing, instead of the *cure itself,* which is Panakeia. The word *Akeso* actually means curing, instead of cure.

Scar tissue provides an interesting metaphor for life's difficulties. Scars are marks left on damaged tissue after it has healed; they are dense, fibrous connective tissue that forms around a healed wound. Scar tissue is a form of protection while the body heals. Scars can form externally, such as on the skin, and more often internally, such as on or around your internal organs. Some people scar more easily in certain places on the body. The amount of scar tissue developed depends upon the size, depth, and location of the wound, age, heredity, and skin. Scar tissue is normal: it develops all of the time. When you pull even the simplest of muscles, some amount of scarring will occur; this is dissipated by normal stretching and activity. More serious scar tissue develops after surgery and it can take time for the tissue to be reabsorbed into the body. Too much scar tissue can cause additional damage, including numbness of the nerves in an area, decreased flexibility, and problems with internal organs working improperly, and ultimately, pain.

Scars represent a polarity. They are evidence that something has invaded the body (e.g. surgery, paper cut), which is negative. But they often result after something positive, such as a cancerous tumor being removed, or a baby being born via C-section. They also represent a record of change. More severe at the start, scars will fade but usually they do not dissolve completely. Thus scars are evidence that an event has happened and change has occurred.

And isn't this an amazing metaphor for our lives! We learn, we grow, and we get hurt. And we must learn to "defend" ourselves while we heal. Some of us respond to injury excessively; we produce tough scars that act as barriers and involve complicated networks of defense. Some of us shut down completely, the scar walls so strong and high that nothing can get in. Some of us form isolated rooms in our mind that no one knows about; these are internal scars below the surface. We are surprised when we find out it is there, just as a surgeon might be surprised to find out that our internal organs are filled with a massive network that won't allow him or her in.

The objects I suggest making to explore issues of scars are what I call emotional healing shawls, similar to prayer shawls. Shawls are beautiful pieces of clothing. They also embrace, envelop, wrap, shelter, and give us comfort. In 1998, Janet Bristow and Victoria Galo, two graduates of the 1997 Women's Leadership Institute at the Hartford Seminary in Hartford, created a Prayer Shawl Ministry. Their program combined knitting and crocheting with prayer by having the shawl creator put blessings into every piece. With Bristow and Galo's approach, the shawl-maker began the knitting or crocheting process by praying and blessing the recipient; positive intentions were continued throughout the creation and then again upon the completion, with a final prayer or blessing offered before the shawl was given away.

My modification of the prayer shawl acknowledges that there are scars left behind from life's trauma and pain. By making the shawl, the client begins to transform her personal scars into an object of beauty, looking for positive associations to the scar tissue. At the same time, there is an emphasis on positive thoughts during the creation process. This provides cognitive reconceptualization of the emotional pain.

Knitting and crocheting are obvious mediums for shawl-making. However, I like to use the process of nuno felting. Originally developed in 1992 by Polly Stirling, a fiber artist from Australia, nuno felt is also called laminate or cobweb felt. It is a transparent, thin felt created by placing small amounts of wool top (preferably merino) onto a sheer fabric, such as silk gauze, nylon, or muslin. The finished fabric has a lightness that is strong, holds its shape, and is filled with color and unique texture. More metaphors for how life's emotional pain has left scars, which bring about our own inner strength, texture, and color.

16. Healing: Milagros bead pouch
PSYCHOLOGICAL ISSUES

There are many alternative health books written about healing that cover a wide spectrum of methodologies, ranging from metaphysics and the occult, to prayer and Christianity, to visualization and imagery, to nutrition and diet. One common thread running through all of these books is that they pick up where modern medicine leaves off. There are too many inexplicable variables that Western medicine cannot control. The placebo effect is one way that physicians are reminded of this. Placebos are actually inactive substances that are given as a control substance during experimental testing for new medicines. This is the gold-standard in medical research, a double-blind placebo-controlled clinical trial where doctor, patient, and research assistants do not know which is the "dummy" pill. When prescribed, placebos are given with the expectation that the person will get better.

Years of research has indicated that, despite having no medical value, the positive expectations given by the prescriber (casually referred to as the placebo) have led to significantly better outcomes. As many as 60 percent to 90 percent of the people who receive placebos show physical improvement, depending on the context of the research (e.g. for analgesia, asthma). Critics believe that the placebos are subsequently associated with positive emotional changes and health behaviors, which impact physical health. Regardless, I think this is a phenomenally large difference that leaves room for biopsychosocial and faith-based explanations.

As a graduate student at UCLA, I had the rare opportunity to know and work with Norman Cousins, director of Psychoneuroimmunology. In the 1970s, Mr. Cousins allegedly healed himself from a rare collagen disease by checking into a luxurious hotel (instead of a hospital), taking mega-doses of Vitamin C, engaging in a positive attitude of love, hope, and faith, and regularly using laughter by watching comedy movies (especially old Marx Brothers films). He then went on to write a number of books featuring alternative medicine, the most famous called *Anatomy of an Illness: As Perceived by the Patient* (Cousins 1979). In *Anatomy of an Illness*, Mr. Cousins reviewed scientific evidence for miracles—and encouraged people to accept the power of their minds in healing. In one of my monthly grant-related meetings with Mr. Cousins before he died, he said this: "Someday, please devise an experiment where you have a group of patients that have the same type of life-threatening illness, such as cancer or coronary artery disease, and have the physician tell one group that they will die in a few weeks and the other that they will be completely healed. What do you think would happen?" I remember nervously looking at him to see if he was actually serious; I think he was. Regardless, his point was well taken, and still is: expectations about physical outcomes can do mysterious things to our bodies.

In the 15 years that I worked in psycho-oncology, many people begged me to use hypnosis and guided imagery for healing. I was fundamentally opposed to doing this, despite my passion for mind–body research; I knew there was no scientific evidence that it worked. I had seen far too many casualties of patients "thinking positively" and using visualization and prayer faithfully, only to have their bodies ravaged, destroyed, and killed by cancer. I didn't want to be the one to bring someone false hope. So I always took a non-committal and cautious stand. The other side of the coin was that I intuitively embraced what Cousins believed, which was why I did the research that I did. I knew that the likelihood was that we (the scientists) had not yet designed the right experiment, but that there was a strong possibility that someday science would discover the mechanisms behind miracles. Maybe not in my day, nor in yours, but it was and is possible.

Knowing what I knew then and now about biology and immunology, I respectfully believe that non-verbal communication occurs at a cellular level between our brains and our bodies. I say non-verbal on purpose; I think that people can influence basic cell functioning with images, not words. And by unlocking how this process works we will find the key for that which looks like miracles or false beliefs now. Then, maybe, it will be more under our direct control. Until that day comes, when someone figures out the mechanism behind healing, we are left only with our intuitions to guide us and influence our bodies.

RELEVANCE OF SYMBOLS, OBJECT, TEXTILE, AND FORM

The most obvious archetype for healing is that of the *Healer*. However, I like to associate the *Jester*, which can also be portrayed as the *Clown* or *Fool*, with healing as well. According to Myss (2002) there are three major characteristics of the Jester archetype: making people laugh, making them cry, and wearing a mask that covers one's own real emotions. The message of the Jester is very serious yet, because a mask is worn, a boundary can be crossed. The Jester disarms the person with humor; in this vulnerable state, the person is more open (and less defensive) about accepting wisdom.

There are many male examples of Jesters in folklore around the world. Two female examples are the Greek goddess *Baubo* and the Japanese goddess *Uzume*. Baubo was seen as a fun, lewd, sexually liberated (and wise) goddess who played a role in healing. As an older goddess or crone, Baubo encouraged people to relish the life force, especially with laughter. Uzume played a similar role in Japanese lore; she was known for her emphasis on laughter and merriment. Again, laughter allows us to relax, whereby we can gain perspective.

Milagros (also known as *ex-votos* or *dijes*) are religious folk charms that are traditionally used for healing purposes in Latin America. The word *Milagro* actually means "miracle." Milagros can be made from a variety of materials and are used to focus attention towards a specific ailment. This could be a concrete body part or a symbolic representation of the malady. Milagros can be carried for protection and luck, or used as components in necklaces, earrings, and other jewelry. More commonly, they are attached to altars, shrines, and sacred objects.

The object I suggest making is a beaded necklace with special Milagros beads. The metaphoric associations of beads were described in Chapter 2. They do have particular significance in healing, as various beads and charms are referred to throughout myths and folklore about their medicinal values. Some cultural traditions even use specific stones for specific ailments. Ancient Egyptians used lapis lazuli for curing eye ailments; rubies and carnelians were used to cure blood disorders; hematite was used for headaches (Cannarella 2005). Quartz crystals were used to balance energy in shamanic rituals. Because of their alleged mysterious properties, many indigenous cultures wrap significant beads, Milagros-type objects, and healing liquids and materials in small pouches, sashes, shoulder bags, charm bags, shells, and bottles for protection (Cannarella 2005). This could be part of the special assemblage that the client makes.

One unique example of how to use beads can be taken from Beads of Courage, founded in 2005 by Jean Baruch while working on her PhD in nursing (see Beads of Courage 2011). The program assists children in coping with serious medical illnesses by using colored beads as a symbolic way to mark treatment milestones. At the beginning of the program, the child is given a length of string and after each milestone (e.g. chemotherapy, bone marrow aspiration, radiation treatment) their health care provider gives them a color-coded bead to reflect acknowledgment of the treatment journey. Beads of Courage could be adapted and tailored to suit your client's needs, especially by having her make personalized beads.

As a fiber addict and textile junkie, I am obviously a proponent of having clients create their own fiber beads. These can be fashioned with the client's personal fabric stash, hand-made fabric remnants from previous projects, hand-made paper, clay, crochet and knitting, kumihimo, and, of course, wool felt. Any of these materials can be further embellished with seed beads, antique beads, and artistic beads. They can also be hardened with different mediums if the texture and softness of the fiber is less desirable. By combining hand-made beads with personalized Milagros and a special bag, an unusual and beautiful adornment can be made for the body or home altar.

17. Physical disability and deterioration:
Don't pull the rug out
PSYCHOLOGICAL ISSUES

In the United States, a person with a "disability" is defined as someone who has a physical or mental impairment that substantially limits one or more major life activities. Physical impairment is "any physiological disorder or condition, cosmetic disfigurement, or anatomical loss affecting one or more of the following body systems: neurological, musculoskeletal, special sense organs, respiratory (including speech organs), cardiovascular, reproductive, digestive, genitourinary, hemic and lymphatic, skin, and endocrine" (Department of Labor 2011). People may experience disability from birth, gradually with onset later in life, or suddenly as a result of trauma or illness (Nosek 2010). Disability is a heterogeneous concept and encompasses extreme variability. Severe disabilities are associated with the use of adaptive equipment or cognitive assistance and the disability significantly interferes with daily life. Milder disabilities may not even be apparent to other people.

In a sense, aging is also a disability, for it represents a progressive decline in functioning. According to the National Center for Health Statistics (NCHS), adults aged 80 and over are 2.5 times as likely to have one or more physical limitations as adults aged 50–59. Census data suggests that over 29 percent of Americans 65 and over suffer some form of physical disability. The majority of limitations for elder people are caused by arthritis, high blood pressure, and heart disease; accidents are the sixth leading cause of death for people 65 and older, with falls the single leading cause of injury mortality in this group.

Women with physical disabilities, regardless of the cause, face unique issues. Nosek *et al.* (2003) reported that women with physical disabilities had significantly lower self-esteem and greater social isolation than women without disabilities. They were also significantly less educated, more overprotected during childhood, had poorer quality of intimate relationships, and had lower rates of salaried employment. Nosek (2010) has also reported that women with disability experience greater violence and abuse, depression, discrimination, employment and income inequities, and disparities in health and access to health care.

Thanks to the work of Reynolds and others, we know that textile-making can have a significantly positive impact on physical disabilities. Reynolds has reported that many women already use their textile arts to symbolically cope with chronic illness (Reynolds 2002). Textile arts have been used to symbolize suffering, change feelings about the illness experience, transform the situation into something more meaningful, master the effects of illness/treatment, and to symbolize religious or spiritual values, transcendence, and a new positive self. Reynolds has also found that textile art-making in women with physical illness enhances their feelings of control, even when done as a leisure pursuit, not just as therapy (Reynolds 2004a). Women with severe physical limitations can produce artwork and adapt their activity to meet their emotional and physical needs (Reynolds 2004b). Textile guilds also provide older women with a group activity that allows for social contact, structure in their lives, cognitive stimulation, and satisfaction at completed projects (Schofield-Tomschin and Littrell 2001).

RELEVANCE OF SYMBOLS, OBJECT, TEXTILE, AND FORM

Over the decades, quite a few symbols have been associated with goddesses. Very common symbols include the labyrinth, spiral, and Celtic knot. The *labyrinth* is a very ancient symbol of both life and death; it is considered a mystical journey into the other realms and then back to Earth. Some see the labyrinth as a journey out of the busy mind back to the spiritual or inner self. The labyrinth is consistent with the themes of weaving and spinning: it is made in the image of Siuhu's house, the creation deity who brought people by way of a spiraling path from the center of the earth to its surface (ARAS 2010). The labyrinth incorporates confusion and clarity, chaos and order. It is said to be restricted and confusing from within, but from above there is artistry and order (ARAS 2010). The *spiral,* an ancient symbol of life, is created by a circle moving forward. It can also be seen as a wheel that turns; you might come back to where you started, but never exactly. The spiral signifies growth and evolution and, again, it does not begin or end. The spiral appears in religion, art, dreams, folktales, and mythology all over the world, and symbolizes transformation, regeneration, and awakening (ARAS 2010). The *Celtic knot* is also known as the endless knot; you can't see the beginning or the end. It can suggest the uninterrupted lifecycle. There are quite a variety of Celtic knots, each with their own meaning. The Triple Celtic knot suggests all trinities, including the Triple Goddess as well as the Holy Trinity.

All three of these symbols suggest the cyclic nature of life, the complexity of life, and the transformation process we go through on our passages. Having a physical disability will definitely change you, but you are still yourself, albeit a changed version. You may have to adapt your textile-making, but it is still *your* textile-making: a changed form of what you already do. These symbols encourage taking perspective from a holistic vantage point.

The rug is suggested as the item to make for coping with disability. First, a rug was chosen because there are so many different ways that rugs can be made. This will be essential in order to allow the client to adapt the activity for her physical disability. As discussed in Chapter 2, rugs can be hand woven on a loom, hand knotted or hand tufted, hand hooked, latch hooked, braided or knotted with rags, and painted on canvas. They can also be made with needlepoint and tapestry techniques.

Second, rugs were chosen because of their symbolic meaning in different cultures. There is an expression: "what happens on the rug, stays on the rug." In the Middle East, rugs have always been the main decoration in a home and the most valued possession, frequently the very heart of the home. In a position of centrality, the rug was (and still is) where people prayed five times a day, ate, slept, held ceremonies, held social events, and even made love. More than mere floor coverings, rugs are very special forms of art. The weaving techniques, range of colors, and details of patterns are all reflections of the culture's values. Even in modern Middle Eastern cultures, rugs are similar to jewelry, gold, and silver, and can be exchanged for hard currency.

That they are of such significance makes it understandable that rugs have been incorporated into many common story tales and fables. The "Magic Carpet," part of the Aladdin's Lamp story, supposedly transported people rapidly to their destination. The seemingly worthless rug of Tangu, also called Prince Housain's carpet, was featured in Aladdin and Arabian Nights, as was a reference to King Solomon's carpet. King Solomon's carpet carried the King, on his throne, when he traveled. The carpet was large enough for his entire coterie to stand upon, and the wind ensured that the King and his possessions would arrive at the proper destination. Whether used to hide something or to provide a ground for stability, rug qualities remain magical in many ways.

Encourage the client to create her "new" space within her "old" space by making a rug(s) to change the atmosphere of her home or favorite room. Simple symbols, as described in the labyrinth, spiral, and Celtic knot, can easily be incorporated into the design, yet they can hold so much personal meaning. The activity is called "Don't pull the rug out," to indicate that you can remain grounded, in touch with a deeper, quieter sense of self, while living with a disability. The rug metaphor can be easily integrated into guided imagery, especially for coping with pain.

18. Cancer: Wigging out

PSYCHOLOGICAL ISSUES

The psychological issues that develop during cancer treatment are multifaceted and different at each stage of the process. Acute anxiety is common upon the diagnosis and initial treatment, and then again after treatment has been completed. During treatment, severe adjustment issues can develop that take the form of anxiety, sadness, or even major depression. During treatment it is common to see learned food aversions, where specific foods become distasteful because of their association with chemotherapy. Similarly, conditioned or anticipatory nausea is common in 30 percent of the people undergoing chemotherapy; anticipatory vomiting occurs in about 11 percent (National Cancer Institute 2011). Anticipatory nausea or vomiting occurs when seemingly random stimuli in the treatment environment become classically conditioned to the chemotherapy, and thereby trigger nausea and vomiting on their own. For example, upon entering the hospital clinic, some patients will feel immediately nauseated by the antiseptic smell of alcohol. This is because the alcohol aroma is associated with the chemotherapy drug, and after a few pairings, the aroma triggered severe nausea and vomiting.

Impaired quality of life, low energy, fatigue, physical changes, and disability incurred from either the disease or its treatment also occur during and afterwards. Sometimes, there are neurological changes from the radiation and chemotherapy that last for years or are even permanent, regardless of whether there was cancer in the central nervous system. "Chemo brain" is common, where attention, concentration, and short-term memory problems abound; it can also take several years for fatigue to dissipate and energy to return.

The net impact for people during and after oncology treatment is that the experience can be miserable. On top of these insults, imagine a person with unfinished psychological business and the picture becomes even more complex. For example, if a person has a history of significant trauma, such as rape or physical abuse, or a history of poor coping including substance abuse, or a previous mental health disorder, or an unstable social network, her overall resilience in coping with the cancer treatment may decline unless her psychological needs are attended to. For almost every woman, there is some amount of sexual dysfunction that occurs due to body image changes and hair loss. Even if treatment is successful, the client will need to have regular tests to monitor cancer recurrence for most of their lives and this can provoke intense anxiety and fear. Some have even suggested that if PTSD develops in cancer survivors, that can bring back all of the psychological memories and associated conditioned responses to the treatment. Finally, if the cancer is terminal, end-of-life issues become pronounced. Again, each of these phases will certainly have an impact on those close to the person with cancer; they must be acknowledged and worked through.

RELEVANCE OF SYMBOLS, OBJECT, TEXTILE, AND FORM

According to the legend that most of us hear, the mortal *Medusa* was originally charming and sensual, especially known for her magnificent, long, enchanting hair. One day, either Medusa seduced Poseidon at the temple of Athena or Medusa bragged that her beauty was superior to Athena's. In both versions, Athena took her fury out on Medusa and turned Medusa's skin green and scaly and her beautiful hair into a bunch of whistle snakes. She also gave Medusa the power to turn into stone any living creature who dared look at her face directly.

The myth of Medusa may seem at first an unlikely image to use for coping with cancer. However, the growth of cancer in one's body might very well feel like the curse of Medusa. The seemingly lovely, healthy body is replaced by a scaly, shedding snake skin with a grayish glow and all hair is lost. Maiden sensuality dissipates with declining libido, fertility gives way to at least temporary sterility, and participation in life as a player is lost as survival forces one to turn inward. There is little to feel beautiful about. In Judeo-Christian symbolism, Medusa most likely represented the enemy and death, and thus becomes an embodiment of the Devil. Anyone who has cancer has had to face their own mortality.

As with all metaphors, working with the image of Medusa can be transformative. Medusa can be envisioned into a new form of beauty. Or the rage associated with Medusa can be borrowed in order to express the anger one may feel about having cancer. Fury at all that is lost, at one's mortality. The snakes in Medusa's hair can be recognized as something not to fear, but the symbol of healing. Hence Medusa's image can be transformed into the guardian of healing energy. Medusa can also represent the bookends of the lifecycle: the one at the beginning is young, pure, and connected with young life; the other at the end is seen as gruesome and connected with death.

Hair is an incredibly important part of how we look. It conveys important information about our values, our profession, our politics, and even our religion (ARAS 2010). The style of our hair can reveal how individualistic we are or how much we conform. Unkempt or unruly hair may tell us someone is in a poor mental state or has unconventional ideas. Biologically, hair carries our ancestral history, coding race, ethnicity, and gender. When women lose their hair during cancer treatment it is no wonder that there is emotional discord. What once provided them with their identity and beauty is now gone. Hair loss becomes symbolic for all of the loss that a life with cancer may bring. Baldness can be experienced as degrading and dehumanizing. Some cultures make criminals shave their heads, or they shave the heads of women as a form of punishment. When bald, people often feel naked and vulnerable.

That is why I have chosen the creation of the wig series as the textile metaphor for cancer. The wig is an artificial head of hair, human or synthetic, that is worn to disguise baldness; most women with cancer are familiar with this. Historically, wigs are part of theatrical or ceremonial dress and can be used for disguise or adornment. The word *wig* originates from *periwig*, meaning "person who wears a wig (professionally)," and dates from 1828.

If your client knows how to spin wool on a spinning wheel, I suggest beginning this project by having her create "hair." Spinning is one of the most calming textile handcraft techniques. The majority of clients in my study who spun indicated that the rhythmic, repetitive motion of spinning relaxed them and brought about a sense of peace (Collier 2011). Guided imagery is especially helpful to control the learned food aversions and nausea and vomiting, but spinning can accomplish similar results. There are quite a few books on creative spinning techniques (e.g. Boeger 2010). The spinner can create interesting thick and thin yarns: yarn that incorporates material such as paper and wire; yarn that is plied and stacked with crochet thread and then spun in thick and thin pieces that look like springs; and hand-dyed merino wool which is then corespun on a cotton weaving thread with mohair locks. Encourage the client to be creative and incorporate a variety of fibers such as alpaca locks, angelina, cormo fleece, top, kid mohair locks, teeswater locks, tussah silk, sari silk threads, and even silk flowers or found objects.

The next step is to have the client create a series of wigs. The wigs can be made to fit by using a wig head mannequin, lace or stocking wig cap, and either thread or glue. Have a look at Christine Marie Davis's wig series; she incorporated the wigs onto unusual objects (see *Yvette Self-Portrait with Pearls*, by Christine Marie Davis, Chapter 10). The objects can have personal significance to reflect working through these issues.

Chapter 9

Spin the Web

CIRCLES OF WOMEN

Introduction

We are raised in families, we attend schools, and we live in communities. We belong to peer groups and sometimes religious groups. We belong to clubs—groups that require formal membership; and sometimes our groups are cliques—groups that have unspoken membership. We belong to sports teams, to interest groups, to political groups; we have social networks and professional groups. Especially women. Why? Because we have an underlying need to affiliate, to have social interactions, and to share interests, values, and kinship. Taylor and associates (as reviewed in Chapter 3) have actually found that there is a biological reason that women need to "tend and befriend."

It is not surprising, then, that art-making has historically occurred in groups. Moon (2010) pointed out that artists have been working in groups for as many as 32,000 years, starting with Paleolithic cave paintings. Most of us have heard of the well-known artist group that included van Gogh, Tanguy, Russell, Bernard, Anquetin, de Toulouse-Lautrec, and Cezanne; they met in the 1880s for support, challenge, and inspiration. Another well-known group *for* artists is the Art Students League, founded by and for artists over 130 years ago. The basic principles of the League are: "emphasizing the importance of artistic creativity, maintaining the greatest respect for artists who devote their lives to art, and educating students in the process of making art in an environment where anyone who wishes to pursue an art education can realize his or her full potential" (Art Students League 2011).

There are many benefits for artists working in groups. Moon (2010) suggested that the process of making art in a group setting, in and of itself, has therapeutic value, even without the explicit directives of a psychotherapist. Moon proposed that group art-making creates a sense of community, is an expression of hope, keeps people present in the here and now, and allows for self-transcendence. Sense of community, hope, existentialism, and transcendence are all therapeutic group factors that Irvin Yalom (2005) has promoted for decades. Simply put, creating art in the presence of others is validating. Moon emphasized that people do not want to feel lonely; loneliness can occur even in the midst of a busy social life. Instead, what is needed is to have close emotional connections with others. Creating art in a circle, presumably with people who share similar values and affinities, allows us to connect and form intimate relationships.

For those of you conducting art-based group psychotherapy, I encourage you to look at Yalom's (2005) *The Theory and Practice of Group Psychotherapy* (5th edition), a classic in the field. In addition, Moon (2010) has a recent publication, *Art-Based Group Psychotherapy: Theory and Practice*, which provides suggestions for incorporating art therapy in groups. This chapter will focus on how textile handcrafters use groups, how they function in groups, both successfully and unsuccessfully, and how to manage groups, especially when they are not intended for therapy.

Textile handcrafters and groups

Textile handcrafters, just like visual and performance artists, create social connections with like-minded people. This can include quilting circles, sewing and weaving guilds, professional art groups, informal and formal craft groups, study groups, self-help art groups, and even small groups that meet at individual stores on a weekly basis. In these settings, handcrafters share and learn from one another, bring in experts to learn specific techniques, and interact while sharing problems and concerns. For example, quilting guilds allow for learning the functionality of how to make a quilt, as well as the aesthetics of quilt-making, how to be part of a craft culture, and how to push and stretch oneself (Dickie 2003).

Textile communities also provide handcrafters with a forum for individual self-expression, which in turn affirms women's uniqueness and individuality (Cerny, Eicher, and DeLong 1993). One study looked at social patterns in three different types of quilting groups: Amish, Appalachian, and Latter Day Saints (Piercy and Cheek 2004). The authors reported that women in each of the quilting groups had both horizontal and vertical connections with one another. During the process of teaching and learning techniques, they also built strong emotional bonds and left meaningful legacies across all generations. Cheek and Piercy (2004) further reported that the quilting groups supported and guided women through managing their own businesses, learning how to teach and mentor others, gaining respect as a skilled artisan, and acting as guardians of family traditions.

Other authors have suggested that guild membership provides women with structure in their lives and a sense of "we" identity. These factors, in turn, allow for positive emotional and cognitive experiences, especially for women who are aging and facing physical and emotional life changes (Schofield-Tomschin and Littrell 2001). With the advent of the internet, thousands of textile artists have also started to join internet community networks such as Ravelry, where they can purchase materials and patterns, and share ideas with women all over the globe.

In my research, I have found that the majority of textile handcrafters belonged to some type of group for textile-making (67.5%). These groups included social groups (such as quilting circles, craft groups) (45%), guilds (41.4%), virtual or on-line networks (40.9%), and professional groups (6.8%). Interestingly, I found that women who participated in any type of textile-related group were significantly more curious, had tried significantly more textiles, had greater mastery over textile techniques, and had made textiles more frequently, than women who did not belong to any type of textile group (Collier and Hahn 2011). There were some interesting differences between the types of textile groups.

First, women who belonged to virtual groups were significantly more depressed than women in any of the other groups. The good news for them is that these virtual networks probably fostered positive, pro-social coping. Even though they may have been more depressed to begin with, the constructive activity would inevitably help them to feel better. Second, women who belonged to guilds and professional groups were overall go-getters. That is, they engaged in significantly more leisure activities (of any type) and displayed higher levels of curiosity than women who belonged to the other types of groups. Finally, the social group attendees were the least depressed, but also the least curious. One could interpret this to mean that textile social group attendees were happier people, and that curiosity did not drive their participation. No doubt, spending time with friends doing an activity they enjoyed was the motivation.

Are textile groups good for everyone?

None of the groups I have discussed above were meant to be therapeutic, yet they had positive benefits for women. Most of these groups have some type of lay leadership, but usually for specific purposes. For example, guilds typically have a director or "president" who is responsible for managing the financial and logistical operations of the group. Sometimes guilds invite teachers (within and outside of the group) to teach specific techniques. But none of the leadership roles are tasked with containing atypical interpersonal behavior, or promoting psychological transcendence. If these groups were offering group psychotherapy, clinical leadership would be critical. Someone would need to monitor the structure, be the gatekeeper for who can or can't enter the group, determine the expected behaviors for group membership, moderate how members interact with one another, and oversee adherence to important tasks. But again, these groups do not offer psychotherapy. From a psychological perspective, these textile groups are essentially leaderless. How can leaderless groups manage effectively if these unspoken functions are not dealt with directly?

As a participant and teacher in various textile groups and workshops, I have seen problems surface quite frequently. Sometimes it is due to the insecurity that people experience when trying something new. Sometimes it is because the person is difficult to get along with in any situation. Sometimes it is because the person is going through very real psychosocial stressors, and experiencing depression or anxiety. And sometimes, it is because the teacher challenges participants to create something that pushes them out of their comfort zone.

Several years ago, I took a workshop from an inspirational teacher who was focusing on knitting without patterns. There were no pre-made designs, just the creation of improvisational knit and crochet functional objects. Most of the students were from the local guild and were coming along for the ride, so to speak, because their guild had brought in the teacher. I had been following this teacher and, whenever she was close enough to Alaska (where I lived at the time), I flew over to take her class. Where some students reveled in the spirit of not staying within the lines, others were extremely uncomfortable with the lack of structure. Over the course of the workshop, several who wanted to stay in the lines became increasingly insecure and needy, eventually taking too much of the instructor's and other students' time. This became a burden for all of us who genuinely wanted occasional assistance. Another workshop I took was probably a magnet for soul-searchers; it was about making a textile object that reflected your values. The teacher was young, smart, and skilled. She was also overly self-confident and critical. Over the course of the class, many of the participants became defensive and angry, and as a group essentially ganged up against her. A few left the class altogether; others spent hours while we were working reveling in their dislike for her. All of this "noise" made it difficult for me to concentrate on what I was making and took away from the joy of my process. My observation was that she had challenged participants to think about important and deep issues, but because it was a competitive environment, it was difficult for them to participate. It was really not the teacher's job to create a safe therapeutic environment. But the issues did begin to fly all over the room and they had a very significant impact on the class. I found the experience to be mentally exhausting; there were just too many psychological process issues occurring and it was not anyone's job to deal with them.

Who does well in leaderless groups?

While certain personality characteristics may be associated with having difficulty in group settings (described later in this chapter), the good news is that some personality factors may serve people well in groups. Over the past 20 years, investigators have relied on what is referred to as the "five-factor model" of personality. These describe people on a continuum with the following five characteristics: extroversion, agreeableness, conscientiousness, neuroticism, and openness to experience. The five factors are meant to be descriptive, not diagnostic. Thus some are more of an asset or a liability, depending on the setting.

Teams seem to function better when most of the people in a group are agreeable and stress negotiation, as opposed to being disengaged and asserting their authority. These characteristics are obviously related to flexibility, cooperativeness, and tolerance (e.g. Mount, Barrick, and Stewart 1998; Neuman and Wright 1999). It becomes even more important when there is any type of conflict or disagreement. Extroverted people also perform better than introverted. This may be because extroverts demonstrate leadership quickly, while introverts have less influence in coping with the immediacy of a problem (Judge and Bono 2000).

Few studies have examined performance in leaderless group discussions. Waldman and associates reported that extroversion and openness to experience were strongly correlated with performance (Waldman, Atwater, and Davidson 2004). Extroversion is related to sociability; people high on extroversion are more assertive, talkative, and active. Openness to experience is associated with being imaginative, curious, broad-minded, and artistically sensitive. Likewise, neuroticism, which is high in people with a great deal of anxiety, depression, anger, embarrassment, or insecurity, was not associated with good performance. This is consistent with what was described in the section on difficult people: individuals with more psychopathology will not do well in any type of group setting, but especially not in a leaderless group setting.

Waldman and associates (2004) found a few other interesting results. If you have previous work experience, you are more effective at participating in leaderless groups. This might suggest that women (and men) who have been active in the workforce gain valuable interpersonal skills that they can bring to group settings to facilitate problem solving. Second, independence in a leaderless group is good, but only to a point. Independence involves emphasis on personal welfare, over the welfare of a greater group. If too many people are highly independent in one group, then there are probably going to be problems—and poorer performance overall. And if there are too few members who are independent, there are also going to be problems. You can't have too many chefs in the kitchen, or everyone may argue about what to make. Likewise, if you don't have enough chefs in the kitchen, no one will know what or how to cook! Extroversion is similar to independence: too many extroverted people in a group can also be detrimental to overall process performance. Too many extroverts appear to have a negative impact on group cohesion and supportiveness.

It is imperative to look at both the individual factors that will make a group successful, as well as the interactive factors. While the individual factors may predict individual performance, any given combination of people may not do well with teamwork. If you find yourself in a group setting that appears to be functioning poorly, or you are teaching a textile class that is very disengaged and critical, you might want to take stock. Sometimes, as in many therapeutic situations, acknowledging differences is the first step towards rectifying the situation. This can be dealt with by using humor. It can also be side-stepped just by recognizing that these differences are there and people need to make more of an effort to cooperate.

Women in leaderless groups

Kees (1999) is one of the few investigators to explore successful leaderless groups with women. During the 1970s a trend started regarding women's consciousness-raising groups. These groups had a socio-political focus, with an emphasis on oppression (Enns 1992). More recently, Kees found that women groups were more focused on providing emotional support during personal change than they were in the past. She interviewed almost 50 women in eight different support groups over the course of one year. Most of the groups were small (between 4 and 15 members) and met very consistently with a stable membership.

For starters, the women's groups typically had some component of ritual in them, such as food, checking in with one another, discussing readings, or celebrating milestones. Most of the groups did not have a structure; instead, there was a flow that was different each time. There were not the usual restrictions as in psychotherapy groups, banning outside social interactions: most of the members met socially outside of the group. The group members were left with the responsibility for asking for what they needed themselves, even if that meant not attending. If they were going through a personal crisis, they were the ones who needed to bring it up if they wanted support. It wasn't the job of the group members to "pull it out of them." And, they made it clear they were not therapy groups and could not provide therapy to one another. The biggest difficulty faced was how to cope with members who had left, especially if that had occurred in a hurtful way. This had even led to the disbanding of some of the groups.

Some feminist authors have suggested that women enjoy leaderless groups the most: they prefer a more democratic, decentralized leadership structure, where men tend to use more autocratic and centralized structures (Meyers *et al.* 2005). Women also tend to use more emotionally oriented communication, and share information more equally, than men (Meyers *et al.* 2005). Thus, the leaderless model works well for the majority of women. This helps to explain why textile groups may be so popular and how easy it is for members to be supportive and focus on each other's emotional needs. But members need to take responsibility for their own well-being, by appropriately asking for what they need, and offering support at other times. And, if there is a great deal of psychopathology or competitiveness, the groups are less likely to work smoothly.

Managing difficult people in textile groups

Who is difficult?

What makes a person difficult? Is it how other people react? From a layman's perspective, anyone who is perceived by others as abrasive, irritating, aggressive, or annoying will most likely have problems functioning well in a group setting (Wepman and Donovan 1984). Litvak (1994) described a "difficult" person in terms of the degree to which others feel uneasy when the person is around. Another indicator of "difficult" would be the extent to which people will engage in avoidance behaviors in order not to be around the person (Litvak 1994). The ideal group participant is someone who is cooperative, uncomplaining, trusting, not demanding, cheerful, and probably grateful. Likewise, the ideal leader and caregiver is loving to everyone, knows everything, cures everything, comforts everyone, and helps to facilitate problem solving for all problems. Of course, neither of these two types actually exists in reality. We are all imperfect.

Research in group psychotherapy suggests that some clients are more difficult than others (Hahn *et al.* 1996). The most difficult clients have proven to be older, female, and have chronic physical or mental health problems. Both in the United States and internationally, one in four adults aged 18 and older suffer from a diagnosable mental disorder in a given year (Kessler *et al.* 2005). Thus it is likely that there will be people in any group setting (therapeutic or not) who have real psychological disturbance including severe depression, anxiety, and eating disorders. Some clients will also have personality disorders and these can be extremely disruptive in group settings. Personality disorders are rigid and unhealthy patterns of thinking and behaving that lead to severe problems in relationships, social situations, work, and school.

For example, if a person has characteristics associated with narcissism, she would consistently be self-centered in a group, to the point where she can monopolize the class. Often this comes with an inflated sense of self-importance, a deep need for admiration by others, and a belief that one is superior. Narcissistic people are typically unaware and unconcerned with other people's feelings. She wants to be the star, *she is the star* in her own mind, and wants you to recognize it—always, over and over again. In a class or social setting, this person can easily bring attention to her own wants and needs; she has been known to hijack the group.

Alternately, other people manipulate groups more quietly, especially if they have dependent personality disorders. People with dependent personality characteristics are described as having a persistent and excessive need to be taken care of, and are frequently submissive and passive. In an art group, these people would be extremely clingy and have difficulty making everyday decisions without excessive advice or reassurance from others. Some dependent people can be called *help-rejecting complainers*; they constantly seek help because they are dependent, but when given suggestions or advice, they reject it. We have all seen these people in classes. They are the ones who come across with a complete lack of confidence and are very self-critical. They want you, as the teacher, and other members of the class, to tell them what to do, exactly, maybe even do it for them.

There are many other temperaments that make it difficult for people to function well in group settings. Even people who are too silent can be difficult; it is hard to get a pulse from them. For example, do quiet people want artistic feedback? Do they need help from the instructor? In psychotherapy, silent clients, or people who provide minimal self-disclosure, are the least likely to benefit in group settings. This makes sense, given that being able to ask for and receive feedback (appropriately) is essential for growth.

What can you do with difficult people?

Of course, the easiest approach to coping with difficult people would be to flat out refuse to have them in your group or class. But that isn't always practical, especially when people sign up ahead of time and there is no pre-screening available.

The very first step is to try to stay objective. Look at the situation from an impartial, non-emotional perspective. Don't internalize their behavior or respond to the person in kind. An angry, hostile person does not have to invite an angry, hostile response. Likewise, you can set limits with a dependent, clingy student or participant. Over and over again, in a non-condescending way, support the client in making her own decisions and clarify that it is not your job to do that.

Another way to cope with difficult people is to try to understand whether the source of the problem is with them, you, or an interaction between the two. In psychotherapy, we use the terms *transference* and *counter-transference*. Freud first coined the term *transference* in his early work on Hysteria. Defined, transference refers to where the client transfers beliefs and feelings from other important figure(s) in his or her life on to the therapist. Thus, regardless of what the therapist does or is like, the client expects and believes that the therapist is a certain way—based on her/ his past experiences (not the therapist's actual behavior). In more recent psychological terminology, transference can be referred to as *schemas*, that is, the client has formed structured beliefs about the world that provide a framework for what he or she expects.

When I was a very new and young-looking therapist, I had a client who related to me as a daughter—one whom she loved very much, thankfully for me! As such, her behavior was extremely complimentary and she agreed with almost everything I said. She was so supportive of me that it interfered with her ability to explore her own issues. Her admiring behavior was actually the result of her maternal transference to me, that is, it had to do with who she was and her life experience, not who I was as a therapist she had just met. Another client of mine, around the same time, was hostile and condescending, dismissing me as ignorant and young. He found ways to belittle my questions and he too refused to explore his issues. I didn't behave very differently with one client compared with the other. But each of these people was *transferring* their own feelings from past relationships to me.

If I had been unaware of these transference processes, I could have unknowingly participated in unhealthy interactions, which is called *counter-transference*. Thus I might enjoy having a kind, older maternal figure, albeit a client, dote over me and tell me how wonderful I was, how cute I was dressed, and what a great counselor I was. Unaware of my own issues, I might need this type of social reward from a maternal figure. Alternately, I might have resented the hostility of the older man, and been critical and negative in response. That would have been a response if I had my own unresolved issues with my father. I could make the situation worse in either of these situations. The transference, if the leader knows how to handle it, can be a positive tool to effect change. But undealt with, transference and counter-transference can lead to unhealthy, destructive behaviors. In each of these situations, I reflected on the disconnection between who I was (as a therapist) and how the person was responding to me (overly nice, excessively hostile). I asked the person to think about past (and current) relationships with other people in their lives that may justifiably provoke these reactions. In a neutral manner, I asked the client to think about what their response to me was all about. I didn't assume that it was truly about me, but it was more about them.

How do you cope with these overwhelming reactions in a group setting? One of the problems with transference in any situation is that it is easy to react to. If someone is hostile to you, you can easily become hostile back. If someone is extremely critical of you, it is easy to get defensive, upset, or frightened, depending on how you tend to react to critical attitudes. If someone is very flattering to you, it is easy to seek more. I want to emphasize that the leaders and co-participants must pay attention to their own reactions. If personal feelings do come up, you should think about whether it truly has to do with you or the other person. Take note if their behavior is truly warranted by the situation. If you don't think it is, you can comment on the process.

Second, you can serve as a "container" for the client. Instead of reacting as one would do in a normal social situation, such as with reciprocal aggression or withdrawal, you can remain calm and objective, and not see the behavior as a personal attack. Instead, the behavior can be seen as how the client or student relates to everyone. The leader or facilitator's reaction is best served if it is one of empathy, not anger or distress.

Third, you can talk to colleagues about the person. Consultation allows you to process your feelings and get a reality check on how others perceive the person. Consulting may also provide you with ideas that you hadn't thought of for how to work with this type of person.

Chapter 10

Psychologically Minded Female Textile Artists

INCREDIBLE EXAMPLES

During the time that I was doing research for this book, I kept coming across remarkable fiber artists who seemed to deeply understand the opportunity for expression that textile mediums allowed. They seemed to "get it," how the metaphors and psychological issues could be integrated with the mediums and the objects. I would often stop in my tracks to examine their work with reverence and ponder how startlingly expressive they were, and wouldn't "this piece" or "that piece" be a magnificent example for my book? Eventually, it dawned on me to ask them if I could use their pictures. And guess what, they were thrilled to participate; it was like singing to the choir.

What follows is profiles of nine female artists, all selected because their artwork is brilliantly metaphoric; their preferred mediums are textile-based; they are female; and they are psychologically sensitive to both their own internal processes and to those of their students. The sample is not random; it is essentially a convenience sample. That is, you could say I stumbled across them haphazardly. Or, you could say that there is some kind of synchronicity in how they came across my path—or in some cases, how I came across their paths. As I started the list, I switched my approach and tried to look for artists more "scientifically." I combed the internet with my key terms looking for more fiber artists who met these criteria. Alas, they would not be found this way. Then, after I started interviewing some artists, I decided to ask them if they could recommend others who worked the way they did. I had gravitated towards their work, so maybe they had other colleagues that were similar in mind. Well, the majority said no, they did not. And if they did, either their colleagues were so similar in style that there was no added benefit to including them, or the dominant mediums of the artists they suggested were not actually textiles.

In any case, here they are. They were an amazing group of women to talk to, and I was humbled by the experience. Here are their stories, after which I summarize the key themes emerging. Their work shows us the land of possibilities for textile-making expression.

1. Neta Amir
Artist statement

> *My work combines the disciplines of traditional textile crafts with the visual arts: sculpture, painting, and photography. After graduating from my fashion design studies in 2003 (Shenkar Institute of Design) and following several years of work in commercial clothing companies I decided, in 2005, to devote myself to a more creative and artistic work-path. At first I created crochet dolls, then the creation of textile dolls extended itself to installation where these dolls were part of a space that I formed. My interest has extended beyond the creative aspects of handcraft and collectables to an intricate language and concentration on cultural and social background of the figure and how these manifest themselves visually. The characters I create are of detailed dress mode and styling that are apparent in the clothing, jewels, and accessories that I design and create especially for them. In order to tell more about each figure / character, I started creating not only fashion articles but also paraphernalia such as bicycles, scooters, pets,*

etc., in this way thickening the plot and the characters that I formed. The selection of materials used in each character is a top priority. I work with fabrics that are recycled, such as old bedding, clothing, and socks. The wear-and-tear of these fabrics adds another dimension to the work and some vestigial essence of previous owners. In some way they, too, tell another chapter in the stories I interweave. As time goes by, my occupation with dolls has spread in numerous different directions. People who saw my dolls on the internet admired and envied the unique style I fashioned for my characters and requested I create these in full scale for their use. This is how I started my accessory collection that includes shoes, slippers, and bags. All these are handmade, and are each a singular blend of sewing, embroidery, and crochet. Beside my artistic work I conduct doll-making workshops for adults, and artistic classes for young children. In these workshops, I place a great emphasis on the development of each participant's unique design and ideas, as well as using up cycled and re-used textiles.

Objects and mediums

Doll-making, with handcrafted and recycled fabrics; clothing, jewels, and accessories for hand-made dolls and people (that match the dolls). Some sculptural work with fabric (e.g. *Geranium*).

Background

Amir makes astonishingly provocative dolls, dolls that have both a human and fantasy-like complexity, dolls that have an enchanting yet dark quality. Born and raised in Israel on a kibbutz, Amir reflected that she began making textile handcrafts when she was a young child. Her passion for art drew her to an art high school in Tel Aviv. The balance between practicality and imagination has always been a dialectic she struggles with; it arose again with her decision to go to fashion school—which she saw as very practical: "In Shenkar College of Engineering and Design, to become a fashion designer involves a very professional, strict training that prepares you to work commercially in the industry." Despite being an alumna of Shenkar College of Engineering and Design, Amir did not enjoy fashion design as a career.

After leaving the fashion industry in 2005, Amir began making dolls until she "found another job." Ironically, the dolls began to sell on international internet sites. Although Amir initially made the dolls for children, she quickly realized that her buyers were adults, people who were buying them for themselves. With time, Amir recognized that her dolls were artistic and sculptural, i.e. art, and that gave meaning to her need for expression. Eventually her artistry extended into making adult-sized versions of the doll accessories, and she began to offer workshops in doll-making. As she was able to support herself more and more with the workshops and accessory sales, Amir was finally able to create art for her "soul and need to express," not just to be successful commercially.

Metaphors

Amir acknowledged that her work has a great deal of personal and symbolic value. "I combine imaginary things with everyday life; this is from the biography of my life, my work, conflicts, and desires. I want to be practical and yet I wish I could be more ordinary; I have a vivid imagination!" Amir carries her own personal biases against being an artist; in some ways, she used to feel it is shameful to be an artist. This dynamic plays itself out in her art. Her doll characters are highly imaginative, yet super-realistic. The dolls do things in everyday life, yet are whimsical and sharp, at times more captivating than beautiful. By having her workshop participants make dolls from their imagination, Amir believes that they always create dolls that have personal metaphoric value. She agreed that not all women were aware of this meaning, but there was meaning nonetheless. Additional symbolic value is added to her doll-making by the use of up-cycled materials, such as old bedding, clothing, and socks. Amir likes using these fabrics because they bring an extra dimension to her work, both from the remaining spirit of the previous and unknown owner, and the historical integrity of the fabric. One type of fabric that Amir frequently uses is cast-off socks.

Psychological processes

When Amir talked about her workshops, it was obvious that she has a true love for teaching. Although she realizes that not everyone will be an "artist," she believes that everyone can find joy in creating. Amir talked a great deal about how her students were frequently astonished at their own ability to make dolls. One requirement Amir has in her workshops is that participants cannot use patterns. Although she does not try to encourage participants to talk about the emotions sparked by their creations, they often do. Amir thinks this is a normal process, because "if you make dolls, it is an integral part of it." She said that she does not press forward on these reflections because it could lead to embarrassment. However, she is usually very touched, emotionally, by what the children and adults have experienced and expressed.

When asked how she becomes inspired to make a piece, Amir said that, more frequently than not, the material she was using inspired her. She typically begins by "playing" with the materials and forms and the piece eventually evolves. Rarely does she begin making dolls by thinking about what she wants to express. The fiber-making process is usually satisfying and makes her feel happy. However, she indicated that it goes in both directions. Sometimes she will become very upset with the process when it is not working well and she is not getting the results she wants. Alternately, when it does go well, she is motivated to keep working and ultimately derives her happiness from the success in the end product. Upon more discussion, Amir reflected that some types of handcrafts are much more relaxing for her, such as crochet and embroidery. During these activities, the repetition of the movement, for example the movement of the needles in and out, leads to a deep sense of relaxation: "My hands go, so my mind is free. Memories come back to me, many different feelings." Thus some textile activities worked better with some types of mood. Amir indicated that fiber art-making and her emotions are intricately related, and a very important part of her daily life. "I create my own world…"

Pieces chosen

Amir chose to share *Geranium*, the fabric geranium plant, as an example of her metaphoric work; it carries a great deal of meaning both personally and internationally. Her father was an arborist, and his gardening skills were truly artistic. One plant that he always grew was the geranium. As a plant, this flower carries symbolic significance. It has "character," it is tough and hard, yet beautiful. It reflects her Mediterranean background. It is also the opposite of feminine, which is seen as delicate. The whiteness of the piece allows it to be more sculptural.

The second creation is titled *Buba*. Buba in Hebrew means doll, soft toy, and puppet. It is used with girls to mean little, cute, and beautiful, and with the same meaning it can be used as a compliment or as an ironic nickname for women as well. "For me, the dolls I create always deal with this word [Buba], and its meanings, in general and for me as a woman in particular. Another aspect I wish to research in my work with textiles and dolls I create is the limits between the dolls which we could consider as toys or decorative items and the sculptural or artistic objects which carry more layers of meanings with it as well. The word Buba in Hebrew describes all of those aspects of the word: different kinds of objects as well as different kinds of girls and women."

Geranium

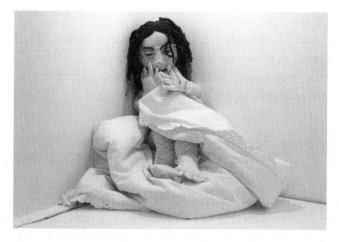

Buba

2. Bo Breda
Artist statement

I am interested in broken images—mosaics, knit patterns, newspaper photographs, pointillist paintings, and the digitized output of computer graphics are some examples. In recent years I have concentrated on beadwork as a way to explore this way of seeing. In loom-woven work I often use metal wire warp because the finished piece can be shaped or distorted and the warp ends manipulated in many ways converting a two-dimensional medium into three dimensions. The beads are strung on invisible monofilament so as not to change their translucent quality or alter the color of the glass. The images that most fascinate me are figurative—human, animal, plant life, and mythic combinations of these. But the texts and frozen moments captured by snapshots which are witness of mundane or intimate human events also find their way into the work. Sometimes I wake up having seen a piece whole in my dreams. Whatever my work is, it is mine; it comes from the inner places in my heart.

Objects and mediums

Breda uses beadwork, embroidery, hand weaving, dyeing, kumihimo, and sewing, with fibers, cotton sheeting, metal, aluminum mesh and screening, soldering, and wire to make figurative garments and sculptures.

Background

Breda is currently the Academic Director of Fashion Design at the Art Institute of California—San Francisco. She received her BA in Linguistics at Queens College in New York City (NYC) and her MFA in Fibers at the University of Illinois at Carbondale, Illinois, and additional fashion training at a number of institutions including the Fashion Institute of Technology (NYC) and Parsons School of Design (NYC). Her work in craft disciplines was done at Penland, Arrowmont, and the Appalachian Center. In addition to teaching, Breda has worked as a clothing designer, fabric designer, in costuming, and as a seamstress and weaver.

Breda came from a family that "always made things." She describes her parents as "sturdy peasant stock," her father of Italian descent and her mother of Cajun descent. Breda's mother was described as someone who always "made everything beautiful." She sewed, embroidered, and cooked, and when she began her own spiritual quest, this influenced Breda. Breda's father was an automobile mechanic and a carpenter. The family was quite poor when Breda was growing up, and taught her to recycle and re-make worn-out pieces into something useful. Although her parents never pushed her to acquire skills, Breda remembers always having something in her hands to make.

Metaphors

Breda is inspired by her spirituality. She has spent considerable time investigating Jungian symbols, folklore, fairy tales, and anthropology. Her spirituality is deeply grounded in who she is, although Breda indicated that most people would not be aware of this because she is quiet about it. Sexuality also plays an important role in Breda's artwork, and she frequently integrates sensuality, femininity, and sexuality, even if they appear frightening or negative to the outsider.

Psychological processes

Breda reported that when extremely depressed, it is difficult to create art. What usually stops this impasse is an energy stream that comes out as a "built-up creative flow," so that her ideas "will burst out." Breda's inspiration frequently comes directly through her dreams, where she will see part of or the entire object that she will then create. When working with clothing and textiles, Breda is deeply moved and inspired by both the color and the quality of the fabric. Breda indicated that she loves color and texture, as well as shape and embellishment.

Pieces chosen

"*The Great Mutha* is a statement about femininity, the earth, nature, and the spirit. My feeling is that women are close to the earth because of their bodies." The second piece, *Veil*, is part of a larger installation entitled *Wedding Night*. "Wedding nights are usually not unalloyed roses and joy, but the dreams, hope, and fantasies of the prospective bride and groom are symbolized by the otherworldly costumes worn during the ceremony. The installation includes trousseau items, the bridal gown and veil, the floral bouquet, and clothing for the groom. These are made of steel and aluminum wire mesh, solder formed into buttons, plus wire, beads, and rhinestones. I am fascinated by the idea that women are often led to marriage with their heads covered, hidden from their prospective husbands—either as a calf is led to slaughter or as a human sacrifice is led to the altar; an altar is originally a place of sacrifice, after all, where animals were killed so that their aromatic smoke might reach the heavens."

The Great Mutha
Photograph © John Lucas

Veil
Photograph © Bill Kipp

3. Rebecca Cross
Artist statement

These lightweight textiles are hung to form various configurations of multiple fabric planes, which are variously dyed, cut, pieced, and embellished. Each piece explores the physical potential of suspension and the possibilities of layering. Suspension from multiple points creates a fluid drape in the fabric that hints at its gravitational pull, but because the fabric is so lightweight, suspension also subjects the work to air currents. The use of transparent and limited hues within each piece, and the creation of negative spaces between and within layers, enhances the work's fragility. The substance and physicality of fabric thus arranged conveys multiplicity, temporality, and complexity. This work is meant to express the spaces between or the spaces just before, or just after, things—spaces that we inhabit temporarily. Scaled to the space a body inhabits, this work engages the viewer both visually and viscerally, encouraging a haptic visual experience in which the viewer imagines, recognizes, or remembers the feeling of these textural elements.

Various processes contribute to the somatic history of the fabric and its multiple transformations; these pieces hold not only the results of the labor that made them, but the memory of that labor as well. As sensuous materials suspended in space, casting shadows on the walls and floors, they confront the viewer differently from different perspectives as they subtly oscillate in response to the atmosphere, becoming, ultimately, communicative memories, that are completed when the viewer receives them.

Although this work has fixed edges, it also functions in relationship to what is absent—between, around, or behind these edges. By creating line as well as openings, and by delineating positive and negative space, the edges frame information—or demarcate the lack of information—caught within, behind, or beyond the edge. Composers of music also point to the "substance" of nothingness: when a silence is created

~

*between sounds, the silence has profound significance, partly
because it resonates with the memory, or the shadow, of sound.*

*These textiles consider how the residue of the past—
whether expressed through layers that are selectively visible and
hidden, through colors that are carefully created or resisted,
through embellishments that enhance formal elements, or
through objects that are cast off from the process of making
the textile—is intrinsic to any renewal. The gossamer layers
of experience, depending upon our perceptual vantage point,
are transient, creating a mutable, translucent skin that keeps
quietly changing as we proceed forward in time.*

Objects and mediums

Cross's recent forays into shibori tying, dyeing, and shape resist
techniques, primarily in silk organza, coupled with nuno-felting
with wool on silk, help her develop reflections on and expressions
of memory. Her shibori and felting processes embed memory in
color and form in fabric, often in collaged layers. Cross prefers to
use silk organza because of how it holds "memory." Cross indicated
that these processes provide a rich metaphor for the ways in
which life experiences create multiple palimpsests as one proceeds
forward in time, while continually registering the accumulations
of the past.

Background

Cross was formally trained as a bel canto singer at the Oberlin
Conservatory, where in 1984 she received both her BM in Voice
and BA in English (Oberlin College, Oberlin, Ohio). Cross earned
her MEd at Kent State University, Kent, Ohio (1987), and then
taught middle school and performed contemporary art music in
a range of venues for almost 20 years. In 1989, during her first
pregnancy, Cross discovered her passion for making quilts that
would eventually lead her to a new career in textiles, including
earning an MFA in Textiles Arts from Kent State University in
2007. Currently, Cross is both a full-time artist and part-time

adjunct professor in Art and English Composition at Kent State University.

During her time as a student, Cross became fascinated with the concepts of functionality and art. What became increasingly important to her was how the tactile and haptic engaged one's senses, and how the creation of handwork allowed a different type of artistic expression.

Cross spent a great deal of time as a child in Oregon, on the coast, as well as Japan and Fairbanks, Alaska. She feels most at home in Oregon, finding that the landscape resonates with her soul. This type of rocky and ocean landscape has been a major part of her work.

Metaphors

Intrigued by how all art must traverse the imagined and the material, Cross believes that the imagined is what resides in our dreams, thoughts, and memories; the material helps us "voice" these. Dreaming her way into artwork allows her to explore what is captivating, troubling, deeply beautiful, or mysterious—sometimes doing so while quite literally holding on by a thread. Cross is fascinated by the sculptural potential of fabric treated with shibori processes, which can suggest aerial landscapes or topographical maps. She has been heavily influenced by her musical background, as well as by her father, who was a geographer. She would describe maps as a central metaphor.

Psychological processes

Cross stated that she is happiest when she is working in her studio. She described herself as an aspiring Buddhist who values being focused and present. Cross works improvisationally, enjoying the unpredictability of results in shibori dye processes. On walks in all seasons, she collects natural objects (such as pods or slate from riverbanks), and then uses these materials to tie different shapes in silk. Cross enjoys these materials because of their metaphorical value: to her, they represent the regenerative potential. Cross is interactive with her work, which requires "listening" to it. For example, she will hang a piece from the ceiling, look at it, think about it, look at it again, and try to further understand it in order to resolve the piece.

When asked if she created objects to reflect her inner emotional issues, Cross said "yes, and no!" Ultimately, Cross stated that her work does reflect her inner concerns at the time, although she may not be aware of it at the moment of creation. One example she gave is some new work she is doing that involves linear transformations. She takes her hanging shibori, flattens them under glass to create a light box tracing, and keeps adding layers of transformations by applying fabric and drawing. Her husband has been undergoing cardiac treatment and recently she realized that his heart films were uncannily similar to her body of recent light box tracings, so she used them as source material for tracing as well as shibori fabric. Again, this is where she emphasized the need to "listen to your work." Her ultimate message was that: "Unless you are trying to repress your issues, you can't avoid expressing them in your work."

Cross was clear that she did not encourage her students to process their psychological issues during class time. Although she sees art as therapeutic, she establishes ground rules to keep them focused on critical discourse. Cross does encourage her students to find a quiet, focused place in which they can work. However, when she teaches, she keeps her students focused on achieving, not feeling.

Pieces chosen

Through layering and tying, *Transformations* creates variations in color relationships and gradations. *Grey Ghosts* represents the interplay of shadow and light and the heaviness of rocks, remembered in the ethereality of fabric. Suspended in space, both pieces are meant to engage the viewer by both their physical size and their subtly shifting layers, as they respond to air currents created by movement around the piece.

Transformations

Grey Ghosts

4. Christine Marie Davis
Artist statement

> *I rescue abandoned things and remake them into small-scale sculptures and body adornment. I love to pair dissimilar objects that were never meant to be together. Imagine Betty White and Iggy Pop having a love child. It's that kind of anomaly I'm after.*
>
> *I haunt old dump sites, thrift stores, and flea markets for that special something that calls to me. It's an inexplicable process but when I find something that is right I know it. I may not know exactly what I will do with the item, but I know I must have it. It might be a battered kitchen pot that has a lovely patina, an ornate Victorian hand mirror, an odd piece of taxidermy, or a rusty outdated tool.*
>
> *Things that are battered, broken, worn, or weathered are rich in history and often layered with earthy patinas that can only evolve over time. I find these kinds of objects the perfect starting point to add softer materials such as hair, fur, or rubber which bring them back to life and contrast with the roughness.*

Objects and mediums

Found (trash and antiques) objects; all kinds of textile materials. Davis does not consider herself to be a fiber artist, even though she typically incorporates fibers into her sculptural pieces. Davis readily acknowledged that textile-making, for example spinning, dyeing, and knitting, is seen as "women's work," and because of this, some art critics and artists still do not take this medium seriously.

Background

Historically, Davis had little to do with fibers. She grew up in the Midwest, from "a long line of junk dealers." When she was bored, her mother gave her art supplies and told her to "make something." Always a bit eccentric, in her younger years Davis started collecting pictures of shrunken heads and scrounged for materials like wallpaper sample books and barn wood. She opened a craft and "antique" shop while in high school in Montana, where she sold crafts made from "dug-up old bottles, rusty pans, and chamber pots from the town dump" to tourists. She went on to train as a studio potter, then ceramic sculptor, and then college teacher and instructional designer in the Denver–Boulder area. Now, Davis continues her love of old junk, antiques, and an oddity of collections by using her found objects in assemblage sculpture.

Metaphors

Davis has themes to her projects that usually involve feminist issues. She also indicated that her work frequently makes social and political commentary. Davis does not try to represent a particular feminist issue in her work, but she acknowledged that the end product usually does.

What originally attracted me to Davis's work was the fact that she made Goddess jewelry. Yet as I started to explore the variety of items that she created, I was taken aback by the sheer quirkiness and idiosyncratic quality of it. One project Davis created is called the *Pet-O-Mat*, or a "Mini museum to tactile delights." The Pet-O-Mat houses 49 touchable, sculptural creatures in a former sandwich-vending machine. The pets are made from found objects and tactile materials and live in "remodeled pet condos," which were formerly designed for sandwiches and fruit. The grant-funded project was designed to allow the public a way in which to interact with art that is not normally allowed in museums and art galleries. Davis stated that the Pet-O-Mat invited social participation, interaction, and inquiry, as well as expanded the public's conception of what art was and how one interacts with it. People were both horrified and entertained by the juxtaposition of the creatures in a place they expected to see snack food.

Davis's current series focuses on wigs. She applies wigs in shocking and sometimes socially inappropriate ways to animal skulls, bones, antique tools, and indescribable scrap metal. Davis acknowledged that hair is a highly personal way in which we identify who we are. Wigs can be used as a disguise, to hide who we are, to hide the shame of baldness, or to cover a body part considered intimate and sexual.

Davis is attracted to objects she finds and then invariably creates something distinctive with them. One can easily say that Davis's creations challenge people to reflect on their sexuality, femininity, and beliefs.

Psychological processes

Davis usually starts with one of her found objects that is intriguing to her and then adds fiber and other tactile materials to it. She explores themes in her work for several years at a time. Davis stated that creating a body of work allows her to fully explore the ideas that evolve.

Making art always helps Davis's mood: "I always feel better in the studio." However, as with other artists, there are times when the construction of objects is difficult and not going as expected. In these cases, the art-making obviously causes her distress. Davis indicated that this has happened less often over time because her techniques and problem-solving skills are more developed. She has found that, over the years, her sense of enjoyment, exploration, and adventure, as well as absorption in the art-making process, has become more profound.

Pieces chosen

Davis's first piece, *Pet-O-Mat*, has been discussed above. The second one is entitled *Yvette Self-Portrait with Pearls*. "In the surrealist manner, I like to place ordinary objects in unusual combinations to give new meaning and insight to familiar things. Yvette began when I spotted a wooden lamp base at a flea market and I knew I had to have it. Adding a wig, a base, and pearls, it was done, and I immediately laughed, so I knew it was a keeper. Later, I realized it referenced the surrealist painter Magritte's *Le Viol*, a shocking and witty commentary on the female body done in the 1930s. Magritte's painting replaced the eyes, nose, and mouth with the female torso. Yvette draws attention to the cultural expectation that a woman's face should always be beautiful. Yvette's face is monstrous, but she does have on a coiffed wig and pearls, so that makes her ironically presentable to the public eye. Yvette was the catalyst for a whole body of work where I used wigs to transform inanimate objects into anthropomorphic creatures that comment on beauty, social norms, and women's roles in society."

Pet-O-Mat

Yvette Self-Portrait with Pearls

5. Elizabeth Harris

Artist statement

> *Most recently I have been concentrating on various textile media as my primary means of expression. I feel drawn to these media for artistic as well as cultural reasons. I find the challenges they represent to my artistic vision stimulating and richly rewarding. I feel a sense of connection as I work on my craft to all of the women who have quilted before me, creating for me a sort of community in time. I vacillate between traditional quilt-making techniques and the more experimental art-quilt format. The most common theme that has appeared in my pieces has been the image of a sun. Permutations of this celestial theme have been appearing in my works recently and range in their representation from realistic to abstract. I see the sun image as a*

metaphor for many things, especially for my own spiritual being as well as my creative life.

Objects and mediums

Quilting is Harris's main textile medium. Although she has a fine arts background, a workshop in quilting opened her eyes to the possibilities of fabric collage. Harris has spent the past 20 years creating functional and nonfunctional fabric collage art.

Background

Harris actually holds a doctorate degree in Botany from Louisiana State University (1991). Her undergraduate degree was a double major in Art and Biology, at the University of Tennessee at Chattanooga (1985). Harris also did a post-doctoral fellowship at the Smithsonian.

Metaphors

Harris's work is heavily influenced by metaphors. She indicated that the metaphors come through by way of a combination of methods from meditation to journaling and dream work. The metaphors evolve as she creates a piece and she often only realizes the complete message upon the completion. Harris is closely connected to the colors and fabrics she works with.

Psychological processes

Harris summed up how psychological issues are involved in her work as follows: "I try to exercise the part of me that needs therapy or work, to get it out there. As I do the art, it becomes less painful, less of an issue, and it is no longer a painful part of me." An early inspiration for Harris was viewing *The Divorce Quilt*, now on display at G Street Fabrics in Washington, DC. Interestingly, Harris does not think the average viewer of many of her Inner Landscape series of quilts would recognize most of the deeper meanings of the images, as they were very personal to her, very much in the tradition of Frida Kahlo with her own uniquely personal iconography. But through the process, Harris is able to non-verbally release the images that tell her story, and because of this release, she becomes "altered" in a positive way.

Harris's work is very spiritual, and she feels grounded and rewarded by the end-product. Harris has also done psychological exploration through journaling, dream work, and groups. When deeply absorbed in her work, Harris feels like a "conduit to another dimension, where unfiltered ideas and images" come through to her. She described the creative process as a "flow state" for her.

Pieces chosen

Harris's first piece is *Our Lady of Creativity*, "As an artist, I am, of course, highly interested in the outcome of creative endeavors, but I am also just as fascinated with the act, the process of creation itself. How does it come about? In one sense, it seems a finite, definable thing since it can be present or not present. Sometimes, it does not happen at all despite all of my best intentions and wishes, and other times I am blessed with a veritable overflow of creativity. Often, new creations appear in my mind fully formed and it seems, almost, that they have arrived there from some other, higher, dimension through some mystical conduit. Other times, the main concept appears and it behooves me to keep the conduit open so that the fine details may be accurately rendered. Here I present an allegory for that concept. The higher plane present beyond and unseen to our everyday reality is represented to the upper left. It is always there but not accessible, except through acts of creativity for those with the inner eye and open heart that can build and maintain that conduit. When that happens, the creations are introduced into our world blessing it and making it a more beautiful place. This is indicated by the rays that emanate forth from the heart and creative conduit of *Our Lady of Creativity*."

The second piece, *Nocturnal Sojourn*, is based on the Russian folk tale of Baba Yaga, a wise but dangerous crone who possesses much magic and knowledge of the natural world, particularly herbs. "Her hut is also formidable and walks about on giant chicken legs and is ringed by a fence made of human bones and skulls. To approach Baba Yaga and entreat her for help one must first locate her hut, no mean feat since it magically appears in a different location throughout the world each morning. It is generally supposed that the hut spends the night walking to each new locale, but I represent an alternative option here. If the hut is so magical in the first place, can it not just appear wherever it is fated to be? I propose that the hut and Baba Yaga replenish their magical powers at night in a mysterious, mountainous land under a thin new moon and at sunrise rush to their next destination restored by their nocturnal sojourn."

Our Lady of Creativity

Nocturnal Sojourn

6. Kathleen Holmes

Artist statement

I incorporate found and self-made pieces of crocheted textiles into my work as metaphors for the particular patterns of my native Southern culture. Of specific interest to me is how these pieces of traditional handwork transcend the mere decorative by creating evocative domestic icons, powerful and often innocently ironic. Rusted, pierced, and shaped metal refers to man-made aspects of our culture and provides the visual and conceptual counterpoint to the woman-made textiles, thereby creating a metaphorical duality.

~

Objects and mediums

Over the past ten years, Holmes has used vintage pie pans with crochet and oils; crochet, felt, and mixed-media for dress sculptures; ceramics with mixed-media; and found objects. Her sculptural work is frequently built onto a multi-media board and foam core.

Background

Holmes currently lives in southern Florida, grew up in the South, and comes from a family rich with textile traditions, artists, and photographers. Holmes remembers her family "always making stuff," including knitting, crocheting, tatting, and embroidery. With this background, it is not surprising that she grew up to become a professional artist, having her first show in 1984.

Holmes reflected that her grandmother was very influential in her desire to become an artist. As homage to her, Holmes incorporated many of her grandmother's hand-crocheted squares on a painting, using gesso and heavy paper to create shadows and texture on the canvas. She worked laboriously to complete it before her grandmother's death. Ironically, her grandmother didn't like it; she was shocked and confused about why Holmes had essentially ruined the crochet squares with paint and gesso!

Metaphors

Over time, however, Holmes realized how much she enjoyed combining the patterns and textures of fabric and paint. She also found meaning when using textile materials, such as cotton, which was prolific in Louisiana. Holmes indicated that cotton had an "ongoing thread heritage that is powerful." She also expressed reverence for the fiber-based domestic arts textiles that so many unnamed women have created over the years. Holmes realized early on that by incorporating the beautiful "found" work of unnamed textile handcrafters, such as that found in thrift shops and garage sales, she would be "memorializing" these anonymous girls and women. She wishes that she knew who made the tablecloths and spreads that she finds and uses.

Psychological processes

On reflecting about psychological issues observed in other females, Holmes stated that many women have had difficulty with seeing their creative textile work as valid art. This has taken different forms but includes outright embarrassment, tears, and actual denial. Holmes recounted that a man approached her once at a show and told her that he had a large box of crochet pieces, or doilies, his mother had made, which were never used anymore. He was an architect and had never thought of these pieces as art. Looking back, he said: "I was so stupid; I didn't get it. I can now see what a profound effect making this had on her. I respect her now and truly undervalued her work."

For herself, Holmes finds inspiration in everything, from current events to "things in the past." For example, she read a book about slaves and then made a series of pieces with this theme. She has found that her work reflects who she is, and does serve a very therapeutic process.

Pieces chosen

The first piece is called *Picking the Blues*. "The crochet I use in the skirt is made from cotton thread; I grew up in cotton country and remember as a child seeing folks out picking cotton bolls by hand. This piece is a tribute to them. It is also a reference to the plight of the slaves and the evolution of guitar blues music, originating from the field chants that the slaves sang as they worked. The 'cotton bolls' in the piece are made from scraps of differently patterned blue cotton fabrics. The metal bodice is hard and tough, like the life of the slaves, and has hash marks in sets of five—counting bags of cotton picked, rows walked, years in slavery, and the five strings on a guitar."

The second piece, *Always a Bridesmaid*, is "a reference to all those bridesmaid dresses that get stuffed away into closets never to be worn again! And the dyed shoes that go with them. The large dress is ceramic and has buttons on the outside and crochet on the inside. The small blue dress is a little crocheted pot holder."

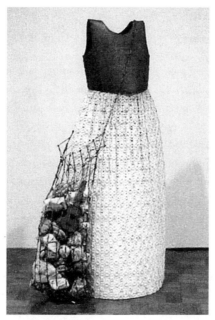

Picking the Blues

Always a Bridesmaid

7. Lisa Klakulak
Artist statement

Creating is a function, inseparable from my person. As are my interactions with the world and implicit expressions in art inseparable from my perspectives and opinions. I am inspired by humanity's age-old relationship with the community and time-involved fiber processes; through which I convey contemporary issues from within a society preoccupied with individuality, time efficiency, and disposability. My reactions to this current psychological and physical condition are expressed by the materials used, the methods employed, and the concepts referenced. Previous to the industrial revolution, a community was necessary to shear animals, wash fleece, and felt wool as well as to spin yarns, thread looms, and weave fabric.

Additionally, humans had forever obtained color through the alchemy of dyeing fiber with gathered and cultivated natural materials until the discovery of synthetic dyes in 1856. My primary use of fiber and natural dyes represents a fight for the threatened values of community responsibility, patience, physical activity, and an intimate relationship with our natural world.

I color, felt, stitch, and bead fiber; manifesting body textiles, accessories, and pieces solely of aesthetic and contemplative function. Recent concepts conveyed in the work reference issues related to human vulnerability, the resulting need for physical security and mental defense, and the unfortunate isolation that often results. I work primarily with protein fibers from silk cocoons and animal fleece as well as natural materials and human-made products that offer a sense of comfort and security through qualities of insulation, durability, convenience, and control.

Objects and mediums

Klakulak is a fiber-based artist who structures her artwork with felting and hand-stitching techniques and employs free motion embroidery to "draw" images as well as to create textural fields on the felt's surface. She pursued the felt medium because it was most receptive to natural dyes, has a supple surface for embellishment, and can be sculpted three-dimensionally. As her artistic voice developed she realized that felt, with its antiquity of use in protecting the human body from the elements, was an ideal material to reference the human condition and began making figurative sculpture in addition to more functional work such as handbags, body textiles, and adornment. "There is security and comfort in the material, there is a protective nature." She indicated that felt is "the ultimate skin." Klakulak finds the processes employed in manipulating felt to be rhythmic, meditative, and comforting in the chaos of modern life.

Background

Klakulak was always a "maker" and was encouraged to explore the arts by her mother who was a watercolorist. As a young child she recalls taping 40-strand macramé bracelets to her social studies book and knotting patterns during class under her desk. When her parents divorced in her third grade year the process of making offered a sense of control when it seemed her "whole world was falling apart." Whether working with fiber, beads, or drawing, she found that detailed art-making has always helped her cope with the challenges of life.

Although self-directed in her exploration of fabric dyeing, sewing, and off-loom bead weaving, Klakulak went on to receive a BFA in art from Colorado State University (1997). She then was accepted as an Artist-in-Residence at the Appalachian Center for Craft, in Smithville, TN. While at ACC from 2002 to 2005, she independently explored the felt medium, designed and produced a body of well-crafted, functional work, and developed a conceptual drive behind her making. Additionally, she earned a teaching certificate in K-12 Visual Arts from Tennessee Tech University

(2004) and has proceeded to educate children and adults in the felt medium, both nationally and, increasingly, internationally.

Metaphors

Klakulak has an idea of the techniques she wants to explore when beginning a new piece, but does not typically start a piece of art with the intention of a specific metaphor, although her work usually evolves into something filled with metaphors about her own life. Thus, she indicated that the full meaning of a piece is not revealed to her until the process has been completed.

Psychological processes

Klakulak still finds the same meditative space she discovered as a child when she creates her fiber-based art today. It is a safe place for her to deeply process life and inevitably resolve the issues on hand. Because of the hypnotic state, when in her studio, "everything drifts away, it is my ideal space. I once heard a quote and wish I could recall the source, but it referenced the ideal space that is created in an artist's studio when no one else is around and went on to say that if you are lucky you [the artist] will leave too! At this point I feel like a conduit of creative energy as I am not mulling over decisions in the making process but simply dancing with the material."

Participants in Klakulak's courses over the past eight years are typically women between the ages of 45 and 75 (older than Klakulak by at least a decade). Many of these women have had years of making with some form of textile technique and are comfortable with detailed hand work, although it is surprising the number of women without textile backgrounds that are drawn to the felting process. "Often workshop participants are skilled in their hand work but don't have the visual design vocabulary or confidence to push a demonstrated technique in a personal direction." Klakulak stated that some participants are inhibited in trying something new by a fear of possible failure or by making a statement that may be interpreted incorrectly. She is surprised by the lack of confidence in many of the women she has taught as they often will reference themselves or their work in a demeaning manner. She encourages participants to accept themselves where they are in their skill level and to recognize that only by being present and stepping forward with a technique will they better themselves. Occasionally, if someone is having a block in class, Klakulak will ask them to think about their own process. For example, she will ask "What attracts you to that color... What do you remember that is red?" to help them develop a personal connection and story with their experience of making. In general, Klakulak reported that she is there to teach textile techniques and although she encourages the participants to develop a personal connection in their work she is cautious when opening psychological doors.

Pieces chosen

Entrapment was inspired by finding an old soap cage (used to allow the soap to dry between uses) at a second-hand store during a time when Klakulak was struggling with issues of the heart. She chose to make a heart organ from felt and to embed the cage in the chest of a figure. While sculpting the figure by stitching pieces of felt together the arms became longer than the height of the figure, which resulted in the arms laying open in front of the figure in a helpless and defeated manner. This gesture spoke to the experience of recognizing our issues and the need for change, but not quite having the tools or ability to alter our emotional and psychological patterns. She then added some rusted keys in the hands to symbolize the unsuccessful efforts of opening up one's heart.

Internal Chaos began by using a ball of tangled wire as a form of resistance to create a sphere, which developed into the earth. Similar to felt (offering a smooth surface, though it is constructed by a web of chaotically matted hairs), the earth from space appears tranquil, but under the surface image, has chaos created by its human inhabitants: social inequality, racism, religious warfare, abuse of natural resources, pollution. In the process of articulating the continental shapes of North America and Africa with partial-felts,

Klakulak recognized that a recent intercultural relationship shared a similar trepidation. The aesthetic and idealism of the union created surface beauty, but the internal strife of navigating cultural, economic, and social differences created a core struggle. As she sculpted the racially split human image by fusing wool through naturally dyed silk to create the texture of worn skin, Klakulak realized that her personal experience with race was occurring on a macrocosmic scale. Obama took office in the making of this piece and, from a distance, it would appear that the USA had reconciled a tumultuous past; but despite topical solutions to suture deep wounds, racism continues to fester under the surface, creating internal chaos within our social structure. Discussing issues of race is a delicate walk, thus the beaded glass feet. The figure's hands are bound behind the back, not able to create meaningful change, and the facial expression is one of sorrowful witnessing of how humans have created seemingly irreparable divisions of understanding based on race.

Entrapment
Photograph © John Lucas

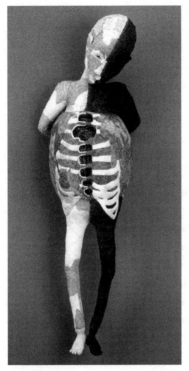

Internal Chaos
Photograph © Steve Mann

8. Elaine Quehl
Artist statement

My art celebrates the visual drama that is present in the natural world and aims to evoke the emotion, awe, and wonder I experience when I first encounter my subjects. Often described as bold and sensual, my work employs contrasts of light and shadow to intensify visual impact. Foliage, trees, flowers, and nature's cycles serve as metaphors for my inner world and for the human condition. I use my art as a means of self-expression and to communicate and connect with the world through universally understood themes of personal growth, wonder, self-acceptance, loss and healing, joy, and the cycles of life.

~

Objects and mediums

Quehl specializes in colorful and intricately stitched pieced and appliquéd art quilts. She focuses almost exclusively on making nature-themed art quilts that use her own hand-dyed fabrics. Her quilts are heavily textured with free-motion machine quilting.

Background

Quehl grew up on a farm in Southern Ontario (Waterloo County). She has little formal art training, except for a few acrylic painting classes and a couple of drawing classes. Quehl has read extensively about composition, design, and color. Quilts were an important part of her heritage; her great-grandmother, grandmother, and mother all made quilts, and as a child she was surrounded by them. When her mother was stricken with Alzheimer's disease and Quehl was suffering emotionally, she decided to take a quilting class at a local high school evening program. Upon reflection, Quehl thinks that making quilts was her way of connecting with her mother. However, it was also a way to focus and calm her mind during a troubling time.

The type of work Quehl makes today is vastly different from the traditional quilts her ancestors made. Eventually it would lead to a career as a full-time artist, teacher, and dyer. Currently, Quehl is an award-winning Canadian quilt artist and teacher; her quilts are known for their depth and contrast, color, and texture. She has participated in juried shows both nationally (in Canada) and internationally. In great demand as a teacher, Quehl travels extensively delivering workshops and lectures to colleges, summer art programs, guilds, conferences, and shops. Her specialties include expertise in free-motion machine quilting, fabric dyeing, and original quilts. Quehl has been selling her hand-dyed fabrics across North America for the past six years.

Metaphors

Quehl stated that she builds metaphors while she is working on a piece (consciously), and then finds more metaphors when she is finished (unconsciously). For example, the hosta leaf has become a special metaphor for personal growth (as a middle-aged woman and in her career). She realizes that artists vary in their awareness of using metaphors, for example some make pointed political statements and some create in a stream of consciousness style. Regardless of their styles, Quehl firmly believes that symbols come through her work (and that of others) time and time again. An interesting point Quehl makes is that those new to art-making might be more likely to choose overworked and common symbols until they start to work deeper, when they become more unique.

Psychological processes

Quehl doesn't think most people always know why they make something when they make it. She indicated that there is usually a strong emotional reaction to the subjects she chooses. Her inspiration frequently comes from her own photographs, and she is very visually reactive. Quehl also reported that there was something "transformative about connecting with a viewer, the relatedness between two human beings, that human bridge that is built when someone gets your work or finds it meaningful."

To Quehl, there is pain and loss in life, but being able to make beauty out of those things through her quilting is transformative. She has found many positive results have come to her from her art, which began with the loss of her mother. Quehl's art has always comforted her during other painful times. Quehl stated that the rejuvenation comes afterwards; during the process, she tends to experience anxiety, doubt, and a lot of hard work. Interestingly, she has been told that regardless of how bad or difficult the time was for her the quilts come across as joyful in appearance despite her troubled mental state. Quehl laughs this off as: "Either I am repressed or I have a need to turn ugliness into beauty. However, I have often been told that work I made during a bad or difficult time is rather joyful in appearance, despite my troubled mental state. I think there is this thing about art...you know that old saying...when life hands you lemons make lemonade. That is what we can do with art."

As with many of the other artists, Quehl noticed that many of her quilting students have low self-esteem. They also set very high standards that they can't meet, coupled with a fear of failure.

Pieces chosen

Femmes FAT-ales, created in 2003, took Third Prize in the Art Quilt category at the 2004 Common Thread Quilt Show, Ottawa. It includes hand-dyed fabrics and commercial batiks, fusible appliqué, and beads, and is free-motion machine quilted. Here is what Quehl had to say about the piece: "In Western society, women are constantly bombarded by a very narrow definition of beauty: thin, tall, and usually white. This quilt celebrates women of all shapes, sizes, and colors. I hope it inspires women to break out of the box of negative body image."

Standing Still, a gnarled and dormant winter tree, is a metaphor for Quehl giving up her day job and being pulled in many directions to focus on her art.

Femmes FAT-ales

Standing Still

9. Erica Spitzer Rasmussen

Artist statement

> *When I was a little girl, a family member told me that eating tomatoes would make me "big, strong, and hairy chested." I avoided eating tomatoes for 20 years. As a general rule, my sculptural work is inspired by childhood myths or adult anxieties regarding my body. Like my childhood association between the consumption of tomatoes and the growth of chest hair, I sometimes find body-stories or body-experiences to be simultaneously comical and horrifying. It is often these extremes in emotional reactions that drive me to produce the work, in an attempt to better comprehend each situation. Recently, the parameter of my work has expanded to include the well-being*

of loved ones. Coping with familiar illness and motherhood has altered my outlook on the world and my responsibilities in life.

I use clothing as subject matter because it allows me a ground on which to investigate identity and corporeality. My garments are metaphors. They can encompass narrative qualities, illustrate and dissolve bodily fears, or act as talismanic devices.

Objects and mediums

Rasmussen creates mixed-media and hand-made paper garments. The base of most of her sculptural work is paper, but all of her art is embellished with "odd-ball" material. Rasmussen indicated that she uses paper because it is the closest thing that she has found to emulate the skin, given its vulnerability and fragility. In addition to utilizing hand made paper, Rasmussen often incorporates non-archival media into her work. She derives great joy from transforming everyday materials into something personal, meaningful, and beautiful. For example, when she sees tomato paste, dog hair, sausage casings, spent tea bags, or dried fish skins, she envisions a work that may be transitory in nature, but rich in surfaces.

Background

Rasmussen is the daughter of a fiber artist and has been making arts and crafts all of her life. She received her BFA at the University of Minnesota (Minneapolis) in 1990 with an emphasis on studio arts (drawing and painting); this included coursework in Mexico and Greece. She then went on to take coursework in fiber arts at the University of Wisconsin, River Falls, Wisconsin, in 1992, and then received her MFA from the University of Minnesota, Minneapolis, in 1997 (studio arts: drawing and painting). It was halfway through her graduate degree that Rasmussen realized she wanted to work three-dimensionally. That is when she turned to paper-making. Rasmussen's thesis show did not have one single drawing or painting on view—just paper garments. She has been making related works ever since.

Rasmussen currently teaches studio arts as an Associate Professor at Metropolitan State University (St. Paul, MN). She is also affiliated with the Minnesota Center for Book Arts and is on the Board of the Textile Center (St. Paul, MN). Rasmussen's sculptural and wearable works are exhibited internationally. Her most recent work explores issues of identity and corporeality, often utilizing clothing as a metaphor for skin.

Metaphors

Rasmussen agreed that she usually uses metaphors in her work. One symbol that she described as her signature is the "tomato myth" (as she describes in her artist statement), which represents her anxieties about being perceived as masculine. To this end, Rasmussen continually explores the polarities between masculinity and femininity, beastliness and humanity, and attraction and repulsion. Often her sculptural works are intended to act as talismanic devices, to protect a feminine identity from psychological harm. Rasmussen quoted the photographer Richard Avedon, who "lays his ghosts to rest" with his art. She materializes her concerns, issues, and fears through her art in order to gain some control over the situation. Like the use of humor, she finds making artwork is a constructive outlet, "and it's cheaper than therapy!"

Psychological processes

Rasmussen is generally moved to create a work when she has something on her mind. For example, if she has a sick loved one whom she hopes to see healed or has a fear of her own that needs to be confronted. She typically starts by making a thumbnail sketch and experimenting with various media that might support the theme of the work. Sometimes the work materializes over a period of months or years to reflect the drawing. At other times it morphs into something similar, when she finds the materials won't behave as she had planned.

Rasmussen is aware that her students frequently grapple with psychological issues great and small. She stated that "everything from the grandeur of nature to homelessness and rape seep into their work." On reflection, Rasmussen thinks that it is because she is so open and honest about her own issues that her students feel permitted to address their own deeply personal content.

Pieces chosen

Rasmussen's first piece is the *Juju Dress*. "As a small child, my girlfriends and I believed that swallowing a watermelon seed resulted in pregnancy. As an adult, I found myself battling infertility. Hence, the dress was constructed of cast and leafed plates of paper, modeled after medieval armor. Watermelon seeds were tied at each juncture. The dress was worn to my monthly 'procedures' as an attempt to enlist magical assistance." The piece is mixed-media with hand-made paper (abaca, cotton, kozo, acrylics, tracing paper, waxed linen thread, gold leaf, and watermelon seeds).

After several years of fighting infertility in Rasmussen's mid-thirties, *Red Hot* (2005) is a celebratory work that marks the conception of her son. The piece is mixed-media with hand-made paper (cotton, acrylics, gold leaf, wax, metal, rubber, and match sticks).

Juju Dress

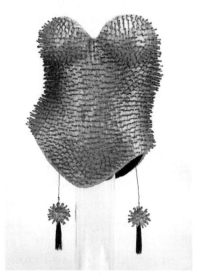

Red Hot

Synthesis of the interviews

You may have noticed that all of these artists are quite different and unique. Their mediums vary, their ages vary, and their chosen objects vary. Some come from families rich in creative and artistic traditions; some don't. Some are professionally trained artists; some are self-taught and had other viable careers. Some started creating with textiles early in life; several did not.

You may also have noticed that there are quite a few similarities amongst the artists. First, almost every one of these women was drawn to fibers and textiles early in their artistic endeavors. The professionally trained artists were aware that this could leave them open to criticism (i.e. not taken as seriously) by their colleagues since it was "women's work." Regardless, each artist eventually accepted that fibers were her destiny and embraced textile mediums whole-heartedly.

Second, most of the artists recognized low self-esteem, insecurity, and sometimes severe emotional problems, in their students. As a group, they were sensitive and supportive of these issues. They acknowledged to their students that it was acceptable to express psychological concerns through their work. However, even with this support, they also strongly conveyed that art education was the priority in the classroom. They recognized that firm boundaries needed to be in place so as not to confuse the creative environment with a therapeutic milieu.

Third, most of the fiber artists I talked to said they started a project with only a vague idea of the metaphor they wanted to explore. Then, after immersing themselves in their creative processes, they found that the metaphor(s) evolved and changed. If they allowed the process to continue, which they all did, then the end product was very different or much more complex than they had originally planned. Thus they did not "over-think" the creative process, nor did they try to create a concrete manifestation of their metaphor (e.g. I need a mother so I will create a mother doll!). Most of the artists kept re-working the metaphors in subsequent projects, creating a series or body of work that fully explored their themes. This allowed them to fully express and work through their own issues, most of the time, to the completion of the dilemma.

This gives credence to the idea not to have your clients over-think how they will apply metaphors in their textile-making. They can choose a metaphor that resonates, but they must let the process evolve. There is discovery in the making; the final story will be exposed when the piece(s) are finished. In addition, making one piece is probably not sufficient to explore an issue. It may take multiple pieces along a theme to fully realize the complexity of an issue.

Fourth, most of these fiber artists believed that all artwork was metaphoric, for professionals and non-professionals alike. They also thought that the majority of textile handcrafters would not be aware of their own symbolic expression, nor would they be *trying* to express metaphors. I agree. Especially when a person creates something uniquely expressive; there will definitely be deeper psychological metaphors, even if she doesn't acknowledge this. Does that mean that if a person goes into a yarn store and buys a pattern to make a sweater or jersey, then that jersey provides an expressive metaphor for the person? If they didn't design the piece, and they followed a pattern, how could it communicate deeper meaning? True, it is probably not *that* symbolic. However, you could say that the object selected to make probably revealed something (e.g. a snuggly blanket, a purse, a hat), that the knitting style probably revealed something (e.g. small, tight, uniform stitches with a smooth strong yarn, vs. big, loose, irregular patterns with a chunky, highly textured yarn), or that the colors probably revealed something (e.g. all shades of black and white, or bright, bold colors). What is revealed may not be as complex as it is for people who use their own muse at every step of the creative process, but psychologically, there is still underlying expression and meaning.

Fifth, each of these artists found that the process of making art was positively transforming. Of course there were frustrations when they weren't happy with how something was turning out. But each one of them felt that they were typically invigorated, refreshed, and rejuvenated by their handcraft-making. The creative process allowed them to enter a meditative, here-and-now state, similar to Buddhist mindfulness. Some described this as spirituality, some as stream of consciousness, some as a connection to all women, some as feeling grounded. They all felt renewed by their work and happiest when making art. I take away from this finding more reason to encourage textile art-making because it just feels good! Creating with metaphors or to psychologically express yourself does not have to be cathartic, mentally exhausting, or over-wrought with negative feelings. In contrast, it just might help you to cope with life better because the process is so enjoyable.

Finally, most of the artists indicated that their materials frequently "spoke" to them about what to make. I found this same artifact in my research on handcrafters. Women indicated that they spent time connecting with their fibers before beginning a project. They would look at what they had in their stash of fabric, yarn, or wool, and see how it could fit together. They would go on-line or to stores to get inspiration. They would play around and get excited about what they were going to do. Sometimes, this was all they could do. They either had no time, no money, or no energy to initiate a project. We need to encourage our clients to honor this as a valuable step in the art-making process. It needs to be completely acceptable to explore the material without knowing where it is going to end up. As Rebecca Cross suggested, she had to learn to "listen" to her work. When she listened to it, she knew where she needed to go next. The listening is the groundwork for the creative process. Encourage your clients to be immersed in the visuals, the tactile, even the smells of the materials before starting. And have her go with what her inner voice moves her to do, not her intellect.

Appendix

Textile Survey

Q1. Tell us about your experience with the textile handcrafts outlined in the table on the following page.

- First, please check all of the textile handcrafts that you have tried.

- For the next two columns (skill, time spent), only answer if you use this technique.

	Check all that you have tried	Rate your skill					How much time do you typically spend when using this technique?				
	Check	Poor	Low	Moderate	Good	Excellent	Less than 1 hr	1–2 hrs	3–4 hrs	5–8 hrs	8+ hrs
Basketry	☐	○	○	○	○	○	○	○	○	○	○
Beadwork	☐	○	○	○	○	○	○	○	○	○	○
Bookcrafts	☐	○	○	○	○	○	○	○	○	○	○
Braiding, macramé, or kumihimo	☐	○	○	○	○	○	○	○	○	○	○
Dyeing fibers	☐	○	○	○	○	○	○	○	○	○	○
Fabric surface design (e.g. dye, paint, embellishments)	☐	○	○	○	○	○	○	○	○	○	○
Felting (e.g. wet, dry, needle)	☐	○	○	○	○	○	○	○	○	○	○
Knitting and crocheting	☐	○	○	○	○	○	○	○	○	○	○
Lace-making (e.g. tatting, needle, cutwork, bobbin, tape, guipure)	☐	○	○	○	○	○	○	○	○	○	○
Mixed-media	☐	○	○	○	○	○	○	○	○	○	○
Needlework (e.g. embroidery, cross-stitch, needlepoint)	☐	○	○	○	○	○	○	○	○	○	○

Paper-making	☐	○	○	○	○	○	○	○	○	○
Rug-making (e.g. braided, woven, hooking, rag, needlepunch, prodded)	☐	○	○	○	○	○	○	○	○	○
Sewing: Clothing and functional objects	☐	○	○	○	○	○	○	○	○	○
Sewing: Quilting	☐	○	○	○	○	○	○	○	○	○
Spinning fibers	☐	○	○	○	○	○	○	○	○	○
Temari balls	☐	○	○	○	○	○	○	○	○	○
Weaving	☐	○	○	○	○	○	○	○	○	○
Other	☐	○	○	○	○	○	○	○	○	○

Q2. What percentage of your handcrafts are "functional" (i.e. art pieces that can be used in your everyday life) compared with "non-functional" (i.e. art pieces that are created purely for aesthetic purposes)? Please make sure your total adds up to 100.

_____ Percentage of items made that are functional
_____ Percentage of items made that are non-functional

Q3. What do you usually make with your textile handcrafts? Please indicate the percentage for each; make sure your total adds up to 100.

_____ General household items (e.g. rugs, curtains, bed coverings)
_____ Wearable items (e.g. clothing, sweaters/jerseys, hats, mittens)
_____ Containers and vessels (e.g. baskets to hold food, bags to hold clothing)
_____ Items for play (e.g. dolls, play cloth)
_____ Items for sports (e.g. tents, backpacks, kites, temari balls)
_____ Materials that can be used for transportation (e.g. nets, kites, sails)
_____ Other (please indicate what it is)

Q4. Use the table on the following page to answer a few more questions about these textile handcrafts:

- Who do you typically make them for?

- How frequently does this involve being with other people?

- How much intellectual focus is required for you to make this handcraft?

- How engaged do you feel in this activity?

Please answer only for those techniques that you have tried.

| Handcraft | for Who do you typically make them for? | | | | | How frequently does this activity involve being around other people? | | | | | How much intellectual focus does this handcraft technique require? | | | | | How "engaged" do you feel when making this handcraft (i.e. how immersed in your activity, lose track of time, how absorbed, completely involved)? | | | | |

Craft	Myself	No one in particular	To sell	My family	My friends	Never	Rarely	Sometimes	Often	Very often	None	A little bit	Some	A lot	Tremendous amount	None	A little bit	Somewhat	A lot	Tremendous amount
Basketry	O	O	O	O	O	O	O	O	O	O	O	O	O	O	O	O	O	O	O	O
Beadwork	O	O	O	O	O	O	O	O	O	O	O	O	O	O	O	O	O	O	O	O
Bookcrafts	O	O	O	O	O	O	O	O	O	O	O	O	O	O	O	O	O	O	O	O
Braiding, macramé, or kumihimo	O	O	O	O	O	O	O	O	O	O	O	O	O	O	O	O	O	O	O	O
Dyeing fibers	O	O	O	O	O	O	O	O	O	O	O	O	O	O	O	O	O	O	O	O
Fabric surface design (e.g. dye, paint, embellishments)	O	O	O	O	O	O	O	O	O	O	O	O	O	O	O	O	O	O	O	O
Felting (e.g. wet, dry, needle)	O	O	O	O	O	O	O	O	O	O	O	O	O	O	O	O	O	O	O	O
Knitting and crocheting	O	O	O	O	O	O	O	O	O	O	O	O	O	O	O	O	O	O	O	O
Lace-making (e.g. tatting, needle, cutwork, bobbin, tape, guipure)	O		O	O	O	O	O	O	O	O	O	O	O	O	O	O	O	O	O	O
Mixed-media	O	O	O	O	O	O	O	O	O	O	O	O	O	O	O	O	O	O	O	O

Handcraft	Who do you typically make them for?					How frequently does this activity involve being around other people?					How much intellectual focus does this handcraft technique require?					How "engaged" do you feel when making this handcraft (i.e. how immersed in your activity, lose track of time, how absorbed, completely involved)?				
	Myself	No one in particular	To sell	My family	My friends	Never	Rarely	Sometimes	Often	Very often	None	A little bit	Some	A lot	Tremendous amount	None	A little bit	Somewhat	A lot	Tremendous amount
Needlework (e.g. embroidery, cross-stitch, needlepoint)	○	○	○	○	○	○	○	○	○	○	○	○	○	○	○	○	○	○	○	○
Paper-making	○	○	○	○	○	○	○	○	○	○	○	○	○	○	○	○	○	○	○	○
Rug-making (e.g. braided, woven, hooking, rag, needlepunch, prodded)	○	○	○	○	○	○	○	○	○	○	○	○	○	○	○	○	○	○	○	○
Sewing: Clothing and functional objects	○	○	○	○	○	○	○	○	○	○	○	○	○	○	○	○	○	○	○	○
Sewing: Quilting	○	○	○	○	○	○	○	○	○	○	○	○	○	○	○	○	○	○	○	○
Spinning fibers	○	○	○	○	○	○	○	○	○	○	○	○	○	○	○	○	○	○	○	○
Temari balls	○	○	○	○	○	○	○	○	○	○	○	○	○	○	○	○	○	○	○	○
Weaving	○	○	○	○	○	○	○	○	○	○	○	○	○	○	○	○	○	○	○	○
Other	○	○	○	○	○	○	○	○	○	○	○	○	○	○	○	○	○	○	○	○

Q5. Before you begin a new project, what do you typically do to get ready or to prepare for it? For example, some people gather all of their materials together and think about what they want to make, others go shopping at a local yarn store for ideas, and others take long walks in nature to get inspired. What do you do?

Q6. Think of a time when you were in a terrible mood (e.g. not clinically depressed or anxious, but worried, upset, angry, sad): Use the questions below and the table on the following page to consider how each of these handcraft techniques affected your mood:

- How did the technique change your arousal or energy level? By arousal, we also mean stimulating, energizing, and activating (as opposed to non-stimulating, calming, fatiguing, or low energy).

- How rejuvenated did you feel after doing this? By rejuvenation we mean restored, re-centered, refreshed, repaired, and ready to start anew.

- How did the technique change your mood in a positive direction?

Again, please answer only for those techniques that you have tried.

Technique	Extreme changes towards positive	Changes it a lot	Somewhat changes it	Changes it a little	Doesn't change mood	Extremely rejuvenated	Very rejuvenated	Somewhat rejuvenated	A little rejuvenated	Not at all rejuvenated	Extreme increase	Some increase	Neutral: no change	Some decrease	Extreme decrease
	How did the technique change your mood in a positive direction?					**How rejuvenated did you feel after doing this?**					**How did the technique change your arousal or energy level?**				
Basketry	O	O	O	O	O	O	O	O	O	O	O	O	O	O	O
Beadwork	O	O	O	O	O	O	O	O	O	O	O	O	O	O	O
Bookcrafts	O	O	O	O	O	O	O	O	O	O	O	O	O	O	O
Braiding, macramé, or kumihimo	O	O	O	O	O	O	O	O	O	O	O	O	O	O	O
Dyeing fibers	O	O	O	O	O	O	O	O	O	O	O	O	O	O	O
Fabric surface design (e.g. dye, paint, embellishments)	O	O	O	O	O	O	O	O	O	O	O	O	O	O	O
Felting (e.g. wet, dry, needle)	O	O	O	O	O	O	O	O	O	O	O	O	O	O	O
Knitting and crocheting	O	O	O	O	O	O	O	O	O	O	O	O	O	O	O
Lace-making (e.g. tatting, needle, cutwork, bobbin, tape, guipure)	O	O	O	O	O	O	O	O	O	O	O	O	O	O	O

	How did the technique change your arousal or energy level?					How rejuvenated did you feel after doing this?					How did the technique change your mood in a positive direction?				
	Extreme decrease	Some decrease	Neutral: no change	Some increase	Extreme increase	Not at all rejuvenated	A little rejuvenated	Somewhat rejuvenated	Very rejuvenated	Extremely rejuvenated	Doesn't change mood	Changes it a little	Somewhat changes it	Changes it a lot	Extreme changes towards positive
Mixed-media	○	○	○	○	○	○	○	○	○	○	○	○	○	○	○
Needlework (e.g. embroidery, cross-stitch, needlepoint)	○	○	○	○	○	○	○	○	○	○	○	○	○	○	○
Needlework (e.g. embroidery, cross-stitch, needlepoint)	○	○	○	○	○	○	○	○	○	○	○	○	○	○	○
Paper-making	○	○	○	○	○	○	○	○	○	○	○	○	○	○	○
Rug-making (e.g. braided, woven, hooking, rag, needlepunch, prodded)	○	○	○	○	○	○	○	○	○	○	○	○	○	○	○
Sewing: Clothing and functional objects	○	○	○	○	○	○	○	○	○	○	○	○	○	○	○
Sewing: Quilting	○	○	○	○	○	○	○	○	○	○	○	○	○	○	○
Spinning fibers	○	○	○	○	○	○	○	○	○	○	○	○	○	○	○
Temari balls	○	○	○	○	○	○	○	○	○	○	○	○	○	○	○
Weaving	○	○	○	○	○	○	○	○	○	○	○	○	○	○	○
Other	○	○	○	○	○	○	○	○	○	○	○	○	○	○	○

Q7. Below are a list of reasons women have given for why they make textiles. Please indicate whether these apply to you.

	Strongly disagree	Disagree	Neither agree nor disagree	Agree	Strongly agree
Aesthetic need: sheer beauty of it; love the color immersion; need and love creative expression; like items of quality that are customized	O	O	O	O	O
Feeling grounded: pleasurable sensations including rhythm and texture; repetition; motion is soothing	O	O	O	O	O
Psychological: Brings out positive feelings: helps me feel rejuvenated, calm, and good about things; positive energy put into creations makes me feel good, increases my self-esteem	O	O	O	O	O
Psychological: Takes away negative feelings: helps me decrease depression, stress, and difficult feelings	O	O	O	O	O
Psychological: Distraction: allows me to forget about problems and escape from situations; avoid problems; offers a distraction	O	O	O	O	O
Psychological: Reframes situation(s): gives me a sense of control or completion or balance in life; makes me unique; gives me a sense of identity	O	O	O	O	O
Psychological: Metaphors create textile handcrafts that symbolize or are a metaphor for important issues	O	O	O	O	O
Like to do for others: enjoy making personal gifts; like to do for others; like to make others happy; people appreciate it	O	O	O	O	O

Social satisfaction: eases my social isolation; enjoy the social organizations; connects me with others with similar interests; enjoy camaraderie	O	O	O	O	O
Financial: use it for donations; good income; too cheap to buy; don't like wasting; have money to spend; have fibers from animals available; costs less to make it; like rewards of selling	O	O	O	O	O
Cognitive: helps me mentally, either by stimulating and challenging me, or by slowing down my thoughts and clearing my thinking; like to learn new things	O	O	O	O	O
Idle hands: "Idle hands are the Devil's work"; don't like doing nothing; something to do while waiting for others; something to show for my time; keeps me from being bored; have lots of time on my hands	O	O	O	O	O
Physical health: helps control pain; helps maintain my dexterity; helps me cope with disability/illness/loss of function; non-verbal way to express feelings about physical problem(s)	O	O	O	O	O
Historical reasons: continues family traditions; enjoy leaving a legacy; gives people something to think of me with; marks special event (e.g. birth, death); continuity with my past; connection to my heritage and/ or ethnic background; keeps history alive; connects me with special person or animal that has died	O	O	O	O	O
Other (please list only if it doesn't fit into one of the above)	O	O	O	O	O

Q8. How important are these design elements to you when you make textile handcrafts?

	Not important	A little important	Neutral	Somewhat important	Extremely important	Does not apply
Content or subject matter (e.g. you make specific objects like handbags, or incorporate themes like animals)	O	O	O	O	O	O
Form, for example attention to organic form (irregularity, asymmetry, asymmetrical naturally occurring shapes) or geometric form (squares, circles, rectangles)	O	O	O	O	O	O
Movement (implied movement via drape, color contrast, texture, and repeating patterns)	O	O	O	O	O	O
Texture such as smooth, rough, grainy, sharp, furry, and bumpy	O	O	O	O	O	O
Shade or value (relative light and darkness)	O	O	O	O	O	O
White space or negative space (incorporate use of open space)	O	O	O	O	O	O
Symmetry in design	O	O	O	O	O	O
Color, general importance	O	O	O	O	O	O
Achromatic color schemes: a combination of black, white, gray	O	O	O	O	O	O

Keyed color schemes: involve achromatic values combined with a single hue (e.g. black, white, red)	O	O	O	O	O	O
Monochromatic color schemes: colors involve different values (shades, tints, and tones) of the same hue (red, pink)	O	O	O	O	O	O
Analogous color schemes: combine hues adjacent to each other on color wheel (e.g. red and orange)	O	O	O	O	O	O
Complementary color schemes: combine colors opposite to each other on color wheel (e.g. red and green)	O	O	O	O	O	O
Details of objects	O	O	O	O	O	O
The Gestalt or whole look	O	O	O	O	O	O
Proportion (relative size within the work; relationship between objects, parts of a whole)	O	O	O	O	O	O
Unity (repetition, rhythm, pattern)	O	O	O	O	O	O
Following patterns, kits, or structure others have designed	O	O	O	O	O	O
Inventing and implementing my own design	O	O	O	O	O	O
Context: what is around it	O	O	O	O	O	O
Other (please explain)	O	O	O	O	O	O

Q9. What is your favorite color(s)?

Q10. What life experiences do you associate with this favorite color(s)?

Q11. What is your least favorite color(s)?

Q12. What life experiences do you associate with this least favorite color(s)?

Q13. If you wanted another person to know about who you really were and what you were really like as a person, which two activities would you tell them about that reflect who you are?

❑ Activity #1 (please describe) _____
❑ Activity #2 (please describe) _____

Note: these do not need to include fiber or textile handcrafts, but they can. If you do indicate a textile activity, please answer all of the following questions, even if your answers above touched on the same issues (only a few are repeats). Thank you!

Q14. What is your usual level of interest experienced when you are engaged in this activity?

	Very low	Low	Somewhat low	Neutral (not high or low)	Somewhat high	High	Very high
Activity #1	○	○	○	○	○	○	○
Activity #2	○	○	○	○	○	○	○

Q15. How frequently have you engaged in this activity over the past year?

Activity #2	Very frequently	O
	Somewhat frequently	O
	In between seldom and frequently	O
	Somewhat seldom	O
	Seldom	O
	Very seldom	O
Activity #1	Very frequently	O
	Frequently	O
	Somewhat frequently	O
	In between seldom and frequently	O
	Somewhat seldom	O
	Seldom	O
	Very seldom	O

Q16. Flow: When I engage in this activity...

Activity #2

	I feel I have clear goals	I feel self-conscious	I feel in control	I lose track of time	I feel I know how well I am doing	I have a high level of concentration	I forget personal problems	I feel fully involved	I feel rejuvenated (e.g. refreshed, restored, revitalized) during and/or afterward	My mood always feels more positive
Very much like me	O	O	O	O	O	O	O	O	O	O
Like me	O	O	O	O	O	O	O	O	O	O
Somewhat like me	O	O	O	O	O	O	O	O	O	O
Neutral	O	O	O	O	O	O	O	O	O	O
Not much like me	O	O	O	O	O	O	O	O	O	O
Not like me	O	O	O	O	O	O	O	O	O	O
Not at all like me	O	O	O	O	O	O	O	O	O	O

Activity #1

	I feel I have clear goals	I feel self-conscious	I feel in control	I lose track of time	I feel I know how well I am doing	I have a high level of concentration	I forget personal problems	I feel fully involved	I feel rejuvenated (e.g. refreshed, restored, revitalized) during and/or afterward	My mood always feels more positive
Very much like me	O	O	O	O	O	O	O	O	O	O
Like me	O	O	O	O	O	O	O	O	O	O
Somewhat like me	O	O	O	O	O	O	O	O	O	O
Neutral	O	O	O	O	O	O	O	O	O	O
Not much like me	O	O	O	O	O	O	O	O	O	O
Not like me	O	O	O	O	O	O	O	O	O	O
Not at all like me	O	O	O	O	O	O	O	O	O	O

Q17. Personal expressiveness: When I engage in this activity...

		It gives me my greatest feeling of really being alive	I feel more intensely involved than I do when engaged in most other activities	It gives me the strongest sense of who I really am	It gives me my strongest sense of enjoyment	I feel that this is what I was meant to do	I feel a special fit or meshing
Activity #2	Strongly agree	O	O	O	O	O	O
	Agree	O	O	O	O	O	O
	Somewhat agree	O	O	O	O	O	O
	Neither agree nor disagree	O	O	O	O	O	O
	Somewhat disagree	O	O	O	O	O	O
	Disagree	O	O	O	O	O	O
	Strongly disagree	O	O	O	O	O	O
Activity #1	Strongly agree	O	O	O	O	O	O
	Agree	O	O	O	O	O	O
	Somewhat agree	O	O	O	O	O	O
	Neither agree nor disagree	O	O	O	O	O	O
	Somewhat disagree	O	O	O	O	O	O
	Disagree	O	O	O	O	O	O
	Strongly disagree	O	O	O	O	O	O

Q18. Self-realization of values: How effective is this activity at giving you the opportunity to...

		Appreciate beauty, in any form	Share my experiences with others	Satisfy my desire for competition	Develop my best potentials	Have spiritual experiences	Increase or decrease my need for stimulation	Make progress toward my goals
Activity #2	Very effective	O	O	O	O	O	O	O
	Effective	O	O	O	O	O	O	O
	Somewhat effective	O	O	O	O	O	O	O
	Neither ineffective nor effective	O	O	O	O	O	O	O
	Somewhat ineffective	O	O	O	O	O	O	O
	Ineffective	O	O	O	O	O	O	O
	Very ineffective	O	O	O	O	O	O	O
Activity #1	Very effective	O	O	O	O	O	O	O
	Effective	O	O	O	O	O	O	O
	Somewhat effective	O	O	O	O	O	O	O
	Neither ineffective nor effective	O	O	O	O	O	O	O
	Somewhat ineffective	O	O	O	O	O	O	O
	Ineffective	O	O	O	O	O	O	O
	Very ineffective	O	O	O	O	O	O	O

Q19. Tell us about the challenge and skill involved in these activities.

		What is the usual level of effort you invest when you engage in this activity?	How challenged do you feel by this activity?
Activity #2	Very high	○	○
	High	○	○
	Somewhat high	○	○
	Neutral	○	○
	Somewhat low	○	○
	Low	○	○
	Very low	○	○
Activity #1	Very high	○	○
	High	○	○
	Somewhat high	○	○
	Neutral	○	○
	Somewhat low	○	○
	Low	○	○
	Very low	○	○

References

Adams, K. (1990). *Journal to the self.* New York: Warner Books..

Adler, G. and Hull, R. F. C. (Eds.) (1970). *The collected works of C.G. Jung.* Ewing, NJ: Princeton University Press.

Ainsworth, R. A., Simpson, L., and Cassell, D. (1993). Effects of three colors in an office interior on mood and performance. *Perceptual and Motor Skills, 76(1),* 235–241.

Aksglaede, L., Sorenson, K., Petersen, J. H., Skakkebaek, N. E., and Anders, J. (2009). Recent decline in age at breast development: The Copenhagen puberty study. *Pediatrics, 123,* 932–939.

American Heritage Dictionary (2009). *The American Heritage Dictionary of the English Language* (4th ed.). Boston, MA: Houghton Mifflin Company.

American Psychiatric Association (2001). *Diagnostic and Statistical Manual of Mental Disorders, Fourth Edition, Text Revision* (DSM-IV-TR). Washington, DC: APA.

American Psychiatric Association (2009). *Women's mental health: Issue paper.* Available at www.psych.org/share/OMNA/Womens-Mental-Health-Issue-Paper.aspx, accessed on 1 September 2011.

American Psychological Association (2003). Guidelines on multicultural education, training, research, practice, and organizational change for psychologists. *American Psychologist, 58(5),* 377–402.

American Psychological Association (2007). *Guidelines for Psychological Practice with Girls and Women: A Joint Task Force of APA Divisions 17 and 35.* Available at www. apa.org/practice/guidelines/girls-and-women.pdf, accessed on 1 September 2011.

American Psychological Association (2011). PsycINFO [Database]. Available at www. apa.org/pubs/databases/psycinfo/index.aspx, accessed on 23 September 2011.

Ammer, C. (2003). *The American Heritage Dictionary of Idioms.* Boston, MA: Houghton Mifflin Harcourt Publishing Company.

ARAS (2010). *The book of symbols: Reflections on archetypal images* (The Archive for Research in Archetypal Symbolism). Germany: Taschen.

Art Students League (2011). The Art Students League of New York. Available at www.theartstudentsleague.org/About/History.aspx, accessed on 1 September 2011.

Baikie, K. A. (2008). Who does expressive writing work for? Examination of alexithymia, splitting, and repressive coping style as moderators of the expressive writing paradigm. *British Journal of Health Psychology, 13(1),* 61–66.

Baikie, K. A., and Wilhelm, K. (2005). Emotional and physical health benefits of expressive writing. *Advances in Psychiatric Treatment, 11,* 338–346.

Barber, E. W. (1994). *Women's work: The first 20,000 years*. New York: W. W. Norton.

Barker, C. (2001). *World weary woman: Her wound and transformation*. Toronto, Canada: Inner City Books.

Barker, P. (1985). *Using metaphors in psychotherapy*. New York: Brunner/Mazel.

Barnard, K. E. and Solchany, J. E. (2002). Mothering. In M. H. Bornstein (Ed.), *Handbook of parenting: Being and becoming a parent* (2nd ed., Vol. 3, pp. 3–25). Mahwah, NJ: Erlbaum.

Batten, S. V., Follette, V. M., Rasmussen Hall, M. L., and Palm, K. M. (2002). Physical and psychological effects of written disclosure among sexual abuse survivors. *Behavior Therapy, 33(1)*, 107–122. Battino, R. (2007). Everyone's life is a story: Guided metaphor in changing global lifestyle. In G. W. Burns (Ed.), *Healing with stories: Your casebook collection for using therapeutic metaphors* (pp. 138–149). Hoboken, NJ: John Wiley and Sons, Inc.

Beads of Courage (2011). Beads of Courage. Available at www.beadsofcourage.org, accessed on 1 September 2011.

Berlo, J. C. (2001). *Quilting lessons: Notes from the scrap bag of a writer and quilter*. Lincoln, NE: University of Nebraska Press.

Bouger, I. (2010). *Intertwined: The Art of Handspun Yarn, Modern Patterns, and Creative Spinning*. Minneapolis, MN: Quarry Books.

Brenner, A. (2007). *Women's rites of passage: How to embrace change and celebrate life*. Maryland: Rowman and Littlefield.

Bridges, W. (2004). *Transitions: Making sense of life's changes*. Cambridge, MA: Da Capo Press.

Burns, G. W. (Ed.) (2007). *Healing with stories: Your casebook collection for using therapeutic metaphors*. Hoboken, NJ: John Wiley and Sons, Inc.

Cannarella, D. (2005). *Beading for the soul: Inspired designs from 23 contemporary artists*. Loveland, CO: Interweave Press, LLC.

CDC (2011). Reproductive Health. Available at www.cdc.gov/reproductivehealth/ Infertility/index.htm, accessed on 23 September 2011.

Cerny, C. A., Eicher, J. B., and DeLong, M. R. (1993). Quiltmaking and the modern guild: A cultural idiom. *Clothing and Textiles Research Journal, 12(1)*, 16–25.

Cheek, C. and Piercy, K. W. (2004). Quilting as age identity expression in traditional women. *The International Journal of Aging and Human Development, 59(4)*, 321–337.

Chinen, A.B. (2003). *Once Upon a Midlife: Classic Stories and Mythic Tales to Illuminate the Middle Years*. Los Angeles, CA: Jeremy P. Tarcher/Perigee.

Chu, B. C. (2007). Considering culture one client at a time: Maximizing the cultural exchange. *Pragmatic Case Studies in Psychotherapy, 3*, 34–43.

Collier, A. D. (2011). The well-being of women who create with textiles: Implications for art therapy. *Art Therapy, 28(3)*, 1–9.

Collier, A. D. and Hahn, K. (2011). Resurgence of textile-making in modern society: Social implications. Paper presented at the Annual Conference of the International Textile and Apparel Association (ITAA), Philadelphia, PA, November 2–6, 2011.

Cousins, N. (1979). *Anatomy of an Illness as Perceived by the Patient: Reflections on Healing and Regeneration*. New York: W. W. Norton & Company, Inc.

Crowther, J. H., Wolf, E. M., and Sherwood, N. (1992). Epidemiology of bulimia nervosa. In M. Crowther, D. L. Tennenbaum, S. E. Hobfoll, and M. A. P. Stephens (Eds.), *The etiology of bulimia nervosa: The individual and familial context* (pp. 1–26). Washington, DC: Taylor and Francis.

Csikszentmihalyi, M. (1990). *Flow: The psychology of optimal experience.* New York: Harper and Row.

Dalebroux, A., Goldstein, T. R., and Winner, E. (2008). Short-term mood repair through art-making: Positive emotion is more effective than venting. *Motivation and Emotion, 32(4),* 288–295. Danoff-Burg, S., Mosher, C. E., Seawell, A. H., and Agee, J. D. (2010). Does narrative writing instruction enhance the benefits of expressive writing? *Anxiety, Stress and Coping: An International Journal, 23(3),* 341–352.

Dayspring, R. (2010). Ethnic minorities to make up one in five Britons by 2015. Available at www.blackmentalhealth.org.uk/index.php?option=com_content&task=view&id=802&Itemid=117, accessed on 1 September 2011.

de Silva, E. C. (2007). Institutional racism and the social work profession: A call to action. *President's Initiative: Weaving the Fabric of Diversity.* Washington, DC: National Association of Social Workers. Available at www.socialworkers.org/diversity/InstitutionalRacism.pdf, accessed on 1 September 2011.

Department of Labor (2011). Office of Disability Employment Policy. Available at www.dol.gov/odep/faqs/federal.htm, accessed on 23 September 2011.

Desjarlais, R., Eisenberg, L., Good, B., and Kleinman, A. (1995). *World mental health: Problems and priorities in low-income countries.* New York: Oxford University Press.

Detrixhe, S. (2005). *Zen and the art of needlecraft: Exploring the links between needlecraft, spirituality, and creativity.* Avon, MA: Adams Media.

Dickie, V. A. (2003). The role of learning in quilt making. *Journal of Occupational Science, 10(3),* 120–129.

Dudek, S. Z. and Marchand, P. (1983). Artistic style and personality in creative painters. *Journal of Personality Assessment, 47(2),* 139–142.

Durand, V. M. and Barlow, D. H. (2009). *Essentials of abnormal psychology* (5th ed.). Belmont, CA: Wadsworth/Thomson Learning.

Earle, S. A. and Harris, P. B. (2007). Developing the Inventory of Color Preference (ICP). American Psychological Association Convention Presentation, 115th Annual Convention, San Francisco, California, August 17–20, 2007.

Earnhardt, J. L., Martz, D. M., Ballard, M. E., and Curtin, L. (2002). A writing intervention for negative body image: Pennebaker fails to surpass the placebo. *Journal of College Student Psychotherapy, 17(1),* 19–35.

Enns, C. Z. (1992). Toward integrating feminist psychotherapy and feminist philosophy. *Professional Psychology: Research and Practice, 23(6),* 453–466.

Esquivel, L. (1989). *Like Water for Chocolate.* London: Black Swan.

Fairburn, C. G., Hay, P. J., and Welch, S. L. (1993). Binge eating and bulimia nervosa: Distribution and determinants. In C. G. Fairburn and G. T. Wilson (Eds.), *Binge eating: Nature, assessment, and treatment* (pp. 123–143). New York: Guilford.

Feist, G. J. and Brady, T. R. (2004). Openness to experience, non-conformity, and the preference for abstract art. *Empirical Studies of the Arts, 22(1),* 77–89.

Fields, A. J. (2010). Multicultural research and practice: Theoretical issues and maximizing cultural exchange. *Professional Psychology Research and Practice, 41(3)*, 196–201.

Firestone, L. (2010). Why Going Back Home Can Leave Us Feeling Lost. Available at www.psychologytoday.com/blog/compassion-matters/201007/why-going-back-home-can-leave-us-feeling-lost, accessed on 1 September 2011.

Foos, L. (1995). *Ex utero*. Minneapolis, MN: Coffee House Press.

Frattaroli, J. (2006). Experimental disclosure and its moderators: A meta-analysis. *Psychological Bulletin, 132(6)*, 823–865.

Freeman, R. (2002). *BodyLove: Learning to like our looks and ourselves*. Carlsbad, CA: Gurze Books.

Friedrich, W. N., Fisher, J. L., Dittner, C. A., Acton, R., Berliner, L., Butler, J., *et al.* (2001). Child Sexual Behavior Inventory: Normative, psychiatric, and sexual abuse comparisons. *Child Maltreatment, 6(1)*, 37–49.

Gallant, M. D. and Lafreniere, K. D. (2003). Effects of an emotional disclosure writing task on the physical and psychological functioning of children of alcoholics. *Alcoholism Treatment Quarterly, 21*, 55–66.

Gallician, M. L. (2004), *Sex, love, and romance in the mass media: Analysis and criticism of unrealistic portrayals and their influence*. Mahwah, NJ. Lawrence Erlbaum Associates.

Geda, J. (2009, April 25–May 2). Exercise your brain to prevent memory loss. Paper presented at the American Academy of Neurology's 61st Annual Meeting, Seattle, WA.

Gehlert, S., Song, I. H., Chang, C-H., and Hartaege, S. A. (2009). The prevalence of premenstrual dysphoric disorder in a randomly selected group of urban and rural women. *Psychological Medicine: A Journal of Research in Psychiatry and the Allied Sciences, 39(1)*, 129–136.

Grandmothers (2011). The Grandmothers Speak. Available at http://grandmothersspeak.com, accessed on 1 September 2011.

Gray, L. (2010). Older Women Recycle More. *The Telegraph*, 31 May 2010. Available at www.telegraph.co.uk/earth/earthnews/7779979/Older-women-recycle-more.html, accessed on 1 September 2011.

Gridley, M. C. (2006). Preferred thinking styles of professional fine artists. *Creativity Research Journal, 18(2)*, 247–248.

Griffin, S.A. (2006). A qualitative inquiry into how romantic love has been portrayed by contemporary media and researchers. *Dissertation Abstracts International Section A: Humanities and Social Sciences*, p.2272.

Griffiths, S. (2008). The experience of creative activity as a treatment medium. *Journal of Mental Health, 17(1)*, 49–63.

Grimes, R. (1995 [1982]). *Beginnings in ritual studies* (revised ed.). South Carolina: University of South Carolina Press.

Hahn, S. R., Kroenke, K., Spitzer, R. L., Brody, D., Williams, J. B., Linzer, M., and deGruy, F. V. (1996). The difficult patient: Prevalence, psychopathology and functional impairment. *Journal of General Internal Medicine, 11(1)*, 1–8.

Harris, P. B., Houston, J. M., Gasparri, J., Skelton, A. D., and Sachau, D. (2009). Color preferences for interior space: State or trait? Paper presented at the American Psychological Association 117th Annual Convention, Toronto, Ontario, Canada, August 6–9, 2009.

Hastings, P. (2003). *Doll Making as a Transformative Process.* Available from www. pamelahastings.com.

Herman-Giddens, M. E., Slora, E. J., Wasserman, R. C., Bourdony, C. J., Bhapkar, M. V., Koch, G. G., and Hasemeier, C. M. (1997). Secondary sexual characteristics and menses in young girls seen in office practice: A study from the pediatric research in office settings network. *Pediatrics, 99*, 505–512.

Hinz, E. J. (1975). A woman speaks: The lectures, seminars, and interviews of Anais Nin. Chicago: Swallow Press.

Hoek, H. W. (1995). The distribution of eating disorders. In K. D. Brownell and C. G. Fairburn (Eds.), *Eating disorders and obesity: A comprehensive handbook* (pp. 207–211). New York: Guilford.

Hoek, H. W. and van Hoeken, D. (2003). Review of the prevalence and incidence of eating disorders. *International Journal of Eating Disorders, 34(4)*, 383–396.

Holmes, B.M. (2004). Romantic partner ideals and dysfunctional relationship beliefs cultivated through popular media messages: Implications for relationship satisfaction. *Dissertation Abstracts International Section B: The Sciences and Engineering*, p. 3222.

Howard, D. (2006). *Repairing the Quilt of Humanity.* Silver Spring, MD: Beckham.

Iwasaki, Y., Mactavish, J., and MacKay, K. (2005). Building on strengths and resilience: Leisure as a stress survival strategy. *British Journal of Guidance and Counselling, 33(1)*, 81–100.

JAMA (1995). Stress Reduction's Common Thread. *Journal of the American Medical Association (Quick Updates), 274(4)*, 291.

Johnson, J. S., and Wilson, J. E. (2005). "It says you really care": Motivational factors of contemporary female handcrafters. *Clothing and Textiles Research Journal, 23(2)*, 115–130.

Johnson, N. (2005). *The invisible woman.* Nashville, TN: Thomas Nelson.

Johnson, R. M., Kotch, J. B., Catellier, D. J., Winsor, J. R., Dufort, V., Hunter, W., and Amaya-Jackson, L. (2002). Adverse behavioral and emotional outcomes from child abuse and witnessed violence. *Child Maltreatment, 7(3)*, 179–186.

Joy, K. (2009). A craft revolution: New generation of do-it-yourselfers churns out goods. *The Columbus Dispatch*, 5 March 2009. Available at www.dispatch.com/live/content/life/stories/2009/03/05/1_HIP_CRAFTS.ART_ART_03-05-09_D1_TOD3G57.html, accessed on 1 September 2011.

Judge, T. A. and Bono, J. E. (2000). Five-factor model of personality and transformational leadership. *Journal of Applied Psychology, 85(5)*, 751–765.

Jung, C. G. (1964). *Man and his symbols.* New York: Doubleday and Company, Inc.

Kees, N. L. (1999). Women together again: A phenomenological study of leaderless women's groups. *Journal for Specialists in Group Work, 24(3)*, 288–305.

Kertzman, S., Spivak, B., Ben-Nahum, Z., Vainder, M., Reznik, I., Weizman, A., and Mester, R. (2003). Variability of color choice in the Lüscher Color Test—Sex differences. *Perceptual and Motor Skills, 97(2)*, 647–656.

Kessler, R. C., Chiu, W. T., Demler, O., and Walters, E. E. (2005). Prevalence, severity, and comorbidity of 12-month DSM-IV disorders in the National Comorbidity Survey replication. *Archives of General Psychiatry, 62(6)*, 617–627.

Kessler, R. C. *et al.* (2007). Lifetime prevalence and age-of-onset distributions of mental disorders in the World Health Organization's World Mental Health Survey Initiative. *World Psychiatry, 6(3)*, 168–176.

Khalsa, J.S. (2007). *Altar Your Space: A Guide to the Restorative Home.* San Rafael, CA: Mandala Publishing.

Klass, P. (2008). Turning 50. *Knitter's Magazine*, Summer 2008. Available at http://perriklass.com/files/KlassK91.pdf, accessed on 23 September 2011.

Kim, M., Kwon, K.-N., and Lee, M. (2009). Psychological Characteristics of Internet Dating Service Users: The Effect of Self-Esteem, Involvement, and Sociability on the Use of Internet Dating Services. *CyberPsychology and Behavior, 12(4)*, 445–449.

Klakulak, L. (2008a). Artist Statement. Available at www.strongfelt.com/artist-statement, accessed on 23 September 2011.

Klakulak, L. (2008b). Gallery. Available at www.strongfelt.com/portfolio/, accessed on 23 September 2011.

Kovac, S. H. and Range, L. M. (2002). Does writing about suicidal thoughts and feelings reduce them? *Suicide and Life-Threatening Behavior, 32*, 428–440.

Kroenke, K., Spitzer, R. L., Williams, J. B. W., and Lowe, B. (2010). The Patient Health Questionnaire somatic, anxiety, and depressive symptom scales: A systematic review. *General Hospital Psychiatry, 32(4)*, 345–359. Available at www.phqscreeners.com/instructions/instructions.pdf, accessed on 1 September 2011.

Kübler-Ross, E. (1969). *On Death and Dying.* New York: Simon and Schuster/Touchstone.

Kwallek, N., Lewis, C. M., Lin-Hsiao, J. W. D., and Woodson, H. (1996). Effects of nine monochromatic office interior colors on clerical tasks and worker mood. *Color Research and Application, 21(6)*, 448–458.

Lakoff, G. and Johnson, M. (1980). *Metaphors we live by.* Chicago: University of Chicago Press.

Lepore, S. J., Greenberg, M. A., Bruno, M., and Smyth, J. M. (2002). Expressive writing and health: Self-regulation of emotion-related experience, physiology, and behavior. In S. J. Lepore and J. M. Smyth (Eds.), *The writing cure: How expressive writing promotes health and emotional well-being* (pp. 99–117). Washington, DC: American Psychological Association.

Lincoln, B. (1991). *Emerging from the chrysalis: Rituals of women's initiation.* New York: Oxford University Press.

Litvak, S. B. (1994). Abrasive personality disorder: Definition and diagnosis. *Journal of Contemporary Psychotherapy, 24(1)*, 7–14. Loomis, M. and Saltz, E. (1984). Cognitive styles as predictors of artistic styles. *Journal of Personality, 52(1)*, 22–35.

López, S. R. and Guarnaccia, P. J. J. (2000). Cultural psychopathology: Uncovering the social world of mental illness. *Annual Review of Psychology, 51*, 571–598.

Ludwig, A. (1998). Method and madness in the arts and sciences. *Creativity Research Journal, 11(2)*, 22–35.

Lynch, R. (2011). Kitchen aprons: A symbol of repression or pride? *McClatchy-Tribune News Service*, January 4 2011.

MacDonald, A. L. (1988). *No Idle Hands: The Social History of American Knitting*. New York, NY: Ballantine Books.

Maltsberger, J. T., and Buie, D. H. (1974). Countertransference hate in the treatment of suicidal patients. *Archives of General Psychiatry, 30(5)*, 625–633.

Martini, J., Wittchen, H-U., Soares, C. N., Rieder, A., and Steiner, M. (2009). New women-specific diagnostic modules: The composite international diagnostic interview for women (CIDI-Venus). *Archives of Women's Mental Health, 12(5)*, 281–289.

Mastandrea, S., Bartoli, G., and Bove, G. (2009). Preferences for ancient and modern art museums: Visitor experiences and personality characteristics. *Psychology of Aesthetics, Creativity, and the Arts, 3(3)*, 164–173.

Masuda, T., Ellsworth, P., Mesquita, B., Leu, J-X., Tanida, S., and van de Veerdon, E. (2008). Placing the face in context: Cultural differences in the perception of facial emotion. *Journal of Personality and Social Psychology, 94*, 365–381.

Masuda, T., Gonzalez, R., Kwan, L., and Nisbett, R. E. (2009). Culture and aesthetic preference: Comparing the attention to context of East Asians and Americans. *Personality and Social Psychology Bulletin, 34(9)*, 1260–1275.

McCauley, J., Kern, D. E., Kolodner, K., Dill, L., and Schroeder, A. F. (1997). Clinical characteristics of women with a history of childhood abuse: Unhealed wounds. *JAMA: Journal of the American Medical Association, 277(17)*, 1362–1368.

Meyers, R. A., Berdahl, J. L., Brashers, D., Considine, J. R., Kelly, J. R., Moore, C., *et al.* (2005). Understanding groups from a feminist perspective. In M. S. Poole and A. B. Hollingshead (Eds.), *Theories of small groups: Interdisciplinary perspectives* (pp. 241–276). Thousand Oaks, CA: Sage Publications.

Moon, B. L. (2007). *The role of metaphor in art therapy: Theory, method, and experience.* Springfield, IL: Charles C. Thomas.

Moon, B.L. (2010). *Art-based group therapy: Theory and practice.* Springfield, IL: Charles C. Thomas.

Mount, M., Barrick, M., and Stewart, G. (1998). Five-factor model of personality and performance in jobs involving interpersonal interactions. *Human Performance, 11*, 145–165.

Mulford, J. (2011). Browngrotta Arts. Available at www.browngrotta.com/pages/mulford.php, accessed on 1 September 2011.

Muszynski, M. N. (2009). Influence of a multidimensional model of antiracism training on white clinicians' positive self-regard, white privilege attitudes and social identity development. Master's thesis, Smith College School for Social Work, Massachusetts.

Myss, C. (2002). *Sacred contracts: Awakening your divine potential.* New York: Three Rivers Press.

Myzelev, A. (2009). Whip your hobby into shape: Knitting, feminism and construction of gender. *Textile: The Journal of Cloth and Culture, 7(2)*, 148–163.

Nakamura, J. and Csikszentmihalyi, M. (2005). The concept of flow. In C. R. Snyder and S. J. Lopez (Eds.), *Handbook of positive psychology* (pp. 89–105). Oxford, UK: Oxford University Press.

NASB (1997). *The new American standard bible.* La Habra, CA: Foundation Publications.

National Cancer Institute (2011). Anticipatory Nausea and Vomiting. *National Cancer Institute at the Institutes of Health.* Available at www.cancer.gov/cancertopics/pdq/ supportivecare/nausea/HealthProfessional/page4, accessed on 1 September 2011.

Nelson, N., LaBat, K., and Williams, G. (2002). Contemporary Irish textile artists: Gender, culture, and medium. *Clothing and Textiles Research Journal, 20(1),* 15–25.

Nelson, N., LaBat, K., and Williams, G. (2005). More than "just a little hobby": Women and textile art in Ireland. *Women's Studies International Forum, 28(4),* 328–342.

Neuman, G. A. and Wright, J. (1999). Team effectiveness: Beyond skills and cognitive ability. *Journal of Applied Psychology, 84(3),* 376–389.

Neville, H. A., Worthington, R. L., and Spanierman, L. B. (2001). Race, power, and multicultural counseling psychology: Understanding white privilege and color-blind racial attitudes. In J. G. Ponterotto, J. M. Casas, L. A. Suzuki, and C. M. Alexander (Eds.), *Handbook of multicultural counseling* (2nd ed., pp. 257–288). Thousand Oaks, CA: Sage Publications.

Nisbett, R. E. (2003). *The geography of thought: How Asians and Westerners think differently…and why.* New York: Free Press.

Nisbett, R. E., Peng, K., Choi, I., and Norenzayan, A. (2001). Culture and systems of thought: Holistic vs. analytic cognition. *Psychological Review, 108,* 291–310.

Nosek, M. A. (2010). Feminism and disability: Synchronous agendas in conflict. In H. Landrine and N.F. Russo (Eds.), *Handbook of diversity in feminist psychology.* New York, NY: Springer Publishing Co.

Nosek, M. A., Hughes, R.B., Swedlund, N., Taylor, H.B., and Swank, P. (2003). Self-esteem and women with disabilities. *Social Science and Medicine, 56(8),* 1737–1747.

Obasi, E. M., Flores, L. Y., and Lindaal, J. M. (2009). Construction and initial validation of the Worldview Analysis Scale (WAS). *Journal of Black Studies, 39(6),* 937–961.

O'Connor, M., Nikoletti, S., Kristjanson, L. J., Loh, R., and Willcock, B. (2003). Writing therapy for the bereaved: Evaluation of an intervention. *Journal of Palliative Medicine, 6,* 195–204.

Office of the Surgeon General, Center for Mental Health Services, and National Institute of Mental Health (2001). *Mental health: Culture, race, and ethnicity.* A Supplement to Mental Health: A Report of the Surgeon General. Rockville, MD: Substance Abuse and Mental Health Services Administration.

Pennebaker, J. W. (1997). Writing about emotional experiences as a therapeutic process. *Psychological Science, 8,* 162–166.

Pennebaker, J. W. and Beall, S. K. (1986). Confronting a traumatic event: Toward an understanding of inhibition and disease. *Journal of Abnormal Psychology, 95,* 274–281.

~

Pennebaker, J. W., Francis, M. E., and Booth, R. J. (2001). *Linguistic inquiry and word count.* Mahwah, NJ: Erlbaum.

Pesta, B., McDaniel, M., and Bertsch, S (2010). Toward an index of well-being for the 50 US states. *Intelligence, 38,* 160–168.

Picco, R. D. and Dzindolet, M. T. (1994). Examining the Lüscher Color Test. *Perceptual and Motor Skills, 79(3, Pt 2),* 1555–1558.

Piercy, K. W. and Cheek, C. (2004). Tending and befriending: The intertwined relationships of quilters. *Journal of Women and Aging, 16(1–2),* 17–33.

Pinterits, E. J., Poteat, V. P., and Spanierman, L. B. (2009). The White Privilege Attitudes Scale: Development and initial validation. *Journal of Consulting Psychology, 56(3),* 417–429.

Pope, A. (2001). *The Wild Genie: The healing power of menstruation.* Bowral, NSW, Australia: Sally Milner Publishing.

Quigley, D. (2010). The Four Stages of a Woman's Life. Available at www.care2.com/greenliving/the-four-stages-of-a-womans-life.html, accessed on 23 September 2011.

Rainer, T. (2004). *The new diary: How to use a journal for self-guidance and expanded creativity.* New York: Tarcher/Penguin.

Range, L.M., Kovac, S.H., and Marion, M.S. (2000). Does writing about the bereavement lessen grief following sudden, unintentional death? *Death Studies, 24,* 115–134.

Rawlings, D. and Bastian, B. (2002). Painting preference and personality, with particular reference to Gray's behavioral inhibition and behavioral approach systems. *Empirical Studies of the Arts, 20(2),* 177–193.

Redman, H. (2011). Birthing the Crone Gallery. Available at www.birthingthecrone.com/pages/crone.html, accessed on 1 September 2011.

Reynolds, F. (1999). Cognitive behavioral counseling of unresolved grief through the therapeutic adjunct of tapestry-making. *The Arts in Psychotherapy, 26(3),* 165–171.

Reynolds, F. (2000). Managing depression through needlecraft creative activities: A qualitative study. *The Arts in Psychotherapy, 27(2),* 107–114.

Reynolds, F. (2002). Symbolic aspects of coping with chronic illness through textile arts. *The Arts in Psychotherapy, 29(2),* 99–106.

Reynolds, F. (2004a). Textile art promoting well-being in long-term illness: Some general and specific influences. *Journal of Occupational Sciences, 11(2),* 58–67.

Reynolds, F. (2004b). Conversations about creativity and chronic illness II: Textile artists coping with long-term health problems reflect on the creative process. *Creativity Research Journal, 16(1),* 79–89.

Reynolds, F., Lim, K. H., and Prior, S. (2008). Images of resistance: A photonarrative enquiry into the meanings of personal artwork for people living with cancer. *Creativity Research Journal, 20(2),* 211–220.

Reynolds, F., Vivat, B., and Prior, S. (2008). Women's experiences of increasing subjective well-being in CFS/ME through leisure-based arts and crafts activities: A qualitative study. *Disability and Rehabilitation: An International, Multidisciplinary Journal, 30(17),* 1279–1288.

Rheinberg, F. (2008). Intrinsic motivation and flow-experience. In H. Heckhausen and J. Heckhausen (Eds.), *Motivation and action* (pp. 323–348). Cambridge, UK: Cambridge University Press.

Richards, S. (2011). Artists explore memories, meaning of aprons. *Inforum*, February 27.

Richards, J.M., Beal, W.E., Seagal, J.D. *et al.* (2000). Effects of disclosure of traumatic events on illness behavior among psychiatric prison inmates. *Journal of Abnormal Psychology, 109*, 156–160.

Riela, S., Rodriguez, G., Aron, A., Xu, X., and Acevedo, B.P. (2010). Experiences of falling in love: Investigating culture, ethnicity, gender, and speed. *Journal of Social and Personal Relationships, 27(4)*, 473–493.

Riley, J. (2008). Weaving an enhanced sense of self and a collective sense of self through creative textile-making. *Journal of Occupational Sciences, 15(2)*, 63–73.

Rosenbloom, T. (2006). Color preferences of high and low sensation seekers. *Creativity Research Journal, 18(2)*, 229–235.

Santa Mina, E. and Gallop, R. (1998). Childhood sexual and physical abuse and adult self-harm and suicidal behaviour: A literature review. *Canadian Journal of Psychiatry, 43*, 793–800.

Schofield-Tomschin, S. and Littrell, M. A. (2001). Textile handcraft guild participation: A conduit to successful aging. *Clothing and Textiles Research Journal, 19(2)*, 41–51.

Schomer, S. (2009). Women Will Be Greener Than Men in 2010. *Fast Company*, 23 December 2009. Available at www.fastcompany.com/blog/stephanie-schomer/write/women-green-men-2010, accessed on 1 September 2011.

Schroeder, B. N. and Gordon, C. S. (2002). *Assessment and Treatment of Childhood Problems: A Clinician's Guide.* New York: Guilford Press.

Schrott, S. (2011). Susan Schrott. Available at www.susanschrottartist.com/index.php, accessed on 1 September 2011.

Schwartz, L. and Drotar, D. (2004). Effects of written emotional disclosure on caregivers of children and adolescents with chronic illness. *Journal of Pediatric Psychology, 29*, 105–118.

Schwartz, M. S., Schwartz, N. M., and Monastra, V. J. (2003). Problems with relaxation and biofeedback-assisted relaxation, and guidelines for management. In M. S. Schwartz and F. Andrasik (Eds.), *Biofeedback: A practitioner's guide* (3rd ed., pp. 251–264). New York: Guilford Press.

Segrin, C. and Nabi, R. L. (2002). Does television viewing cultivate unrealistic expectations about marriage? *Journal of Communication, 52*, 247–263.

Sexton, J. D. and Pennebaker, J. W. (2009). The healing powers of expressive writing. In S. B. Kaufman and J. C. Kaufman (Eds.), *The psychology of creative writing* (pp. 264–273). New York: Cambridge University Press.

Shisslak, C. M., Crago, M., and Estes, L. S. (1995). The spectrum of eating disturbances. *International Journal of Eating Disorders, 18(3)*, 209–219.

Siegel, D. J. (2007). *The mindful brain: Reflection and attunement in the cultivation of well-being.* New York: W. W. Norton and Co.

Silverman, Y. (2004). The story within—myth and fairy tale in therapy. *The Arts in Psychotherapy, 31(3)*, 127–135.

Smolak, L. (1996). *National Eating Disorders Association/Next Door Neighbors puppet guide book.*

Smyth, J. M. (1998). Written emotional expression: Effect sizes, outcome types, and moderating variables. *Journal of Consulting and Clinical Psychology, 66*, 174–184.

Smyth, J. M., Hockemeyer, J., Anderson, C., Strandberg, K., Koch, M., O'Neill, H. K., and McCammon, S. (2002). Structured writing about a natural disaster buffers the effect of intrusive thoughts on negative affect and physical symptoms. *Australasian Journal of Disaster and Trauma Studies, 6(1)*, no pagination specified.

Snowden, L. R. and Cheung, F. K. (1990). Use of inpatient mental health services by members of ethnic minority groups. *American Psychologist, 45(3)*, 347–355.

Soule, A.B. (2009). *Handmade Home: Simple Ways to Repurpose Old Materials into New Family Treasures.* Boston, MA: Shambhala Publications.

Sue, D. W. (1998). In search of cultural competence in psychotherapy and counseling. *American Psychologist, 43*, 440–448.

Sue, D. W. and Torino, G. C. (2005). Racial-cultural competence: Awareness, knowledge, and skills. In R. T. Carter (Ed.), *Handbook of racial-cultural psychology and counseling: Training and practice* (Vol. 2, pp. 3–18). Hoboken, NJ: Wiley.

Surgeon General's Workshop on Women's Mental Health (2005). Workshop report. US Department of Health and Human Services. Available at www.surgeongeneral. gov/topics/womensmentalhealth, accessed on 1 September 2011.

Taylor, S. E. and Gonzaga, G. C. (2007). Affiliative responses to stress: A social neuroscience model. In E. Harmon-Jones and P. Winkielman (Eds.), *Social neuroscience: Integrating biological and psychological explanations of social behavior* (pp. 454–473). New York: Guilford Press.

Taylor, S. E., Klein, L. C., Lewis, B. P., Gruenewald, T. L., Gurung, R. A. R., and Updegraff, J. A. (2000). Biobehavioral responses to stress in females: Tend-and-befriend, not fight-or-flight. *Psychological Review, 107(3)*, 411–429.

Trivett, T. (2007). Grandma's Apron. *The Poetry of Tina Trivett.* Available at http:// tinatrivett.blogspot.com/2007/08/grandmas-apron.html?showComment=13 16740911286#c1466041758006698926, accessed on 23 September 2011.

Turney, J. (2004). Here's one I made earlier: Making and living with home crafts in contemporary Britain. *Journal of Design History, 17(3)*, 267–281.

Turney, J. (2009). *The culture of knitting.* Oxford, UK: Berg.

United Nations (2000). World Marriage Patterns. Available at www.un.org/esa/ population/publications/worldmarriage/worldmarriage.htm, accessed on 1 September 2011.

US Census Bureau (2003). *Language use and English-speaking ability: 2000.* Washington, DC: US Census Bureau.

US Census Bureau (2006). Nation's Population One-Third Minority. Available at www.census.gov/newsroom/releases/archives/population/cb06-72.html, accessed 1 September 2011.

Valoma, D. (2010). Dust chronicles. *Textile: The Journal of Cloth and Culture, 8(3)*, 260–269.

Van Eyk McCain, M. (Ed.) (2010). *GreenSpirit: Path to a New Consciousness*. Hampshire: John Hunt Publishing.

Van Gennep, A. (1960). *The rites of passage*. Chicago: University of Chicago Press.

Waldman, D. A., Atwater, L. E., and Davidson, R. A. (2004). The role of individualism and the five-factor model in the prediction of performance in a leaderless group discussion. *Journal of Personality, 72(1)*, 1–28.

Weinman, J., Ebrecht, M., Scott, S., Walburn, J., and Dyson, M. (2008). Enhanced wound healing after emotional disclosure intervention. *British Journal of Health Psychology, 13(1)*, 95–102.

Wepman, B. J. and Donovan, M. W. (1984). Abrasiveness: Descriptive and dynamic issues. *Psychotherapy Patient, 1(1)*, 11–19.

Whaley, A. L. and Davis, K. E. (2007). Cultural competence and evidence-based practice in mental health services: A complementary perspective. *American Psychologist, 62*, 563–574.

World Health Organization (WHO) (1992). *The International Statistical Classification of Diseases and Related Health Problems, Tenth Revision* (ICD-10). Geneva: WHO.

WHO (2011a). Gender and women's mental health. Available at www.who.int/ mental_health/prevention/genderwomen/en, accessed on 1 September 2011.

WHO (2011b). Violence against women fact sheet. Available at www.who.int/ mediacentre/factsheets/fs239/en, accessed on 1 September 2011.

Wills, A. (2009). Study Finds Women Are "Recycling Enforcers." Available at http://earth911.com/news/2009/11/18/study-finds-women-are-recycling-enforcers, accessed on 1 September 2011.

Wittchen, H. (2010). Women-specific mental disorders in DSM-V: Are we failing again? *Archives of Women's Mental Health, 13*, 51–55.

Wolff, T. (1985). Structural Forms of the Feminine Psyche (Trans. P. Watzlawik.). C.G. Jung Institute, Zurich.

Workman, J. (2010). Repurpose Materials to Use for Sewing and Crafts. Available at www.suite101.com/content/repurpose-materials-to-use-for-sewing-and-crafts-a295967, accessed on 1 September 2011.

Yalom, I.D. (2005). *The Theory and Practice of Group Psychotherapy* (5th ed.). New York: Basic Books.

Young, J. (Ed.) (1996). *Saga: Best New Writings on Mythology, Volume 1*. Ashland, OR: White Cloud Press.

Young, J. (Ed.) (2001). *Saga: Best New Writings on Mythology, Volume 2*. Ashland, OR: White Cloud Press.

Zhang, A. Y., Snowden, L. R., and Sue, S. (1998). Differences between Asian and White Americans' help seeking and utilization patterns in the Los Angeles area. *Journal of Community Psychology, 26(4)*, 317–326.

Zuckerman, D. (2009). Early puberty in girls. *National Research Center (NRC) for Women and Families*. Available at www.center4research.org/2010/04/girls-to-women, accessed on 1 September 2011.

Zurbriggen, E. L., Collins, R. L., Lamb, S., Roberts, T., Tolman, D. L., and Ward, L. M. (2007). *Report of the APA Task Force on the sexualization of girls*. Available at www.apa.org/pi/women/programs/girls/report.aspx, accessed on 1 September 2011.

Subject Index

Author Index